The Hard and Soft Sides of **Change Management**

Tools for Managing Process and People

Kathryn Zukof

D1557335

PRESS

ATD Press is an internationally renowned source of insightful and practical information on talent development, training, and professional development.

ATD Press
1640 King Street
Alexandria, VA 22314 USA

Ordering information: Books published by ATD Press can be purchased by visiting ATD's website at td.org/books or by calling 800.628.2783 or 703.683.8100.

Library of Congress Control Number: 2020951580

ISBN-10: 1-95049-687-2
ISBN-13: 978-1-95049-687-7
e-ISBN: 978-1-95049-688-4

ATD Press Editorial Staff
Director: Sarah Halgas
Manager: Melissa Jones
Community of Practice Manager, Change Management: Lisa Spinelli
Developmental Editor: Jack Harlow
Production Editor: Hannah Sternberg
Text Design: Shirley E.M. Raybuck
Cover Design: Rose Richey

Printed by BR Printers, San Jose, CA

For Max and Will

Contents

Introduction.. vii

Chapter 1. The Challenge of Change Management 1

Section 1. Defining What's Changing and the Path to Get There

Chapter 2. The DBZ Applicant Tracking System Case........................... 23

Chapter 3. Determining What's Changing 31

Chapter 4. Creating the Path.. 45

Section 2. Involving the Right People in the Right Way

Chapter 5. The JCo Acquisition Case 63

Chapter 6. Leading and Managing the Change 71

Chapter 7. Generating Advocacy on the Ground 91

Chapter 8. Listening to Opposing Views.. 103

Chapter 9. Accounting for Key Stakeholders... 115

Chapter 10. Designating Roles, Responsibilities, and Authority......... 131

Section 3. Building Awareness, Understanding, and Support

Chapter 11. The PCo Business Transformation Case............................ 143

Chapter 12. Communicating About Change 153

Chapter 13. Developing Knowledge, Skills, and Attitudes
  Needed to Support the Change.. 191

Chapter 14. Anticipating and Addressing Resistance 225

Section 4. Assessing Progress and Making Adjustments

Chapter 15. The TCW Relocation Case.. 251

Chapter 16. Learning From Successes and Mistakes 255

Chapter 17. Dealing With Thorny Issues 279

Chapter 18. And Then Everything Changed..297

Acknowledgments 301

Appendix..303

References 315

Index...319

About the Author...325

Introduction

It's quite a predicament, isn't it? At work, and maybe even in our personal lives, we hear that change is the only constant. We live in a wild, wild world, characterized by volatility, unpredictability, chaos, and ambiguity. To adapt to this ever-changing environment, our organizations introduce even more change. We implement new technology, policies, and procedures. Employees transition to working from home, or they transition back to a brick-and-mortar office environment. New leaders join our organizations and introduce different ideas about how to interact with customers. They change the structure of our workplace, establishing new departments one day and eliminating entire divisions the next. Sometimes these changes produce the kinds of results our organizations are striving to attain. Employees embrace the new technology, and productivity levels increase. The new customer interaction protocol really works, and fewer customers leave.

And yet, far too often, our change efforts come up short. Change is introduced, and we don't achieve the outcome our organization is looking for. Productivity remains the same—or gets worse. Customers continue to leave, perhaps in greater numbers. We try to figure out what went wrong, what we missed, and we're told that we shouldn't be surprised by our lack of results. People just don't like change, we hear. Change is hard. It's painful. And most change efforts fail anyway, don't they? You might conclude that implementing change is a hit or miss affair. Sometimes changes work. Often they don't.

So why do we keep at it? Why do we keep introducing changes in the workplace when it's something we may not really want to do, when it's so challenging, when we do it so badly anyway? Why do we keep trying if we haven't figured out how to do it right—or at least, how to do it right more consistently? If our chances of success are just hit or miss, is this really something we should keep on doing?

The easy answer is, we keep at it because we have to. Much of the change happening in today's workplace is driven by factors outside our organizations—by variables that fall, at least in part, outside our control. Customers want less expensive and more personalized products and services, and that means changing what we offer to clients and implementing new forms of delivery. With globalization, companies face increased competition; our workforce is more diverse, and the co-workers we collaborate with may be all around the world, instead of just down the hall or across the street. Rapid advances in technology mean that our business processes may now incorporate artificial intelligence or robotics. We've had to adjust—both at work and at home—as we take steps to protect our data and ourselves from cyberterrorism. Government regulations that we need to comply with change—and then they change again. Add in a global pandemic, and we may find ourselves reeling.

To respond to all of these external factors, maybe your company has decided to overhaul its business model, like so many retail firms and companies in the hospitality, food, and dining industry did during the COVID-19 crisis of 2020. Maybe your organization is implementing new technologies and work processes. Perhaps you've started to adopt new safety protocols or you're introducing new guidelines for setting up telemedicine appointments. Maybe your workplace is relocating some or all of its employees. Maybe you are relocating. Perhaps you are in the midst of an organizational restructure, in which job roles, responsibilities, and reporting relationships are changing. Maybe your company has acquired a new business, and you now need to figure out how to merge two distinct organizations into one. Or maybe your employer has been acquired, and you have to figure out how to work well with the new parent company. Your organization may be facing financial losses and may be downsizing its workforce. Or business may be booming and you find that the employee population is growing by leaps and bounds. Perhaps new leaders have joined your organization and have announced new ideas they plan to introduce in your company right away.

Maybe change in your workplace truly is the only constant.

How We Respond to Change

The external sources of change—and the steps our organizations take in response—may seem endless and continuous. In fact, in a recent study conducted by *Harvard Business Review* in partnership with the consulting firm Strativity, 86 percent of the organizations studied reported that they were conducting multiple change initiatives simultaneously (Percy 2019). That is, "different business functions—from operations and IT to marketing and finance—[were] trying to tackle different issues concurrently." And that study was conducted prior to COVID-

19, when suddenly everything—from the technology we used to stay connected to our customers and co-workers to our business priorities to simple procedures we needed to follow to enter our places of business—changed and then changed again and then changed yet again. We're facing lots of changes, constantly, all over the place, and all at once.

Sadly, research also shows that we really aren't handling all that change all that well. One often-cited study found that 70 percent of change initiatives fail to deliver on the objectives that were set for them (Ewenstein, Smith, and Sologar 2015). In another, 91 percent of respondents reported that a change initiative had failed in their organizations (Percy 2019). And although some companies successfully navigated the changes that were required to survive during the crisis of 2020, far too many organizations saw their efforts fall short. Research by the consulting firm McKinsey (Blackburn et. al 2020) suggests that companies that will struggle the most to deal with the COVID-19 crisis are reticent to test out new approaches. They aren't willing to try something new, fail, learn from their mistakes, and then quickly try a different approach. Change fatigue, defined as "the exhaustion that comes from excessive change," may be just one reason employees are reluctant to try something new (Carucci 2019). Our change initiatives also fail when we neglect those affected most by the change and fail to secure their buy-in, when we underestimate the scale and scope of the change as we create project plans, when communications regarding the change are inadequate, and when support from senior leadership is insufficient (Dickson 2019; Sirkin, Keenan, and Jackson 2005).

All that said, some workplace change initiatives are stunning successes. Some companies change their leadership team, organizational structure, processes, and technology—even all at once—and it just seems to work. They grow dramatically. Employees describe the company as a "best place to work." Consider Google, which figured out how to help employees focus on the change initiatives that really mattered, and weed out projects that were unlikely to succeed. As a result, 80 percent of Google's employees said that they understood the changes the company planned to implement (up from 50 percent before the company changed the way it managed change) and employee adoption of changes increased to 90 percent (Mautz 2018). Or take Deloitte auditors, who quickly pivoted to a 100 percent work-from-home environment to cope with COVID-19. They reported that executive-level attention, training, communication, and open dialogue with stakeholders was key to their success (Shannon 2020). And as Corning Cable Systems made changes to its corporate structure, executives met with managers to solicit their input, and provided multiple vehicles for employees to express opinions. They found that establishing mechanisms for two-way communication was essential to helping Corning implement rapid change (Robson 2020).

Apparently, some organizations have figured out how to implement change in a way that works.

But just because these companies have found ways to successfully navigate through change doesn't mean their employees immediately embraced change when they encountered it. It turns out there really is some truth to the old adage that people just don't like change. When change is coming, our natural tendency may be to resist a bit—possibly a lot. Research on the neuropsychology of change finds that our brain is hardwired to conserve energy. In comfortable, familiar situations, such as when we're using technology that we have mastered, or when we collaborate with co-workers we know really well, our brain operates on a kind of autopilot. It's just easy to get lots of stuff done that way. But when we encounter ambiguous and confusing situations, such as when we need to begin using a new technology at work or when we're unexpectedly assigned a new task, our brain interprets this as an error condition. It suddenly needs to process more and work harder, and we become, at least temporarily, less efficient. "That is why people crave certainty," explains David Rock of the NeuroLeadership Institute (2009). "Not knowing what will happen next can be profoundly debilitating because it requires extra neural energy." Change really can be difficult, at least for our brain.

And yet despite our neuropsychology, we don't always resist change at work. Many times we actively seek it out. We apply for promotions. We hire new teammates. We try new skills. From a neurological perspective, mild uncertainty actually energizes us. Our curiosity, focus, and interest are sparked by situations that seem just new and challenging enough—that trigger a mild threat response, but not one that is completely debilitating. We seem to have a sweet spot. If there's too much uncertainty—in our personal lives or at work—we get overwhelmed and panic. But if there's just enough change and challenge, we are energized and we engage (Rock 2009).

Why We Need to Handle Change Better

So change is coming at us from all angles, and our organizations make even more changes as they try to adapt. In the workplace, employees sometimes show a real willingness to support what's changing; other times, they find the change to be too overwhelming and debilitating, and they resist. Some change efforts succeed; others fall short. How do we make sense out of all this? Is it really all just hit or miss? Or is there something we can do to help our organizations and employees successfully navigate through change?

Well, there are steps you and your organization can take to achieve more consistently positive results. There are practices you can deploy that will help your company increase the odds of achieving the outcomes you're seeking as you begin a change initiative. And there are strategies you can use to help employees understand why the change is happening, feel less threatened by it, and find the sweet spot where they're excited and energized by the change that's coming. You can use a systematic approach to help the people in your organization change what they're doing today and begin to do something new so your organization achieves the results it's seeking. You can make change less of a hit or miss affair. You can manage change.

In this book, we'll take a look at those practices and approaches you can use to help manage change and produce more consistently positive results for your organization and its employees. You'll see that some of these practices involve using sound project management discipline, such as clearly defining project deliverables; assigning roles, responsibilities, and authorities; establishing a team with the right skill set; and making adjustments as your project proceeds. That's right. There's a "hard," process-oriented side to managing change—a side that's focused on helping your change initiative achieve the business outcomes you're seeking. And you'll see that other practices help you establish an environment of inclusion, trust, and open communication that helps mitigate the sense of threat and destabilization employees may experience as they deal with change. These practices and approaches help you address the "soft," people side of change. In this book, you'll learn that for a change initiative to succeed, you can't just focus on one side or the other—the hard or the soft. You need to integrate both.

That might sound like a tall order—attending to both the hard and soft sides. Can any one person really do all of that as you try to help your organization navigate through change? In this book, we'll figure out how you can meet that challenge. If your organization is about to begin a change initiative and you're helping to manage the soft, people side of change—perhaps you're responsible for leading communication, training, or stakeholder engagement—this book will help you understand and attend to the hard side of change as you execute your change management role. Or maybe you're the project leader, focused on managing project planning and execution. This book will help you learn how to focus on the soft side of change as you perform your hard-side, project management role. Whether you're primarily responsible for managing the hard side of change or the soft, this book will show you how establishing a strong partnership between project leaders and change management leaders is key. You can focus on the hard and the soft simultaneously—you need to—but it helps to have help.

We Can Manage Change

I'm no stranger to experiencing the disorientation—and the energy—that workplace change can bring. For many years, I led the learning and organizational development function in several multinational organizations, ranging from a family-owned conglomerate, to a global manufacturer and service provider, to one of the largest universities based in the US with sites all over the world. Before that, I held jobs in client services, product development, and marketing in the technology-services industry. I worked in these organizations during periods when they were undergoing radical transformation. Over the years, I saw—and led—some changes in these workplaces that really hit the mark and, admittedly, a few that were spectacular disasters.

I've participated in acquisitions, mergers, and divestitures during which employees felt included, informed, and respected as the company's governance, structure, and jobs were profoundly altered.

I've seen software implementations and process re-engineering during which employees felt left out, confused, and resentful, and the company failed to realize the efficiency and cost savings it sought when it initiated these changes.

I've led a relocation during which most everyone moved to their new work site with a sense of optimism and enthusiasm, as well as an organizational restructuring that was met with fear and distrust.

As an employee in these organizations, I experienced changes that I hadn't been asked to help implement but that I advocated for anyway. And there were changes I actively resisted. There were also changes I saw that confused me. And changes that I knew put my job—or my sense of autonomy, status, and prestige—at risk.

I know what it's like, and you may know what it's like, to work in an organization that's pursuing a change that's exciting, where you might—just might—end up on the winning side. And I know, and perhaps you know too, what it feels like when you fear that a change happening in your workplace means that you'll lose something that matters—something that's important to you.

Along the way, I watched my co-workers use tools and processes to lead and manage change that really worked. I learned more about these tools and adopted them myself as I helped lead change initiatives in the workplace. And I used some approaches that I now recognize aren't effective at all. What I discovered most is that managing change is a skill I could develop. I learned that I could build real competence in managing change, my co-workers could become more proficient, and the organizations I worked with could develop a real aptitude for managing change too. It took time, but I came to realize that while change may be challenging, we can begin to manage it.

This book introduces some of the tools I came to rely on when managing change in the workplace. In each section, we'll review a fictional case study that shows one or more tools in practice. We'll look at the key change management challenges that these tools help address, and we'll take a deeper dive to explore how you can apply these tools in your own organization. We'll see how these tools and approaches can be used to generate the business outcomes your organization seeks as you embark on change initiatives—to help you manage the hard side of change. And we'll examine how you can use these tools to build trust, engagement, and a real sense of change competence in yourself and among your co-workers. These are tools that help you manage the soft side.

Table 1 shows the tools and approaches we will cover in this book.

Table 1. Tools and Approaches in This Book

Section	Challenge	Tool
1	Defining what's changing and the path to get there	• Project charter • Project plan
2	Involving the right people in the right way	• Core project team • Change management team • Transition monitoring team • Red team • Stakeholder analysis • RACI matrix
3	Building awareness, understanding, and support	• Communication plan • Training plan • Resistance management plan
4	Assessing progress and making adjustments	• Action review

I'll note that this isn't an exhaustive set of tools and approaches. As you continue to build competence in managing change, you may find yourself using other tools too. But I'm certain this is a great place to start.

You and your organization can manage change. You can thrive in an environment where change is a constant. This book will help you get there.

But first, let's consider two organizations that got it right—at least part of the way. In chapter 1, we're going to look at two workplaces that managed change pretty skillfully, except that they still got it lopsided. Let's find out what we can learn from their experience. Let's see how we can manage change more effectively by focusing on the hard and the soft simultaneously.

1

The Challenge of Change Management

Managing Change From the Hard Side With Bervin Cares

To Mary, vice president of administration, the plan to restructure finance jobs at Bervin Cares seemed perfect. Bervin was a large social service agency with more than two dozen sites across the county. Each site employed a junior accountant who handled routine financial transactions, such as reviewing and approving invoices, submitting payroll hours for processing, and responding to finance-related inquiries from the agency's social workers and staff. The idea was to create a centralized finance service center that would manage these tasks for the entire agency. The junior accountant position at each site would be eliminated, and the employees who currently held these jobs would transfer into newly created roles in the service center. Junior accountants with less experience would be assigned to finance service representative jobs, fielding incoming calls from social workers and staff. Those with more experience would process transactions and research and address complex inquiries that service representatives were unable to resolve. And one junior accountant would be promoted to the job of service center leader, charged with managing the newly assembled team.

The idea made so much sense from a business perspective. According to reports from other social service agencies that had implemented the same structure, after deploying a service center Bervin could expect to resolve routine financial inquiries with greater speed, consistency, and accuracy, as questions would now be handled by a dedicated team that focused exclusively on responding to incoming calls. Bervin would process financial transactions faster and more accurately too, because the employees handling these tasks would no longer feel distracted by social workers and staff who stopped by with simple questions.

The plan ensured better coverage during periods of vacation and sick time, because service would be provided by a service center team, rather than by a lone individual responsible for supporting an entire site. And there might be opportunities for cost savings as service center operations became more efficient. Although no one would lose their job due to the restructure, the agency expected that over time it might be able to reduce overall headcount through attrition.

Convinced that this was the right path, the Bervin executive team set an aggressive schedule to begin service center operations. They asked Mary to act as project manager for the initiative, and she assembled a small team, comprising the agency's financial controller, a space planner, and her assistant, to get the job done. Mary's assistant created detailed project plans that helped them track progress. Table 1-1 provides a summary.

Table 1-1. Mary's Action Plan for Change

Action	Completed?
Announce the plan to the administrative director at each site, and let them know that the junior accountant who currently reported to them will transfer into the service center.	✓
Decide which junior accountant will be assigned to which job.	✓
Notify the junior accountants about the new structure and the new jobs they will be moving into.	✓
Renovate the physical space where the service center will operate.	✓
Configure the new phone system.	✓
Train service center staff on the new phone system.	✓
Send an email to social workers and staff announcing the service center and the new phone number they should call for service.	✓
Brief the executive team on a weekly basis to keep them up to speed.	✓

Despite the aggressive schedule and the need to coordinate so many moving parts, the finance service center launched right on time and without a hitch. And everyone involved seemed so supportive and accepting. No one voiced any pushback. In fact, the junior accountants and administrative directors said nothing at all to Mary as they were informed of the changes. Not a peep.

And yet, one year later, Mary and the Bervin executive team wished that they had never heard of the service center concept. Since the day the center launched, social workers and staff groused about being forced to call "an anonymous hotline" just to get a simple answer to their questions.

"Why would you think it's more efficient for me to call the hotline?" Anisa complained when she ran into Mary at a Bervin fundraising event. Mary knew she needed to keep Anisa happy. Just last year alone, Anisa had raised

more than $500,000 in donations. "I used to just stop by Ernie's desk," Anisa continued. "He knew what I needed. He understood how we worked here." Mary surmised that Ernie was the junior accountant who had been assigned to Anisa's site before the restructure. "Now I call the hotline," Anisa grumbled. "I'm put on hold, and when some stranger finally gets on the line, they have no idea what I'm talking about. I have to explain everything to them. They say they need to research my questions. They'll call me back. And that takes hours. Ernie used to have an answer for me in minutes. How is this better?" Mary had to admit, she had heard this objection from staff at some of the other sites.

Complaints from the administrative directors at each site had reached a fever pitch too. Apparently, some social workers and staff refused to call the service center, turning instead to their administrative directors for answers to even the most basic questions. "I can't get any work done anymore," an administrative director griped to Mary during a biweekly status call. "I don't know what you think service center staff are doing," he continued, "because no one here is calling them. I get all their questions now. I can't do my job when I have to play junior accountant too." The other administrative directors on the call murmured their assent. "That's happening here too," one reported. "Here too," yet another concurred.

Mary was worried. Absenteeism among service center staff was through the roof, and almost 40 percent of the original service center staff had already resigned. The first resignation came just one month after launch, when Ava, the new service center leader, a real up-and-comer handpicked by Mary herself, explained in her exit interview that managing a service center just didn't fit with her career plans. "I love Bervin," Ava explained. "But I want to be the CFO of a nonprofit someday. I'm not getting the kind of experience I need managing the service center." Mary wasn't sure she agreed with Ava's assessment, but Ava's decision was firm. So she left.

The grumbling quickly extended into other areas across the agency too. As soon as the finance service center was announced, rumors started circulating about more "shoes to drop." After all, if Bervin was setting up a finance service center today, could an HR service center, or an IT service center, be far behind? And forget accuracy. New service center employees had been hired to replace exiting team members, and these rookies were making mistakes—big ones. Just last month the agency had to shell out more than $10,000 to fix an error made by a new hire on the service center team. "How could things go so wrong," Mary sighed, "when every step in the project rollout seemed to go so well?"

Mary was right. In some respects, the project was executed flawlessly. There was a clear vision of what was supposed to be accomplished and a convincing rationale for moving forward with that vision. Executive leaders supported the change and were kept up-to-date throughout the entire rollout. The assembled project team seemed to have all the right technical competencies required to get the job done. And even with an aggressive schedule, the project team plotted out all the key tasks and managed them closely to ensure they were completed right on time. There was a training plan, and that worked without a hitch. There was a communications plan, and at least some of the people who needed to know about the change were notified right on schedule. When viewed purely from a perspective of planning, assigning resources, and managing project tasks and deliverables in a disciplined way, the initiative was a spectacular success. Except, of course, it wasn't.

Unfortunately, the project team failed to consider the pervasive sense of loss, threat, and uncertainty that members of the Bervin community might experience as the finance service center launched. They didn't stop to think:

- Will junior accountants feel like they've been demoted when we assign them their new service representative job titles? Will they resent losing the opportunity to perform a variety of job tasks as they transfer into roles where the work is more focused and specialized? And will they feel like they have lost their sense of self-determination and control when they are merely informed of the positions they have been assigned, rather than being offered the chance to apply to service center roles that fit with their career interests and aspirations?

- Will the administrative directors at each site balk at losing direct reports? And will they experience a loss of job status and lose precious time in their busy workday if social workers and staff start directing basic inquiries to them?

- How will social workers and staff feel when we tell them they will no longer receive personalized attention on-site and instead need to call a hotline? Will they become less efficient? Will they lose their sense of status?

- Will staff across the agency feel threatened as they speculate that more restructuring might be planned? Will they question how we made the decision to proceed with the service center approach in the first place? Will it feel "top-down" to them? Will they wonder how that fits with the culture of collaboration and inclusiveness they previously have enjoyed at the agency?

In short, when viewed from the perspective of anticipating and accounting for the sense of loss, threat, and uncertainty the new structure might present, the initiative at Bervin Cares was a spectacular failure.

What the project team at Bervin Cares seemed to miss is a lesson I figured out over the course of many years helping to lead change initiatives at work. There's a hard side to change management and a soft side, and you need to address both, simultaneously, for your change initiative to succeed.

Fundamental project management principles need to be in place to drive your change initiative forward. These are hard-side practices, such as setting achievable deliverables and timelines; securing the right resources; establishing clear roles, responsibilities, and authority; and putting in place sound mechanisms for monitoring progress and making adjustments. And steps need to be taken to establish an environment of psychological safety, trust, and predictability, wherein the sense of threat and loss associated with the change is acknowledged and appropriately addressed. These are soft-side practices, such as engaging with and involving those most affected by the change, establishing frank dialogue and discussion, and providing multiple channels for expressing ideas and concerns. The project team at Bervin Cares seemed to master the hard side of change as they implemented the finance service center, but they flubbed the soft side. And it cost Bervin dearly as a result.

Now, let's consider an organization that focused effectively on the soft side of managing change and see how well it fared.

Managing Change From the Soft Side With ProxyCo

When ProxyCo hired Anil to serve as director of the company's newly formed learning and development team, Anil understood that the situation was sensitive. The company didn't have a professional L&D function to speak of. Sure, there were Patty and Nasma, both engineers by training, who led technical and compliance education programs for the company, but neither of them had any formal L&D background or expertise. That didn't stop them from applying for the director position when the opening was posted on ProxyCo's employment website. But the company needed someone with leadership development and learning technology experience, so ProxyCo hired Anil away from the top L&D position at one of its competitors.

Anil knew that Patty and Nasma might resent not being selected for the director role and might even feel scared that they lacked the skills ProxyCo seemed to value now in the L&D function. So, Anil wanted to make sure Patty and Nasma felt appreciated and recognized for the knowledge and experience they did bring to the department. Although neither was selected to be the director, Anil wanted them to have plenty of opportunities to lead anyway.

Now, as part of the L&D transformation, ProxyCo executives wanted to launch a leadership development curriculum and introduce some new learning technologies to their compliance training programs. "This is your chance to really shine," ProxyCo's vice president of HR, Marisol, announced to Anil one afternoon, about two months into his tenure with the company. Anil reported directly to Marisol, and he appreciated how much space she had provided to him so far to explore what ProxyCo employees might need from L&D.

Anil was surprised to see Marisol being unusually direct with him that afternoon. "There's a lot of pent-up demand for leadership development at all levels," Marisol explained. "The entire executive team is behind this. Start with frontline supervisors. Then expand the program to include midlevel managers. Then move on to the senior executive team." Anil nodded as he listened to Marisol. "And we need to get moving with the compliance programs," Marisol continued. "Your background is perfect for all this. We'd love to see you convert the compliance program to an e-learning platform, maybe develop some microlearning sessions. And we need online performance support tools too. This is important to us. And you'll be great." Anil appreciated Marisol's encouragement. He had to agree with her—his background was perfect. And he knew just where to start.

Anil met one-on-one with Patty and Nasma and summarized the conversation he'd just had with Marisol. "This is a terrific opportunity for you to broaden your L&D skills," he counseled each of them. "We're—you're—going to transform L&D! Go out and research ideas for leadership development programs and learning technologies, and then let's talk." Excited by the opportunity to contribute to real transformation at their company, Patty and Nasma reached out to organizations known for their L&D best practices. They interviewed L&D leaders in these companies and enthusiastically reported their findings to Anil each week.

Meanwhile, Anil embarked on what he affectionately dubbed his one-year grand listening tour. He met with leaders at all levels across the company and solicited their ideas for establishing a leadership development curriculum. He set up a supervisory task force comprising new supervisors and asked them to research and brainstorm ideas for frontline supervisory training. And he established a technology committee with the company's engineers and asked them to investigate and recommend technology-assisted learning programs.

Marisol checked in with Anil from time to time, typically asking him how he was adjusting to work at ProxyCo. Anil reassured Marisol that things were moving along well and that the L&D transformation was under control, so Marisol never asked for details. After all, they could cover specifics during Anil's annual performance review.

Initially, the buzz was incredibly positive. ProxyCo wanted to transform its L&D function, and here was everyone across the company eagerly participating in that change. Everyone had ideas to share, and it was clear that all suggestions were welcome.

Of course, there were a few collisions. The supervisory task force contacted a company known for its leadership development best practices, and was surprised to learn that Patty had met with representatives from the same company just a week earlier. And one day during her one-on-one meeting with Anil, Nasma complained bitterly: Apparently, the technology committee had recommended an e-learning vendor, and Nasma disagreed with their selection. "Who do they think they are?" Nasma protested. "They don't work in L&D. We do. We get to pick. Not them."

Still, for the most part, Patty, Nasma, and the various committee members welcomed the opportunity Anil had provided to contribute ideas. And Patty and Nasma seemed to support Anil's leadership and the direction he said he was taking the ProxyCo L&D department. They wondered when the company would get there. But things still looked and felt good . . . or at least OK.

Looking back at his first year with the company, Anil sighed with a mixture of satisfaction and relief. He had handled a delicate situation, one he had seen other leaders stumble through, with finesse. So Anil was stunned when he received what seemed to be a barrage of critical feedback during his annual review. Marisol told Anil she was deeply disappointed that the company still wasn't offering training to its frontline supervisors. In fact, there weren't any new programs to speak of—nothing for supervisors, midlevel managers, or executives, and no movement on technology-assisted learning either. "We have new supervisors making rookie mistakes, and it's our fault we haven't provided them with the tools they need to succeed," Marisol complained. "You haven't

even announced that there's a program coming. Sure, there are lots of commit-
tees. But we're just spinning here. Nothing is actually moving forward."

> *Anil objected to the feedback about nothing happening. "You wanted*
> *transformation," Anil argued. "Just look around you. I have everyone talking*
> *about leadership development. Everyone is talking about technology. Everyone*
> *feels included. Everyone is participating."*

> *"But what are they participating in?" Marisol snapped back. "There's all*
> *talk and no action. That's not what we needed at all."*

What did Anil miss in his efforts to transform the L&D function at ProxyCo, especially when on the surface he seemed to get so much so right? After all, Anil solicited input and ideas from across the ProxyCo community, and he knew that effort would help build buy-in and support as the L&D transformation unfolded. Anil understood that ProxyCo supervisors and managers had valuable information to share about the challenges they faced as leaders, and he focused on listening to these key stakeholders' needs and concerns. Anil created opportunities for the company's engineers to get involved; he wanted to make sure they felt excited about, and included in, what was changing too.

Within his own department, Anil focused considerable attention on addressing and minimizing the sense of threat and loss that the change initiative might represent for Patty and Nasma. Anil understood that Patty and Namsa might resent not being selected for the director role, so he found ways for them to lead anyway. Anil sensed that they might feel like their jobs were at risk, because they lacked the kind of experience and expertise ProxyCo needed in its new and improved L&D organization, so he provided them with opportunities to contribute and build needed skills.

Anil did an admirable job managing the L&D transformation from the soft side. He created an environment of inclusion, involvement, and psychological safety. He ensured that those most affected by the change had opportunities to contribute, felt like they knew what was going on, and had the chance to develop competencies needed to succeed in the new L&D organization.

Unfortunately, Anil—and his manager, Marisol—ignored the hard side of change management, and that led to an unacceptable delay in producing needed results. At its core, the L&D transformation could have been viewed like any initiative that needs oversight from a project management perspective. Anil, in his role as project leader, and Marisol, as project sponsor, could have clearly defined expectations and deliverables—what exactly needed to be accomplished, by when, and what steps needed to be taken to get there. Marisol provided a hint about what was needed, but she didn't really explain the rationale behind her directives to Anil, nor was she clear about expected timeframes. And Anil didn't seem to ask either. That led to confusion and disappointment as Anil and his team failed to move the transformation forward fast enough for ProxyCo's executive team.

Anil could have set clearer roles, responsibilities, and decision-making authority for the various employees and teams contributing to the transformation effort. But he didn't, and team members were understandably annoyed when they discovered that multiple people were working on the same thing.

Anil could have assembled a project team with enough expertise to develop and deliver supervisory training—perhaps hiring a vendor to supplement Patty and Nasma's developing skills. But he didn't, and so Anil's project team lacked the skill set it needed to deliver results in the expected—albeit fuzzy—timeframe.

Marisol could have required that Anil provide periodic updates on the status of the leadership development and learning technology implementation, so they could discuss adjustments Anil needed to make to meet expectations. But she didn't, and so Anil was blindsided by the feedback he received during his annual performance review.

When viewed from the hard side, the L&D transformation at ProxyCo failed. Sure, people felt good, at least for a little while. But that feeling began to fade as employees realized they weren't receiving the L&D services they expected and deserved.

Change Management—A Dance of Hard and Soft

A lesson we can learn from Bervin Cares and ProxyCo is that effective change management requires focus on both the hard side and the soft side of change. We can manage an initiative like clockwork—clearly defining project deliverables; assigning roles, responsibilities, and authorities; establishing a team with the right skill set; and tracking and monitoring progress—and still stumble with our change management efforts. And we can focus purely on managing the people issues—finding ways to minimize the sense of loss that change might present for others, ensuring that those most affected by the change understand what is going on and why, and providing opportunities for people to be heard and to contribute—and stumble here too. Change management, done effectively, requires us to integrate the hard and the soft.

But let's take a step back. What is change management anyway?

We can find many definitions by doing a quick search on the internet. Here are just a few:

- "Change management is the capability for enabling change within an organization by using structured approaches to shift individuals, teams, and organizations from a current state to a future state. Once initiated, change follows its own nonlinear path in response to uncertainties, reactions, and guidance from those involved. There are tools, resources, processes, skills, and principles for managing the people side of change that practitioners should understand and implement in order to achieve preferred outcomes" (Association for Training Development 2019).
- "Change management is the process, tools and techniques to manage the people side of change to achieve its required business outcomes. It is the systematic management of employee engagement and adoption when the organization changes how work will be done" (ProSci 2020).
- "Change management is the systematic approach and application of knowledge, tools and resources to deal with change. It involves defining and adopting corporate strategies, structures, procedures and technologies to handle changes in external conditions and the business environment. Effective change management goes beyond project management and technical tasks undertaken to enact organizational changes and involves leading the 'people side' of major change within an organization. The primary goal of change management is to successfully implement new processes, products and business strategies while minimizing negative outcomes" (Society for Human Resources Management 2020).

Whichever definition you prefer, some common themes appear. Change management in the workplace focuses on people, processes, and organizational outcomes (Figure 1-1).

Figure 1-1. The Three Themes of Change Management

People	Processes	Organizational Outcomes
Understanding what happens to individuals as they encounter and deal with change at work	Using a systematic approach and set of tools, techniques, and processes to help people navigate that change	Embarking on change to achieve a desired end goal for the organization

Put simply: When we manage change in the workplace, we use a systematic approach to ensure we address both the soft, people side of change, and the hard, organizational-outcome side of change.

But addressing the soft side and the hard side, and integrating the two, present their own challenges. Let's look at each in turn.

The Challenge of the Soft Side

I bet there are times when you and your co-workers have felt optimistic and enthusiastic about a change that was coming. Maybe your organization had been using outdated software that didn't have all the functionality employees needed to get their jobs done. Now new software was finally on its way. It's exciting, right? But as you and your co-workers got closer to actually using the new software, you might have noticed people feeling anxious and a bit unsettled. That's normal, too. After all, your co-workers might be thinking:

- "I really knew what I was doing using the old software. How long will it take me to get up to speed on the new? Will I be able to learn it?"
- "Is it going to take me longer to do my job while I am getting up to speed on the new software? Are things going to get harder here for some period of time while I figure this out?"
- "I know I didn't like the old software, but why did the company pick this new product to replace it? What other options were considered? Why didn't they ask for my opinion?"

I certainly have been in this spot before. I was working for an organization that was about to make a huge acquisition. We were going to purchase one of our major competitors, and as a result our company would double in size. I was excited for my company and thrilled that I had been asked to work on the acquisition integration team. This was the right move for our business and could mean big things for all of us. Maybe big things for me too. And yet I wondered, "When the merger is complete, will I still lead learning and organizational development for the company? Or will the head of L&OD at the company we're buying end up in the top spot?" I googled the other company and checked out the leadership development programs they described on their corporate website. They looked good—really good. Were they better than ours? Hmmm. Forget heading up L&OD. Will I even have a job when all of this is over?

That's the challenge of the soft side of change. When things are changing at work, it's natural for people to feel apprehensive and unsettled. After all, despite all the positives that change can bring, there are risks too. When change is happening in the workplace, employees might feel anxious about:

- **Loss of competence:** Will I be able to learn how to do the work that's now required of me? Can I learn fast enough?

- **Loss of efficiency:** Will my work take more time now? Will I lose free time?
- **Job insecurity and instability:** Is my job at risk? Will I like my job after the changes go into effect? Will I still have a job?
- **Loss of feeling "in the know":** Do I know what's going on here at work?
- **Loss of feeling included:** Do my opinions matter? Is my expertise valued?
- **Loss of status:** Will the level of respect I receive at work diminish because of this change?
- **Loss of relationships:** Will I still have friends here and get to interact with them?
- **Loss of connection to the organization's larger culture and mission:** Does this change really reflect the company I thought I worked for? Do I still fit in here?

That's right. Change, even its most positive form, can also usher in a real sense of loss. And as a result, it's not unusual for people to feel anxious and apprehensive. They may even question the value of the change and begin to actively resist it. Perhaps it's not so much that people don't like change. It's that they don't like loss.

The challenge for the soft side of change management is to be sensitive to that potential for loss—to understand that feelings of loss and threat are a natural, and possibly even appropriate, response to change. The challenge is to find ways to minimize the real or perceived sense of loss employees may experience, where that is possible. And the challenge is to acknowledge and help employees navigate through the unavoidable losses, whether they are temporary or permanent.

We do this by:

- Communicating honestly, openly, and frequently so employees understand what's going on—so they feel like they can anticipate and predict what will happen day to day.
- Acknowledging that work might feel more challenging and less efficient while people are adjusting to the new way things are done. We look for ways to shorten that period of inefficiency as much as possible.
- Helping employees build the knowledge, skills, and attitudes they need to successfully perform their work as their jobs and work tasks are changing. We look for ways to shorten, as much as possible, the period of incompetence they may be feeling.
- Providing lots of opportunities for employees to contribute their ideas and their expertise, so they feel like they still matter at work.

In the chapters that follow, we'll look at tools and approaches that can help you address the challenges of the soft side of change. These tools include:

- The change management team (chapter 6)
- The transition monitoring team (chapter 7)
- Stakeholder analysis (chapter 9)
- The communications plan (chapter 12)
- The training plan (chapter 13)
- The resistance management plan (chapter 14)

That's the soft side. What challenges does the hard side present?

Your Organization and the Soft Side of Change

What do you do in your organization to address the soft side of change?

- Do you have a culture of open communication? Do employees trust that leaders are being honest and transparent about changes that are planned? What do you do to nurture this kind of environment?
- When you're about to embark on a change initiative, do you consider the tangible and intangible sense of loss the changes may create for employees? What do you do to help employees navigate through that period of loss?
- Do you have a learning culture in which people embrace opportunities to change on the job? What does your organization do to help employees develop and refresh their knowledge and skill set?
- What mechanisms does your organization provide for employees to contribute their ideas and expertise during change initiatives? How does your organization help employees feel included and involved?
- Which tools for addressing the soft side of change do you use in your organization? Which ones might you consider implementing for your next change initiative?

The Challenge of the Hard Side

As difficult as it might seem to address change from the soft side, it can be just as challenging to get the hard side right. I was working with an organization that restructured one of its business units. The directive from senior leadership was clear: Cut headcount. Streamline processes. So they brought in an external consultant—fortunately this person wasn't me—who created elegant organizational diagrams and provided compelling research about what other companies had done. But the consultant, and the organization, never gathered input from anyone who actually worked in the unit targeted for restructuring. They failed to account for key tasks employees in the unit performed—work that didn't appear in the consultant's diagrams and research. They failed to comprehend the scope of the work the business unit actually performed and they underestimated what needed to happen to transform how that work got done. In the end, after the restructure was complete, the company discovered it needed to increase headcount, not decrease staffing. And for some time, while we untangled the mess that had been created, work in the unit proceeded at a much slower pace. Processes hadn't been streamlined at all.

Plenty of times, we seem to lose focus on why we're embarking on the change in the first place, what it is that we are trying to accomplish, the scope of what needs to change, and who has the expertise to help us get there. And when we lose that focus, we fail to achieve the organizational outcomes we were shooting for. Here are some of the missteps organizations make as they struggle with the hard side of change:

- **Failing to clearly articulate the end goal or provide a convincing rationale about why the goal is important for the organization.** I once worked with a company whose leaders said they were "going global" because real estate was so expensive in the northeastern United States. Employees dragged their feet and understandably questioned the stated rationale. After all, if land was too expensive in the Northeast, why couldn't they just open up operations in other parts of the country where real-estate prices were more moderate? That certainly seemed easier and less risky. If wasn't until the organization more clearly defined and communicated the market opportunities the company could tap into by "going global" that employees finally got on board and started moving the initiative forward.
- **Underestimating the scale and scope of the change.** I worked on a project for replacing outdated technology in an organization. The project team created a plan that clearly defined all the steps involved in swapping out the software. But they failed to consider the business processes that needed to change for the new software to work effectively. And once they realized the extent to which business processes had to change, it became clear that new jobs needed to be created and that some jobs should be eliminated, too. So the organization needed to be restructured. The project

was like an onion—as soon as one layer of issues was addressed, another was revealed.

- **Failing to include people with the right skills and experience on the project team.** Have you ever seen a project fail, where people said, "I knew this wasn't going to work. All they had to do was ask me. But they didn't." Sometimes this happens when the organization fails to include on the project team people who have a deep understanding of the current state—people who know how things currently operate and why things are done the way they are. Or this sometimes happens when the organization fails to accurately define the scope of the project. People who have the skills needed to address the missing components are simply left out. It's disappointing when a project fails even though people with the right knowledge and expertise are readily available to help set the project on a more successful course.

- **Failure to account for the amount of extra effort employees must exert to cope with the change.** Many times on a change initiative, things become a lot harder before they finally become easier. It just takes longer to get work done, because the new way of doing things is, well, new. Sometimes change initiatives fail when employees get frustrated by how inefficient they've suddenly become. So they drop the new procedures and develop workarounds, saying, "This change just isn't working." This happens most often when project leaders fail to honestly communicate to people that work will become harder for a while, that the difficulties are temporary, and that the end state will make the period of inefficiency worth muddling through. And this also happens when organizational leaders fail to plan for and make adjustments for the extra burden navigating through the change placed on employees.

- **Failure to monitor results and adjust as lessons are learned.** So often, especially when we face the crush of project deliverables and looming deadlines, we fail to take a step back to see what's working, what isn't working, and what we need to adjust so we can meet our goals. Instead, we keep working the plan, moving things forward, even if it's clear that the plan ultimately won't help us accomplish what we really need to achieve. Change initiatives fail when we don't pause often enough to review the project and make needed adjustments.

You can think of change from a project management perspective. Like a project, change requires defined end goals, the right people, manageable workloads, and pauses for reflection and adjustment. The challenge for the hard side of change is to focus, stay organized, secure the right resources and use them in the right way, and keep things moving forward, while at the same time remaining flexible and open to learning.

We do this by:

- **Clearly defining what needs to be accomplished:** What is the end state everyone should be working toward? We need to provide a convincing rationale for why that end state matters.
- **Accounting for the entire scope of the change as we map out the steps we'll take to reach the end goals:** For the organization to reach its desired outcome, we need to consider how a change in one part of the organizational system will affect other parts.
- **Including people with the right skills and experience on the project team:** We need to define the skills that are needed to work on each step of the initiative, and we need to enlist people with those skills to work on the project. And we need to make sure we clarify roles, responsibilities, and the authority of those working on the project.
- **Considering the extra effort employees need to exert to work in the changing environment, and adjusting what's expected to what can actually get done:** We need to make sure project schedules and expected deliverables are realistic. And we need to limit change fatigue by planning changes at a realistic pace and frequency.
- **Pausing periodically, considering what's working and what isn't, and adjusting our efforts so we keep on track:** We need to view our change initiative for what it is—an opportunity for the organization to learn. Our organizations will try some things that won't work. We need to stop, acknowledge that, and move on with something different. And our organizations will try some things that work spectacularly well. We need to recognize that too, and weave more of that throughout our change initiative.

In the chapters that follow, we'll look at tools and approaches that can help you address the challenges of the hard side of change. These tools include:

- Project charters (chapter 3)
- Project plans (chapter 4)
- The core project team (chapter 6)
- The red team (chapter 8)

- The RACI matrix (chapter 10)
- Action reviews (chapter 16)

That's the hard side. But the experiences at Bervin Cares and ProxyCo, the two organizations you read about at the beginning of this chapter, show that there's a third challenge we need to address as we try to help our organizations manage change.

Your Organization and the Hard Side of Change

What do you do in your organization to address the hard side of change?

- When you begin work on a change initiative, do you have a clearly articulated goal you're shooting for? Do you understand the outcomes the change is expected to produce and why this is so important for your organization?
- What steps do you take to make sure you understand the scope of what's changing, and that you've considered how a change to one component in your organization might affect other components?
- How do you make sure you've enlisted the right people with the right skills to work on the change initiative?
- Are project schedules realistic? Is your organization experiencing change fatigue?
- What steps do you take in your organization to pause periodically, examine what's working and what isn't, and make needed adjustments to your project plans? How are you learning from your organization's successes and mistakes?
- Which tools for addressing the hard side of change do you use in your organization? Which ones might you consider implementing for your next change initiative?

The Challenge of Integrating the Hard and the Soft

Here's something else I learned from leading successful change initiatives and from reflecting on those that were less successful. It's not enough to use soft-side practices to deal with people issues associated with change, and hard-side practices to focus on the project management component of change. Things turn out much better when we find a way to integrate the two. That is, people are much more likely to adopt and embrace a change when we focus on soft-side issues while we are using hard-side tools. And likewise, we're far more likely to make progress on the business outcomes we're striving for when we focus on hard-side issues while we are using soft-side tools.

Change management requires us to effectively integrate both the hard and the soft. Effective change management requires a dance of sorts—rigorous project management practices (hard-side tools) deployed in a soft way, and care and concern for people (soft-side practices) executed in a hard way.

Competencies for Managing Change

As you learn more about managing the hard and soft side of change, you probably will discover that you already have lots of relevant knowledge and experience you can draw from.

- Have you ever worked on a project for which you needed to draft a clear statement about what you would deliver—the outcome you were shooting for?
- Did you create a detailed action plan that described the steps you would take along the way to help you get there?
- Have you ever taken the lead on a project and needed to figure out who else should be on your project team—who could you work with that could help you achieve the project goal?
- As you worked on your project, did you pause periodically to think about what was working and what wasn't—and did you make adjustments along the way to keep your initiative on track?
- Did you keep your manager and other leaders up-to-date on how the project was proceeding to make sure you had their support?

Congratulations. You already have demonstrated many of the skills needed to manage the hard side of change. In this book, we'll cover tools and processes you can use to apply these skills in a more structured way. You may find that using these tools and processes will help you achieve more consistently positive results as you work on change initiatives in your workplace.

And how about these skills and experiences?

- Are you empathetic and a good listener?
- Do you communicate clearly and transparently in a way that inspires others to get involved?
- Are you skilled at helping people voice their ideas and concerns—either one-on-one or in group settings?
- Have you helped negotiate and resolve conflict in your organization?
- Have you helped people build new skills and capabilities?

- Have you coached anyone to help them make a change in their personal life or at work?

Congratulations, again. You've already demonstrated many of the skills needed to manage the soft side of change. In this book, we'll cover tools and processes for applying these skills in a more systematic way as you work through your change projects. You'll find that using these tools and processes will help you create an environment in which your colleagues begin to feel more comfortable with, and supportive of, changes as they occur at work.

About to Begin?

Are you about to begin working on a change initiative in your organization? Think about:

- What are some of the soft, people-side challenges you might encounter as you work on this project? Which approaches and tools can you use to help people understand what's changing, and why and how they're affected; develop the knowledge, skills, and attitudes needed to succeed in the changed environment; and feel like they were listened to and that their needs and concerns matter?
- What are some of the hard, project-management-related challenges you might encounter? What do you plan to do to ensure you clearly define the outcomes you're shooting for and the rationale for those outcomes; establish a comprehensive and realistic path for moving the project forward; clarify the roles, responsibilities, and authorities of those working on the project; and continuously adjust your plans based on lessons you learn along the way?
- How can you make sure you stay focused on the overall business goals you're shooting for as you address the soft, people-side of change? And how can you ensure you maintain an environment of inclusion, trust, and psychological safety as you address the hard, project management side of change?

Are you ready to get started? Let's begin by looking at the end. To manage change—actually, to manage just about anything—we need to clearly articulate the outcome, the business result, we're trying to accomplish. And we need to create a realistic plan for achieving that outcome. We need to clearly define the target we're shooting for and the path to get there.

That's what we'll look at in section 1. We're going to learn how to create a project charter that describes what's changing, what isn't changing, and the rationale for embarking on our change initiative in the first place. And we'll see how we can create project plans that help us achieve that desired outcome. We'll learn how to use hard-side tools to launch our project and set it moving in the right direction. And we'll see how we can apply these tools in a soft way.

Learn more. Check out:

Sanchez, P. 2019. "The Secret to Leading Organizational Change is Empathy." *Harvard Business Review,* December 20. hbr.org/2018/12/the-secret-to-leading-organizational-change-is-empathy.

Sirkin, H.L., P. Keenan, and A. Jackson. 2005. "The Hard Side of Change Management." In *Harvard Business Review* 83:108–18.

Defining What's Changing and the Path to Get There

2
The DBZ Applicant Tracking System Case

When Max, a training and development associate at DBZ Corporation, was asked by Bonita, the company's vice president of human resources, to lead change management for an HR systems project the company was about to launch, he was thrilled. Now was his chance to apply some of the change management techniques and tools he'd recently learned to a real live change initiative at his company.

Bonita explained that the company intended to replace the old online applicant tracking system that job seekers used to apply to open positions at DBZ. The new system would be more appealing to job applicants and would help the company's 100-plus recruiters around the globe perform their jobs more efficiently.

"That sounds like an easy win," Max thought to himself as Bonita provided a quick project overview. Max knew that the company's recruiters—the key people inside DBZ whom the project would touch—despised the outdated technology they currently relied on to do their jobs. He anticipated that building support and buy-in for the project among these key stakeholders would be a snap.

"I'm putting together the project team," Bonita explained. She would serve as project sponsor, establishing the overall vision for the applicant tracking system project and coordinating with the company's executive team to ensure the right resources were assigned. Kevin, DBZ's director of talent acquisition, would act as project leader, and would oversee project planning and execution. The project team also included some of the company's recruiters and IT staff, who would serve as subject matter experts, and some consultants assigned by their applicant tracking system vendor.

"I'd like you to head up change management on the project," Bonita continued. *"Think you're ready for that?"*

Bonita didn't need to ask twice. Max couldn't wait to get involved.

So Max was eager to help when Kevin reached out the next day and asked him to review the draft project charter and project plan that Kevin and Bonita had prepared (Table 2-1).

Table 2-1. DBZ Applicant Tracking System Project Charter

Project Name	Applicant Tracking System Phase 1: US
Start Date	March 1, 2021
End Date	December 1, 2021
Objective	Implement an online applicant tracking system that will provide job applicants with an easier, streamlined process for applying to DBZ job vacancies, and that will provide US recruiters with a more efficient process for managing recruitment, from posting job vacancies online and managing candidate information through to extending and tracking acceptance of job offers.
Deliverables	
In Scope	• All US locations • Online system for posting job vacancies and managing candidate information • Integration with job-advertising systems (e.g., Indeed) • Online application forms for job candidates, including résumé parsing • Online system for generating offer letters and tracking acceptance of offers • Mobile enabled for job applicants and recruiters • Revised recruitment workflow and processes • Redesigned jobs for some recruiters
Out of Scope	• Locations outside the US • Integration with reference check vendor
Benefits	• Improved ability to attract qualified job applicants • Reduced time to fill job vacancies (expect reduction of 10 days in time to fill) • Reduced cost to fill job vacancies (expect reduction of $235 per vacancy)

Key Deliverables and Timeline

Major Milestone or Deliverable	Estimated Timeline
Stakeholder analysis	3/1/21–4/15/21
Configuration / integration design and development	3/8/21–7/8/21
Workflow process redesign	3/22/21–4/9/21
Recruiter job redesign	4/10/21–4/30/21
Create stakeholder engagement plan	4/10/21–4/17/21
Create communication materials	4/18/21–7/8/21
Create training materials	5/18/21–7/8/21
System testing	7/9/21–8/10/21
User acceptance testing	8/10/21–8/21/21

User training	8/21/21–9/30/21
Migration from old system	10/1/21–10/31/21
Go live new with system	11/1/2021
Advanced user training	11/15/2021–12/1/2021

Project Team and Key Stakeholders

Project Sponsor	Bonita Lopez
Project Leader	Kevin Louis
Core Project Team Members	East Coast Recruiter TBD
	West Coast Recruiter TBD
	Southwest Recruiter TBD
	Southeast Recruiter TBD
	Midwest Recruiter TBD
	IT Staff Member TBD
	IT Staff Member TBD
	Vendor Staff Member TBD
	Vendor Staff Member TBD
Change Management Leader	Max Williams
Key Stakeholders	US Recruiters
	US Hiring Managers
	Job Applicants
	Recruiters Outside the US

Attachments:
- Statement of Work
- Stakeholder Analysis
- Project Plan
- Stakeholder Engagement Plan
- Communication Plan
- Training Plan
- Budget

Signatures

Project Sponsor:	
Project Leader:	
Change Management Leader:	

"Take a look and fill in some of the missing details," Kevin requested of Max. "And let me know if you see any problems."

"Sure thing," Max responded with enthusiasm. "No problem at all."

But Max felt a bit of a jolt as he began to read through the documents Kevin shared with him. Max began to realize that perhaps the project wouldn't be so easy after all. According to the project charter, the initiative not only involved replacing the outdated applicant tracking system, but also would entail changing some of the processes hiring managers and recruiters used to post job vacancies, review résumés, identify candidates to be interviewed, and send job offers. Because these processes were changing, the initiative also involved redefining and restructuring some of the jobs currently held by DBZ's recruitment staff. Changing the technology meant changing work processes, which meant changing the organizational structure.

Max sighed. This was big. Not only would Max need to help the company's recruiters learn how to use new software, but he would also have to help them understand why and how their work processes were changing and how this affected their job roles, responsibilities, and reporting relationships.

And yet, as Max continued reading through the draft charter, he realized that in some ways the project was also smaller than he originally thought. From his conversations with colleagues in DBZ's offices outside the US, Max understood that DBZ recruiters across the globe were frustrated by the company's current applicant tracking system. But the project charter made it clear that the current initiative focused on replacing the software only in the US DBZ locations outside the US would be addressed in a subsequent project to be launched after the US initiative was completed.

"They're going to be upset," Max groaned to himself as he contemplated the disappointment and ruffled feathers he would need to deal with because of this decision. Part of his change management responsibilities would involve helping his colleagues outside the US understand how the current project affected them and ensure they developed realistic expectations about what was coming in the future.

"Well, at least I know about this now," Max considered as he thought more about the conversations he'd need to have with these colleagues. "Better for them to know what's happening right from the start."

Max wrapped up his review of the project charter and turned to the project plan. As he flipped through, he spotted trouble when he got to the *section on page 9, where Kevin had asked him to enter details related to training (Table 2-2).*

Table 2-2

Page 1 of 9						
Task Name	**Start**	**Finish**	**Duration**	**Percent Complete**	**Owner**	**Comments**
Analysis/Planning						
• Project kickoff meeting and scope confirmation	2/1/2021	2/2/2021	1		Kevin Louis	
• Conduct systems analysis	2/2/2021	2/8/2021	6		Kevin Louis	
• Create project plan	2/6/2021	2/8/2021	2		Kevin Louis	
• Schedule weekly implementation meetings	2/8/2021	2/9/2021	1		Kevin Louis	
• Conduct stakeholder analysis	3/1/2021	4/15/2021	45		Max Williams	
Configuration						
Application Form						
• Design application form	3/8/2021	3/10/2021	2		Kevin Louis	
• Build application form	3/11/2021	4/5/2021	25		Vendor	
• Review/approve application form	4/6/2021	4/13/2021	7		Kevin Louis	
• Revise application form based on feedback	4/14/2021	4/18/2021	4		Vendor	
• Final review/ approval of application form	4/19/2021	4/21/2021			Kevin Louis	
Cover Letter Form						
• Design cover letter form	4/1/2021	4/3/2021	2		Kevin Louis	
• Build cover letter form	4/4/2021	4/14/2021	10		Vendor	
• Review/approve cover letter form	4/15/2021	4/22/2021	7		Kevin Louis	
• Revise cover letter form based on feedback	4/23/2021	4/27/2021	4		Vendor	
• Final review/ approval of cover letter form	4/28/2021	4/30/2021	2		Kevin Louis	

Page 9 of 9						
Task Name	Start	Finish	Duration	Percent Complete	Owner	Comments
• User Training	8/21/2021	9/30/2021	40		Max Williams	
• Communications						

According to the dates Kevin and Bonita had included in the project plan, most of the training for the new system would occur during the late summer. In the past, Max had heard recruiters in DBZ's western and southern US divisions complain about how busy they were during the summer months, when hiring for these locations was at its peak. That probably wouldn't be the best time for DBZ to pull recruiters off the job and ask them to learn new work processes and software.

"That could be a problem," Max thought to himself as he made a mental note to check in with Kevin. "But we can ask recruiters what they think. We'll work together and figure out when it makes the most sense for training to occur."

Max continued to read through the project plan. He was pleased to see sections where Kevin and Bonita wanted him to fill in details regarding training and communications. "It's on their radar," Max recognized. "And I'm on their radar too."

As he finished looking at the documents Kevin asked him to review, Max pondered some of the tough conversations he'd need to have over the ensuing months. This project would require a lot of work, Max realized, but based on what he was seeing in the project charter and project plan, he felt confident the initiative would get off to a good start.

"Let the fun begin," Max announced to himself. He started typing comments into the plan.

What's happening here? We see Max, in his role as change management leader for DBZ's applicant tracking system project, review a project charter and project plan. Max recognizes that by defining the overall objective, scale, and scope of the project, the charter provides him with invaluable information he can use to help employees understand how the project would—and wouldn't—affect them. He also recognizes that by laying out all the tasks he and his project team needed to complete, and the dates by which each of these activities needed to occur, the project plan can help him coordinate with stakeholders to prevent conflicts between project-related activities and the other work key stakeholders needed to perform. By seeking input from stakeholders regarding details contained in the project plan, Max knows he can secure their buy-in and support.

In the chapters that follow in this section, we'll take a deeper look at each of the tools Kevin asked Max to review. We'll see that while the project charter and project plan are essential for addressing the hard side of change—we use them to define project objectives and deliverables, assign responsibilities, and track and monitor progress—they're essential for addressing the soft side of change too. In chapter 3, we'll review how you can use the project charter to build a shared understanding among stakeholders about what's changing and what isn't. You'll see that it's important to consider the full scope of the change your organization is embarking on, so you can speak accurately and honestly with stakeholders about what the change means for them. Then, in chapter 4, we'll look at the key components of the project plan. You'll see why it's so important to integrate training and communications into your plan, and seek feedback about the plan from those who are most affected by it. And as we discuss both tools, you'll see how the project leader and change management leader need to work hand in hand.

But first, think about a recent change initiative you were a part of, or perhaps you're just starting one. Did you have a project charter and a project plan? What documentation did you have that outlined the key details about the project? Was there agreement on what was to be done, in what timeframe, and by whom? What challenges did the absence of this up-front work present not just for the project, but for how well you were able to manage the change?

3

Determining
What's Changing

Twenty of us crowded around a conference table intended to seat only 12. The room was hot. But emotions that afternoon grew even hotter. We had just reviewed a scathing report prepared by our company's auditors. Apparently a series of missteps had occurred—along with some malfeasance in one division. Our job now was to redesign each and every process employees used to order parts and supplies and to ensure that more appropriate controls were in place. We needed to educate employees about these new processes and restrictions, help them understand why the new rules were important, and set up mechanisms for monitoring and reporting on employees' compliance. We also needed to make sure employees could still complete their work effectively and efficiently, despite all the additional layers of authorization. This wasn't the kind of change anyone would have chosen for our organization. But there we were. We were all clear about what we needed to accomplish, and we certainly understood why. If we were confused, all we needed to do was look back at the project charter our vice president had drafted for our project.

But our project team was in the weeds that day, and the bickering was getting intense. A supervisor whose area hadn't been implicated in the scandal questioned why she needed to change anything. After all, no one did anything wrong in her department. And another manager groaned as he reviewed all the times he would now be required to approve parts orders before his employees could submit them. "I'll never get any work done," he complained.

The vice president sponsoring our project shot me an angry look. When the auditors first issued their report, he had decided to make the changes by fiat, redesign all the processes himself, and just issue an edict stating that everyone needed to immediately comply. I convinced him to reconsider, to engage in a

> *more participatory process where supervisors and managers would redesign the*
> *process for the specific area they led. But with all the bickering, the project was*
> *going off the rails.*
>
> *"Guys, guys," I interrupted. "Let's take a step back. We're in the weeds*
> *here. Let's remember what we've set out to accomplish and why it's so import-*
> *ant." I redirected the team back to the project charter. I reminded everyone*
> *about the objectives we needed to accomplish over the next two months, and*
> *the rationale the vice president—and our company's auditors—provided for*
> *achieving those goals.*
>
> *The room quieted. "OK, let's keep going," one of my colleagues concurred.*

Over the next eight weeks, as we finalized new processes, explained them to employees, and monitored adherence, we'd refer back to that project charter numerous times. We'd use it to remind our team and employees across the company about what needed to change and why the change was important. And we'd use it to reinforce to supervisors and managers who participated on the project team that they owned responsibility for implementing and ensuring adherence to the change in the part of the organization they led.

Sometimes your organization will implement changes that employees welcome—like DBZ did in the applicant tracking system case you read in chapter 2. And sometimes your organization will implement changes that aren't welcome at all—like my company did as we responded to our auditors' report. In either case, you and your team need to have a clear sense of the outcome your organization wants to achieve and you need to know the reason why that outcome is so important. Armed with that information—the information provided by your project charter—you can motivate and guide employees to take steps they need to take to support the change, even when those steps are unwelcome.

In this chapter, we'll explore how a project charter can help you and your organization define the target you're shooting for in your change initiative and the reason for hitting that target. You'll see that the project charter addresses the hard side of change by defining expected outcomes and project deliverables. And it addresses the soft side of change by helping you build a shared understanding about what the change means for employees and why they should support it.

The Reasons for a Project Charter

What is a project charter, anyway, and why is it so critically important for your change initiative? When you create a project charter, you formally document the objectives that have been set for your project, its scope, and the roles and responsibilities of the key parties who will be involved. You'll define why your organization is embarking on the change initiative in the first place. You'll describe the outcomes your organization is shooting for—the overall business purpose and objective of the change. And you'll describe the scope of the change. What will change? What won't change? In the charter, you'll summarize the key players who are involved in the change. Who in your organization's leadership is authorizing the change initiative, whom will it affect, and who are the key people who will bring it to fruition? And you'll summarize key milestones and expected delivery dates.

Why is this so essential? Simply put, a project charter motivates action, creates shared understanding, and instills accountability.

Motivating Action

When you have a goal and understand why it's important, you're more likely to act. That's especially true when the steps you need to take to achieve the goal are onerous and unappealing. Trust me, when my organization needed to revise processes in response to a scathing report from our auditors, no one in the affected departments wanted to introduce more rigorous controls or additional layers of approval. But we had a project charter that clearly described the problem we needed to address. There were financial risks we needed to minimize and opportunities for fraud we needed to clamp shut.

Yet all too often, organizations launch change initiatives for which the goals are murky and employees question why their company is making them suffer through all the pain and disruption the change is bringing about. Employees may refer to change initiatives as "the flavor of the month," something they just have to endure until the winds shift and company leadership begins to focus on something else that's new.

Author and speaker Scott Mautz describes how leaders at Google have combated this problem. When Google leaders propose a new project, they're now required to clearly define: "What is the desired future state? . . . What will success . . . look like? . . . Why is change necessary? . . . What problem are you trying to solve?" If the project team is unable to provide clear answers to these questions, Google's leadership won't allow the project to proceed (Mautz 2018).

The project charter provides you with a vehicle for answering these critically important questions. The charter ensures you have defined the overall objective for your change initiative and the business purpose behind it before work begins.

Having that clear definition of the outcome you are shooting for and the rationale for achieving it will help inspire others to modify their behavior to bring that change about.

Creating Shared Understanding

The project charter also helps you create a shared understanding about what's in and out of scope for the initiative—that is, what is or isn't changing. Clarifying that up front, as your change initiative is just starting, helps you avoid misunderstandings and disappointment later on. It helps you create an environment in which people feel like your organization is being honest and forthright about how the change will affect them. And it helps you defend against scope creep, in which the project team may feel pressured to modify or expand project requirements as the initiative unfolds.

Consider the charter that Max reviewed in the DBZ applicant tracking system case you read in chapter 2. Max, in his role as change management leader for the project, experienced both surprise and relief when he saw what was in scope and out of scope for his project. On the one hand, Max saw that the scope of the project was larger than he had anticipated. Not only was DBZ implementing new technology; work processes and job roles would also change. Max appreciated seeing this early on. That way he could accurately communicate with DBZ employees about how the change would affect them. DBZ recruiters wouldn't learn late in the game that their jobs might change. Max could prepare them for that possibility right from the start. And that would help him build trust.

Max also learned that the scope of the project was somewhat smaller than he had anticipated. The current project would touch only recruitment staff based in the US. Max understood that recruiters based outside the U.S. would be disappointed when they learned they would have to wait for their outdated software to be replaced. But it was better for Max to address this head-on at the start of the project, rather than for recruiters to build up false hopes that Max would have to deal with later.

By clearly defining what is in and out of scope for a project, the charter provides information you can use to help stakeholders develop accurate expectations about what the change will mean for them.

Instilling Accountability

And finally, the project charter helps you create accountability for the change initiative. By defining the key players working on your project—the project leader and members of the core project team—the charter communicates to them and to the rest of your organization the work the team is expected to perform and the deliverables they are expected to produce. The charter puts the project leader and core project team on notice for doing the day-to-day work that's needed to make the change a reality.

That's what happened in my organization as project team members were charged with modifying the parts-and-supplies ordering process for the area they led, explaining the new process to employees, and monitoring employee adherence. The project charter made it clear to supervisors and managers on our project team that this was their responsibility. They needed to decide how to implement the change in their own departments, and they were accountable for making that happen.

By defining who is sponsoring the project—who in your organization's leadership has authorized the change initiative—the project charter communicates that leadership actively endorses the change. It creates a contract of sorts with senior leadership. It signals to them, and to everyone else, that senior leadership will actively and visibly do what's needed to bring the change about. It commits senior leaders to providing the decision making, budget, and people power needed for the initiative to succeed. By physically signing the project charter, project sponsors indicate that they are willing to put their names and reputations on the line.

Active and visible leadership provided from the top can be key to getting your project started on the right foot and to sustaining momentum throughout the initiative. If leaders aren't seen as advocates for the change initiative, employees likely won't get on board. You can use the project charter to commit senior leaders to their role and responsibilities as project sponsors. And you can use the charter to communicate to the rest of the organization that senior leadership supports the change.

As You Begin Work on Your Change Initiative, Ask . . .

- Does everyone working on the change initiative understand the objectives that have been established for the project and the outcomes it's intended to produce?
- Can we explain the problem our organization is experiencing and how the change will address it? Can we articulate why the change is necessary?
- Does everyone agree on what's in and out of scope for the project? Have we clarified what will change and what won't?

- Does everyone on the project team understand their role and what they're responsible for delivering?

 Creating a project charter can help you and your organization answer these questions with a resounding "yes."

Creating a Project Charter

Ideally, the project sponsor for your change initiative will take the lead in creating the project charter. This is their opportunity to clearly articulate what they expect the change initiative will deliver and why the initiative is so important for your organization to pursue. In practice, the project sponsor, project leader, change management leader, and a few key stakeholders affected by your change initiative may meet first to discuss the overall goals and purpose for the project. Then, based on that discussion, the project sponsor and project leader may collaborate to prepare a first draft that will be reviewed and possibly revised by others. If your project sponsor is a senior executive in your organization, they may ask someone on their staff—or the project leader—to draft the charter. That's OK, but the sponsor still needs to carefully review the draft to make sure it accurately reflects their vision, goals, and rationale for the project. They'll be signing the charter, which means their name—literally and figuratively—is on the line.

But what if you've been asked to help create a project charter? What should you include? If your organization already has a standard format or template for creating project charters, by all means use it! It helps to have consistent practices and processes across an organization. If your company doesn't have a standard format, here are the basic components you can include in the project charter you create.

Project Name

What's the name you have assigned to your change initiative? How can you refer to your change initiative in a few short words so most stakeholders will quickly understand what your project is about? For example, in the DBZ applicant tracking system case, the project leader assigned his project the name "Applicant Tracking System Phase 1: US." He did that so most people at DBZ would understand that the project involved implementing a system for tracking applicants, applied to the US only, and was the first phase of a multiphase initiative. As an alternative, you can give your project a name that conveys something about the tangible or intangible benefits the change will bring to your organization—something that might even inspire employees to get involved. For example, you could name a change initiative that involves overhauling the IT service model in your organization "Reimagining IT."

Start and End Date

When do you expect work, including planning, to begin? When do you expect work on the project to conclude?

Objective

What does the project accomplish for your organization? What will you have delivered when your project is complete? The objective should not be a lengthy, detailed description of the initiative. Just describe—in a few short sentences— what your project is about and why your organization is embarking on it. If your project involves something complex—like a large-scale system implementation— you can always include an attachment, such as a statement of work, that provides a more detailed description of the initiative.

For example, in the DBZ applicant tracking system case, the project charter (Table 2-1) stated that the objective was to "implement an online applicant tracking system that will provide job applicants with an easier, streamlined process for applying to DBZ job vacancies, and that will provide US recruiters with a more efficient process for managing recruitment, from posting job vacancies online and managing candidate information through to extending and tracking acceptance of job offers." The "what" of the project was to implement an online system to be used by applicants and recruiters. The "why" was to make things easier and more streamlined for applicants and more efficient for recruiters. The details of how that would be accomplished was provided in a statement of work that was listed as an attachment to the charter.

Deliverables in Scope and Out of Scope

What main products, services, features, or processes does your initiative address? What results will be delivered by the end of the project? And what won't be addressed? For example, in the DBZ applicant tracking system case, some of the deliverables included "integration with job-advertising systems," "online system for generating offer letters," and "revised recruitment workflow and processes."

As you think about what is in and out of scope for your change initiative, consider how your organization is a system made up of many interrelated and interdependent parts. A change in one place may affect many other parts of the organization. Just like at DBZ, when you change technology, you may need to change underlying work processes, and that may affect job roles and responsibilities too. If your project potentially involves changing job roles and responsibilities, be honest and say that. And if you aren't sure what the impact might be, it's OK to say that the project involves reviewing certain areas and that decisions will be made as the project unfolds. You want to avoid having people feel deceived when they realize, late in the game, that the project affected them to a greater extent than they anticipated. Likewise, you can avoid unnecessary anxiety by clearly communicating what is out of scope. If an organizational restructure is off the table, say so.

Use the project charter, and the description of what's in scope and what's out of scope, to be honest and up front with people about all of the elements the project entails and doesn't entail. The project charter can help you create a foundation of trust on which to build the rest of your change initiative.

Purpose and Benefits

Why is your organization embarking on the change initiative? What benefits does your project deliver, or what pain points does the initiative alleviate? Focus here on identifying the impact the change initiative will have on your organization as a whole. Why is senior leadership authorizing this project? Why are they committing resources to it? Will revenue increase? Will costs decrease? Will service improve or processes become more efficient? Does the initiative help your organization comply with new government regulations?

As the project unfolds, you can tailor the list of benefits to the unique needs and interests of each stakeholder group affected by the project. For example, in the communications and training you create for each stakeholder group, you can describe "What's in it for me?" customized to each specific audience. But in the project charter, focus on identifying the benefits your overall organization will receive by completing the project. And if the expected benefits can be quantified, provide those measurements too. For example, in the DBZ applicant tracking system case, the project charter listed the following benefits: "Improved ability to attract qualified job applicants," "Reduced time to fill job vacancies (expect reduction of 10 days in time to fill)," and "Reduced cost to fill job vacancies (expect reduction of $235 per vacancy)."

Key Milestones or Deliverables and Timeframe

What are the major tasks to complete for your initiative, and when will work on each of these tasks begin and end? For example, the charter for the DBZ applicant tracking system case listed these:

Major Milestone or Deliverable	Estimated Timeline
Stakeholder analysis	3/1/21–4/15/21
Configuration / integration design and development	3/8/21–7/8/21
Workflow process redesign	3/22/21–4/9/21
Recruiter job redesign	4/10/21–4/30/21
Create stakeholder engagement plan	4/10/21–4/17/21
Create communication materials	4/18/21–7/8/21
Create training materials	5/18/21–7/8/21
System testing	7/9/21–8/10/21
User acceptance testing	8/10/21–8/21/21
User training	8/21/21–9/30/21
Migration from old system	10/1/21–10/31/21
Go live with new system	11/1/2021
Advanced user training	11/15/2021–12/1/2021

Note that you probably won't fill in this section until you've created at least the first draft of your project plan. That's OK.

Sponsor

Who has established the vision for the initiative and is ensuring that appropriate resources and leadership focus are maintained throughout the project? Who in the organization's senior leadership ranks has authorized this initiative to take place? This may be a single individual or a committee comprising multiple senior leaders who have a key stake in the project outcome. We'll explore the role of the project sponsor in more depth in chapter 6.

Project Leader

Who will oversee the project as it moves through its various phases, from planning to execution and project close? Who will set priorities and manage day-to-day activities for the project, so that project activities occur on time and within budget? We'll explore the role of the project leader in chapter 6.

Core Project Team

Who will work on the project deliverables and key tasks? What role will they play? We'll explore more about the core project team in chapter 6.

Change Management Leader

Who will create and execute plans for engaging stakeholders affected by the project? Who will prepare communication and training plans? Who will ensure that the change initiative not only focuses on the business outcomes that need to be achieved, but addresses the needs and concerns of the people affected by the change? We'll explore the role of the change management leader in chapter 6.

Key Stakeholders

Who will be affected by the change? Who needs to buy into or support the change for it to succeed? Who might resist the change? Who will need help navigating through it? You'll likely fill in the details of this section as you complete your stakeholder analysis. We'll explore the stakeholder analysis in chapter 9.

Miscellanea

Some organizations include additional information in the project charter, including constraints and assumptions, key risks and steps for mitigating those risks, and a description of how the change initiative aligns with other organizational goals and priorities. Capturing all of this extra detail in the charter allows stakeholders to better understand the change initiative.

Attachments

What other details regarding your project will people reading the project charter want to see? What other documents can you attach to answer those questions? Readers of your project charter may want more details about project deliverables, who will be affected by the project and how, the project schedule, components of your communication and training plans, and the project budget. To help meet those needs, it may be useful to attach the following documents, most of which are described elsewhere in this book:

- Statement of work
- Budget
- Stakeholder analysis (see chapter 9)
- Project plan (see chapter 4)

- Communication plan (see chapter 12)
- Training plan (see chapter 13)

When you prepare the initial draft of your charter, some of these documents won't be complete. Your project leader and sponsor probably won't sign the project charter until they're absolutely clear about what the project will deliver (these details may be found in the statement of work) and how much it will cost (those details can be found in the budget). But at this point, the project plan and stakeholder analysis might be just a rough sketch. And you probably haven't even begun preparing the communication and training plans. You can attach these additional documents later on, even after the charter has been signed.

Signatures

Provide a space for the project sponsor, project leader, and change management leader to sign the charter. The project charter represents the shared understanding about what the project will deliver, the benefits it will produce, and the timeframe in which the project will proceed. By signing the charter, these people indicate that they agree to these goals, and are committed to doing the hard work—and providing the needed resources—to bring the change initiative to its successful conclusion.

Use an inclusive and iterative approach to refine your project charter. If your project sponsor and project leader prepared the initial draft, review what they created. Does the draft clearly explain what's changing and why your organization is embarking on the change initiative? Was enough thought given to what's in scope and what is out of scope? Does the timeline seem reasonable?

Recommend changes that can help make the project charter clearer and more comprehensive, so others can better understand what the project is about. Then review the draft charter with the rest of the core project team and incorporate their feedback. Likewise, present the draft charter to key stakeholders who will be affected by the initiative, and revise the plan to reflect their input, where applicable.

By using an inclusive process to create the project charter, sharing drafts with key stakeholders, and incorporating their feedback before the charter is finalized, you can increase the odds that your project will produce the intended results and that organizational members will support and endorse the change.

Questions to Ask Your Project Sponsor and Key Stakeholders as You Create a Project Charter

- What will the future look like when the project reaches its successful conclusion? How will work be different? Who will it be different for?
- What will people see or experience that will signal to them that the project is a success?
- What business benefits will the change produce? Why should the organization invest people, time, and financial resources on the project?
- For the project to succeed, what else needs to change? How will the change affect job roles, responsibilities, work processes, technology, the organizational structure, key policies? What falls within the scope of this project?
- What's off the table and out of scope for this project? What do we need to make sure we don't touch?
- Who will be affected by this project? Whom do we need to get involved and how?

Using the Project Charter

The charter has value only if you use it to guide planning and decision making as your project unfolds. As your team creates the project plan (see chapter 4), refer back to the charter. Does your plan address all of the elements that fall within the scope of the project? Have you strayed and started incorporating items that fall out of the scope? Are the actions you and the project team are taking contributing to the overall objective of the initiative? Are you producing the benefits and value you committed to the organization? The project charter provides the target your project team may need to stay focused as they work. And it also provides safety rails—here's what you're not supposed to touch.

Of course, after your charter is finalized and work on your project begins, your team may realize that a deliverable needs to be added, or that your team can't deliver something that you've committed to. For example, in the DBZ applicant tracking system case, after Max and his team begin working on the project, they may discover that it's just too complicated to integrate the new technology with their job-advertising system. Assuming their project sponsor agrees, they can amend the project charter to remove that deliverable. But usually, the key components that you've included in your project charter—the overall objective of your project, its purpose, and expected benefits—won't change as your project proceeds.

Use the project charter to help share information about the initiative with stakeholders. Share the charter with stakeholders during status-update meetings. Consider posting the charter in a cloud-based space your organization uses to support collaboration, such as Google Drive, Dropbox, or Microsoft OneDrive. Give stakeholders read-level access so they can check the details of the charter whenever they feel the need. In communications and training, keep referring back to the objectives, deliverables, and benefits described in the project charter. Use the charter as an anchor to direct stakeholders back to: This is what the organization is attempting to accomplish and why.

About to Begin?

Are you about to begin working on a change initiative in your organization? Reflect on the topics we addressed in this chapter. Ask yourself:

- Do we have a clear sense of the outcome we need to reach? Do we know what we're expected to deliver? Do people agree on what's in and out of scope for this project?
- Do we know why we're embarking on this change? Do we understand what the problem is that we're trying to solve?
- Do we understand how other parts of the organization will be affected when we make this change? For this change to work, what else—such as processes or organizational structure—needs to change?
- Do we have leadership commitment to proceed? Are leaders committed to assigning appropriate resources to support the change? Are leaders ready to serve as champions and advocates for the change?

Of course, you'll also need a project plan to guide your work. That's another tool that helps you address the hard side of change. But you may be surprised by how much you need to consider the soft side of change to create an effective project plan. We'll explore that further in chapter 4.

Learn More. Check Out:

Aston, B. 2019. "Write a Project Charter: How-To Guide, Examples & Template." *The Digital Project Manager,* July 5. thedigitalprojectmanager. com/project-charter.

Mautz, S. 2018. "Want to Better Manage Change in Your Workplace? Learn From Google and Start With These Questions." *Inc.*, August 2. inc.com /scott-mautz/google-is-revolutionizing-how-to-manage-change-starting -with-these-4-questions.html.

4

Creating the Path

At work, and outside work, you've probably seen and created lots of project plans. In your organization, you may have participated in or even led projects with a plan that laid out tasks to be completed, assigned people to each task, and set due dates. Or at school, you may have worked on a group project for which you sketched out a simple plan for how your team would get the assignment done. In your community, you may have collaborated on a project for which the steps, responsibilities, and timeframe were outlined. And you may have created your own simple plans for projects you've worked on independently—something you were expected to deliver by yourself at work, or an assignment you needed to complete on your own for school, or even a job you just wanted to get done around the house. You probably saw how these plans helped you focus on the goal you were working toward and organize the actions you needed to complete to achieve that goal. Maybe you used the plans to monitor your progress and figure out when you needed to make adjustments to get things done on time.

In this chapter, we're going to take a look at the project plans you and your team create to support change initiatives at work and the components you can include in them. You'll see that the project plan focuses on the hard side of change. It helps guide your organization forward in a disciplined way toward the outcome you're shooting for. But the steps you take to create your project plan can determine the extent to which employees buy into and support your project. In other words, as you create your project plan, you need to keep your eyes focused on the soft side of change.

Later in this chapter, we'll explore how you and your project team can address the soft side of change as you help prepare the project plan for your initiative. But first, it's worth stressing why the project charter and the project plan are so important.

Don't Skip the Project Charter or Project Plan

Are you and your team eager to get started with your change initiative? Are you tempted to skip past the project charter and jump right into creating a project plan? Maybe you think that everyone already knows what your project is trying to accomplish and why it's so important. Why waste the time building a charter when you're ready to dive right in?

Resist that temptation. For your change initiative to succeed, and for the project plan to serve its purpose of guiding you to your project outcome, you need to have a clear sense of the goal you are shooting for and the business purpose for reaching that goal. You need to have a shared understanding of what the change initiative will deliver, what will change, and what won't change. And you need to secure senior leadership support for the change and ensure they understand their role and responsibilities as it relates to the project. Before you begin creating your project plan, create a project charter. A simple one will do. If you're in doubt, reread chapter 3 before proceeding here.

Or maybe you're tempted to skip creating a project plan too. Avoid that mistake. As project management expert Andrew Conrad (2019) writes, "Starting a project without a plan is like taking a trip without a map. You might eventually get where you're trying to go, but not without wasting a lot of time and money." Without a well-constructed plan, your project team risks straying, and beginning work on tasks, features, and functionality that fall outside the scope of what you and your organization are trying to accomplish. You may end up missing deadlines and blowing budgets.

A project plan provides you with a structure and a road map for proceeding with your project. It helps you clarify the steps needed to get to your goal and the order in which these steps need to be taken. It helps you track progress and figure out where adjustments may be needed. It helps you create accountability and ownership for work that needs to be performed. And it helps you communicate the progress your organization is making. Have a plan.

Let me share a brief story of learning the hard way about the value a project charter and project plan can provide. I was working with a vice president of HR who'd asked me to head up a project to "fix new employee onboarding." Eager to help out, I assembled a project team, and we dove right in without a project charter or plan to guide us. At first our team discussions seemed pleasant and productive enough. But as the months progressed, team members began to express frustration over our lack of focus and started skipping project meetings. Apparently, some had joined the team expecting that they'd create an orientation program that would help new hires understand their medical and retirement bene-fits. Others assumed they'd be addressing the role that supervisors play during a new hire's first year of employment. Still others thought they'd be working on logistical gaps in the onboarding process; they wanted to make sure new hires received laptops and appropriate systems access their first day on the job. By not articulating a clear sense of what our team was expected to deliver, by when, and with what value to our organization, I had allowed our team to just wander. We weren't accomplishing anything. And as project leader, this was all my fault.

Trust me, the vice president of HR noticed. I had the same tense discussion with my VP as Anil, whom we met in chapter 1, did with his. Our conversation wasn't pretty. But fortunately, I was given an opportunity to recover. I realized our project needed to proceed in two phases—one focused on assessing the organiza-tion's issues with new employee onboarding, and a second focused on addressing the highest-priority needs we uncovered through this needs assessment. And I also realized, with the help of the VP, that I needed to prepare a project charter and project plan that would spell out what our team committed to deliver, the steps we'd complete to help get us there, who was responsible for each task, and expected completion dates. Once that was clear, I reassembled the team. And this time, we produced results that really did address our organization's needs and interests. We were late, because I first needed to learn my lesson about the importance of having a clear project charter and project plan. But eventually, we did help improve the new employee onboarding experience.

What's in Your Plan?

OK, perhaps you're convinced that you need a plan for your change initiative. But you still may think, why spend time looking at how the plan is created or what goes into it? Isn't that a project management function? Shouldn't the project leader create the project plan?

Well, yes they should. Usually, your project leader, with input from the proj-ect sponsor, project team members, and key stakeholders, will create the plan. Your role, as you lead and support change management for the initiative, is to review and provide input for that plan—and for the steps your team takes to create it—so the plan adequately addresses the soft side of change. You'll make sure your project team provides stakeholders with the opportunity to review and provide input for the plan. And you'll make sure that tasks related to stakeholder engagement, communication, and training are included in the plan so they align with everything else that's happening on the project. You probably won't take the lead creating the project plan, but you do need to understand what's in it, why, and the implications for building employee buy-in.

Let's take a quick look at the general components included in most project plans. Then we'll talk more about what you can do to ensure that the plan addresses the soft side of change.

Project Tasks

The project plan for your change initiative should list all the work that needs to be performed from the time the project begins to when it is completed. As your project leader drafts the plan, they may break down the project into its key elements and include steps for planning or designing each of these elements, creating them, reviewing them, making revisions, and finalizing them. For example, in the case study found in chapter 2, we saw a project plan that included steps for configuring a new job application (see Table 2-2). The tasks included:

- Design the application form.
- Build the application form.
- Review and approve the application form.
- Revise the application form based on feedback.
- Conduct a final review and approval of the application form.

In the project plan your project leader creates, you also may see tasks related to project planning and project management. For example, the project plan presented in chapter 2 included tasks like:

- A project kickoff meeting and scope confirmation
- Scheduling weekly implementation meetings

To make it easier to track and manage the status of your project, your project leader may organize tasks into milestones. A milestone is an event or interim stage that signals that a group of related tasks has been completed. It's still important to finish each individual task by its due date. But the milestone gives you an overarching target date to work toward for a group of tasks that belong together. It serves as a marker that you have advanced the project through a key stage.

For example, when you were in college, you may have considered the end of your freshman year to be a milestone. During your freshman year, you worked on tasks—in the form of completing classes—that helped you achieve the milestone of ending your status as a freshman. Finishing the requirements for your freshman year and advancing to sophomore status served as a marker that you were making progress toward completing your degree.

In the DBZ applicant tracking system case, the project plan grouped tasks related to initial project planning under the milestone of Analysis/Planning. Likewise, the plan grouped tasks related to designing, building, reviewing, revising, and finalizing the application and cover letter forms under the milestone of Configuration. Although the case study just shows pages 1 and 9 of the project plan, the full plan likely included many other milestones, such as System Testing, User Training, and Migration From the Old System. Each of these milestones served as a marker that Max and the team were making headway with the applicant tracking system project.

Milestones help you keep tasks organized. But they also help show your project team, organizational leaders, and project stakeholders that you are making progress. A milestone provides a marker to take notice of. You are partway there. Your hard work is beginning to pay off. You've achieved something that you can celebrate.

Timeframe

When does each task need to be finished by? For simple, short projects, your project plan may just indicate the date when each task needs to be completed. For more complex and lengthy projects, the plan may include other information in addition to the finish date, such as the start date, duration (expressed in days or weeks), and percent complete. These additional elements can help you and your team better track progress as you work on the many steps needed to bring the project to its conclusion. That's what Max saw in the project plan he reviewed in the DBZ case. The project was expected to take about nine months to complete.

As your project leader assigns timeframes to the tasks listed in the project plan, they'll consider task order and task dependencies. Some tasks need to be completed in a certain order to make sense. For example, in the DBZ case, it probably makes sense to notify recruiters about the upcoming project before notifying hiring managers. Although both recruiters and hiring managers are affected by the change initiative, the impact on recruiters is far more significant. So the project plan should show an earlier completion date for the task of informing recruiters than the task of informing hiring managers.

Likewise, certain tasks must be completed before work on another task can begin. In other words, one task may be dependent on another. The start date and finish dates included in the project plan need to reflect those dependencies. For example, at DBZ, the task of designing how recruiters will post vacancies to the new system likely needs to be completed before Max can begin the task of developing training for that new process. As your project leader assigns a time-frame to each task in the project plan, they'll think about task order and task dependencies, and make sure the dates they assign make sense.

Owner

Who is responsible for ensuring each task is completed? To build ownership and accountability, the plan should list the name of the specific person responsible for getting each task done. For example, in the DBZ case, instead of saying that the training plan will be prepared by the "change management team," Max is listed by name as the person responsible for getting that work done.

Some organizations include additional elements—such as status or comments—in their project plans. If your organization provides a standard format or template for creating project plans, become familiar with it. A template can help you save time as you define the change management tasks related to stakeholder analysis, communication, and training, which need to be incorporated into the overall project plan. By using the format that others in your organization are already used to seeing, you can help them save time as they read and review the part of the plan that you're responsible for providing. Of course, you and your team can create a project plan using a simple spreadsheet. And there are lots of software packages available that can help you build one too. If your organization provides you with access to one of these software packages, use it! By using a tool your organization already endorses, you'll build credibility and make it that much easier for everyone to get on board with your change initiative.

Does Your Organization Use Agile?

Some organizations use an approach to project planning and project management called Agile. A hallmark of the Agile method is that projects proceed in short iterations, often called sprints. In each iteration, a small portion of the project that will provide value to the end user—some feature or function—is completed. Then users try out the feature and provide immediate feedback about changes they'd like to see. The team prioritizes the changes, and work continues on the feature in a series of short bursts until the feature is complete. The goal is to create a solution that better meets user needs and provides users with something of value sooner, rather than having them wait until the very end of a project, when the entire solution is complete. The goal is also to shorten the overall amount of time needed to complete a project.

When a project team uses Agile methodology, they don't create a detailed plan for the entire initiative at the outset. Instead, details are laid out at the beginning of each sprint. If you work for an organization that uses the Agile approach for project management, follow the guidelines your organization provides.

To learn more, read the chapter "Applying Agile Techniques to Change Management Projects," written by Bob Tarne, in the book *How Successful Organizations Implement Change: Integrating Organizational Change Management and Project Management to Deliver Strategic Value.*

Have You Been Asked to Create a Project Plan?

- Make sure you're clear on the outcomes you're shooting for. What key deliverables are you expected to produce, by when, and why? What's in your project charter?
- Break down the project into its core elements, phases, or key outputs—such as needs assessment, programming, testing, and rollout—then identify the steps that need to be completed in each.
- Include tasks for project and change management activities, such as "schedule weekly project-update meetings" or "conduct stakeholder analysis."
- Group tasks into key milestones so you can show that you and your team are making progress and can celebrate their success.
- As you assign target completion dates, consider the order in which tasks need to be completed and make sure you've accounted for task dependencies.
- To build accountability and ownership, specify by name the person responsible for completing each task.
- Before you finalize the plan, ask for input from your project sponsor, project team members, and key stakeholders and incorporate their feedback.

Addressing the Soft Side

Much of what we've discussed so far in this chapter addresses the hard side of change. We've looked at how you can create a project plan that helps you make progress on the outcomes you're supposed to deliver. But for the project plan to really serve its purpose of guiding your organization to its desired future state, you and your team need to organize project deliverables and tasks in a way that show people that their hard work and sacrifices are paying off. You need to provide opportunities for stakeholders to contribute to the development of the plan so they feel like it is relevant and realistic. And you need to incorporate activities related to engaging with stakeholders, communicating, and training into the plan so actions that address stakeholder needs and concerns are given priority and not considered a mere afterthought. As you and your project team create the project plan, you need to focus on the soft side of change. Let's take a closer look at how.

Create Short-Term Wins

As you plan how your project will unfold—identifying tasks and organizing them into milestones—one of the most significant actions you and your team can take is to plan ways for the project to deliver short-term wins. A short-term win is a benefit your project delivers before the project has reached its conclusion. It's an outcome that produces some value to your organization while your project is still ongoing. It's an interim result that stakeholders can experience for themselves and lets them know that the project is beginning to yield benefits before it's even complete.

Why are short-term wins so important? According to change management guru John Kotter (1996), they provide people with concrete evidence that the organization is embarking on a successful endeavor. This is especially important if other change initiatives conducted in your organization have recently failed. Short-term wins help you demonstrate that this change initiative will be different, because it's already producing valuable results. They show those who doubt the value or viability of your change initiative that the project can and will benefit your organization. They can help quell the cynics and naysayers and turn people who are sitting on the fence into supporters. And they can provide the evidence people need to get on board—or at least to stop actively resisting.

Ideally, your project team will find a way to structure your project so that it delivers multiple short-term wins over the course of the entire project. This may come in the form of introducing the change to a small portion of your organization before the change is rolled out enterprise-wide. Perhaps you can implement the change initiative department by department or region by region. If the change initiative involves implementing new technology, you may be able to introduce new features and functionality over the course of the system implementation, rather than waiting until the end of the project, when all the functionality is live. Or maybe you can introduce some new work processes first, before the associated new technology comes on board, so employees can experience a more streamlined workflow before they begin using the updated systems. However you do it, look for ways to plan your change initiative so people can see and experience the project generating value before the project reaches its end.

For example, a large university wanted to change the approach it used to staff temporary positions, so that significantly more employment opportunities were provided to students. The university released new guidelines that required managers to post most temporary jobs on the university's student employment website for one week. If they weren't able to find a student with the appropriate qualifications during that week, only then could the manager approach a temporary staffing agency to fill the vacancy with a nonstudent. The university announced that the plan was to initially launch these new guidelines in three administrative departments, which would test the approach. Following that pilot test, the new guidelines would be phased in over a three-month period across the rest of the university.

Many managers initially balked at the announcement. Although they supported the idea of providing employment opportunities to students, they doubted whether the approach would work in their part of the university. After all, they complained, the work performed in their area was unique. When they hired a temporary worker, they needed to bring on board someone who had specialized skills—the kinds of skills not typically found in student workers. And yet, within weeks of launching the test, news started circulating across the university about how well the plan was working. Managers in the three administrative departments where the approach first launched started to share glowing testimonials about the student workers they'd brought on board. These student employees had sorely needed software skills and administrative capabilities that the managers quickly pressed into service. And because the student workers were paid through the university payroll system, managers avoided paying overhead fees to the temporary staffing firms too. The new approach gave managers temporary staff who had the right skills at a reduced cost. And it helped the university make progress toward achieving its overall goal of increasing student employment. Based on news of these early wins, managers in several departments not included in the early rollout began to implement the idea in their part of the university before it was required. The early evidence convinced them to try out the idea.

Planning for short term wins also can help you test out strategies and refine them as your project unfolds (Kotter 1996). For example, when the university tested the new temporary staffing guidelines in three departments, it quickly discovered that its procedures for handling student-worker timesheets were cumbersome and needed to be updated. The university changed these procedures before the new guidelines were rolled out university-wide. During the test, the university also found that the guidelines worked well for certain kinds of temporary staffing needs, but didn't work as well for other kinds of positions. So, it refined the guidelines to identify the specific types of temporary positions managers should seek student workers to fill. Managers could continue to rely on temporary agencies to fill vacancies that were not listed in the guidelines. Planning for a short-term win helped the university uncover and address issues before they were experienced on a larger scale. It helped the university avoid unnecessary, but valid, pushback and complaints.

Short-term wins let people know that the sacrifices they're making to implement your change initiative are worth it. It helps people see that their hard work is beginning to pay off (Kotter 1996). For example, when organizations implement large-scale enterprise resource planning (ERP) systems that affect employees in just about every functional area across the organization, they typically plan their rollout to occur in a series of phases that unfold over several years. During these years, day-to-day work can become more challenging—at least temporarily—for employees. All the planning and disruption that goes into switching processes and technology can feel like a real slog, and employees may stress over having to relearn tools required for them to perform their jobs. Organizations that are most successful at implementing these systems find ways to engineer into their plans multiple short-term wins that unfold throughout the course of the project. They implement one or two features or functions at a time—something that makes work better or easier for employees—so employees begin experiencing the benefits that the new system is intended to provide as soon as possible. (Think Agile!) The ERP implementation may still take years to complete, and may still be disruptive, but employees see early on that their struggles are worth it.

And finally, short-term wins help keep senior leaders engaged, and their active and visible support is critically important to keeping others across the organization on board (Kotter 1996). Project sponsors and senior leaders usually focus on the business outcomes that change initiatives are expected to deliver. A short-term win can provide leaders with the concrete evidence they need to confirm that their organization is on the right path. Armed with this evidence, leaders are more willing to advocate for the initiative as they communicate with the larger organization.

So whether you're preparing a project plan—or reviewing and providing input on a plan created by your project leader—look for opportunities to incorporate short-term wins. They can help you increase stakeholders' sense of confidence that the change initiative will succeed. They'll help you build support and quiet resistance, so people will be more likely to try out the change. They'll help you fine-tune plans and avoid unnecessary errors. And they'll help you keep senior leaders and project sponsors engaged, so they're more likely to demonstrate active support for your project (Kotter 1996).

Involve Stakeholders

For people to feel like the project plan is viable and realistic—that it provides a good path to help the organization reach its goal—they need to see that input and guidance was sought from those who will be most significantly affected by the change. People need to see that the plan is based on credible knowledge and insight—that the leaders and team members planning the change have an accurate sense of the way things currently function before they begin to change things. For people to believe that your project plan is workable, they need to know that you and your team involved stakeholders appropriately in developing the plan. And quite honestly, you need to involve stakeholders for your plan to actually be workable too.

Encourage your project leader to use an iterative approach when they create the project plan, wherein multiple drafts are prepared and then refined based on input gathered from an ever-widening circle of people who are affected by the project. For example, your project leader may collaborate with the project sponsor to prepare an initial draft. Next, they might ask you to review the plan from a change management perspective. That's your opportunity to add in details related to stakeholder engagement, communication, and training. At the same time, your project leader may ask the core project team for their review from a functional and technical perspective. Your project leader then may share a version of the plan that's been updated to incorporate all this feedback with key stakeholders—perhaps supervisors of the areas most affected by the change. And later you have an opportunity to share a further modified version of the plan with additional stakeholders—for example, members of the transition monitoring team, if your organization is using that approach (see chapter 7 for more information about creating a transition monitoring team), and members of your red team (see chapter 8 to learn why and how to create a red team). Each time the plan is reviewed by another group of stakeholders, you, your project leader, and the project team should be gathering and incorporating information that makes the project plan more complete and realistic. Gaps in the plan should be addressed. Missing steps should be added. Unworkable timeframes should be changed.

That's the approach that Kevin, Bonita, and Max may have used in the DBZ case you read in chapter 2. We know that Kevin, in his role as project leader, and Bonita, in her role as project sponsor, collaborated to create an initial draft of a project plan. They shared the first draft with Max, who was serving as change management leader on the project, to gather his input. Kevin and Bonita also may have planned to share the project plan with members of their core project team, after the plan was updated to reflect Max's input. And after that, they may have shared the plan with recruiters most affected by the system implementation to secure their feedback and guidance. By using an iterative approach, gathering input from additional groups of stakeholders and refining the project plan to reflect their guidance, DBZ could create a more complete and realistic plan. With each iteration, they could identify and incorporate improvements that would increase the odds that their project would succeed.

By involving stakeholders in the process of creating the project plan, DBZ also would send an early signal that the company intended to follow an inclusive process as the project unfolded. It would let recruiters know that their input and ideas mattered—that their involvement was in fact essential for getting the project started on the right foot. Including stakeholders in the development of the project plan would help DBZ create a more workable plan and help the company secure the support of those most significantly affected by the initiative.

One final comment here: As you, your project leader, and team prepare draft versions of the project plan, avoid accidently disrespecting stakeholders by specifying details about tasks you need them to complete when you really don't know anything about the work involved. Don't make assumptions about how they'll perform a task or about the amount of time they'll need to complete it. Just let stakeholders know what you need them to accomplish and ask them to provide the detailed steps.

For example, if you know that a website needs to be created by your organization's IT team, but you are unfamiliar with the work entailed to get that done, just include in the project plan the expected outcome ("website created") and ask the IT team to provide the detailed tasks—such as design, programming, and testing—and due dates associated with that outcome. Then update your plan to include the details the stakeholder provided. Likewise, don't assume that you know the amount of effort an area needs to complete a task. If you don't know how long it will take a stakeholder to get work done, just list the task on the project plan with an expected due date, and ask the stakeholder to provide the date that work on the task will need to begin for them to get the work done on time. For more information about involving stakeholders in the process of creating a project plan, check out Lou Russell's insightful book *Project Management for Trainers.*

Incorporate Soft-Side Tasks Into the Project Plan

Your project plan should spell out *all* of the work that needs to be completed to bring your change initiative to fruition. And that means that activities such as creating the stakeholder analysis, creating and executing a communications plan, and preparing and delivering training need to be incorporated into your overall project plan. It's OK to have the details of these activities described in separate documents. But the key tasks and due dates defined in these plans need to be listed in your main project plan too. Tasks that address the soft side of change—actions that focus on building awareness, knowledge, and support for your change initiative—need to be planned, executed, and monitored just like any other task in your plan. Make sure these tasks aren't included as an afterthought. They need to be listed as important steps in your overall plan, just like any other task.

Why is this so important? Well, all too often, when organizations plan major change initiatives, activities that address the people side of change are given short shrift. In the rush to get things done, organizations focus on activities needed to install new technology or relocate people and equipment or redefine job descriptions and reporting relationships. They lose sight of the activities needed to help people navigate through these changes—actions that address communications, training, support building, and resistance. And yet, many change initiatives fail when the team ignores these soft-side actions.

Including activities related to stakeholder analysis, communications, and training in your overall project plan gives these tasks visibility, and visibility creates accountability. As your organization implements its project plan, project sponsors and project leaders want to see progress being made on all of the tasks listed there. Including tasks that address the soft side of change in your plan creates the expectation that these tasks will be completed too. These tasks need resources assigned to them. They need to be monitored and tracked. They need to be discussed and reported on. Including soft-side tasks in your overall project plan signals that they are key to the success of the project, just like everything else.

So when you're asked to lead or support change management for a project that's happening in your organization, ask to get involved right from the start. Let your project leader know that you want to—you need to—review the project plan and provide input. You want the opportunity to ensure that the plan appropriately addresses the soft, people side of change. You want to ensure that tasks related to stakeholder engagement, communication, and training are included so they align with and support all the other tasks that are specified in the plan. And you're willing to be held accountable for those tasks, just like everyone else on the project team.

Ensure That Your Project Plan Addresses the Soft Side of Change
- Build in short-term wins that help stakeholders experience benefits early on as the initiative proceeds.
- Encourage your project leader and team to use an iterative approach as you create drafts of the plan. Incorporate input and feedback from organizational leaders, key stakeholders, supervisors, and managers of areas affected by the change, and members of your transition monitoring and red teams.
- Build visibility and accountability for change management activities by including details regarding stakeholder analysis, communication, training, and other stakeholder engagement activities in the overall plan.

About to Begin?

Have you been asked to lead or support change management for a project in your organization? Build credibility as a change leader by demonstrating your project management skills—by showing that you can not only support the organization through the soft side of change, but also contribute to managing the hard side of change. Learn how to speak the language of project management, and how to use project management tools such as the project charter and project plan. Find out what templates, tools, or software your organization uses to create project plans, and then use those same tools as you create the communications and training plans needed to support the change initiative. Having a consistent approach will make it easier to incorporate all the elements into the main project plan. And you'll also show that you are a key part of the team, speaking the same "language" and using the same tools as everyone else who is working on the project.

To continue building your skill, create formal project charters and project plans for your own work-related initiatives. Practice on your own projects. And if you work in an organization that uses the Agile methodology to plan and execute projects, see if it makes sense to apply that same approach to your own work.

This chapter wraps up section 1. In it, we addressed the steps you can take to create a project charter and project plan. We discussed why it's so important to clearly define the outcome your organization is shooting for—what's changing and what isn't—and to build a clear path that will lead your organization to that outcome. We discussed how there are lots of people that you and your team will need to get involved to develop and execute project charters and project plans that really work. Along the way, I mentioned project sponsors and project leaders, core project teams, change management leaders, stakeholders, and transition monitoring and red teams. A lot of people are involved in a change initiative. In section 2, we take a much closer look at all these people—and a few others too—who are so critical to the success of your change initiative. We'll look at how you can help identify the right people to include in your change initiative and how you can involve them in the right way. Are you ready to meet them? Read on.

Learn more. Check out:

Project Management Institute. 2017. *A Guide to the Project Management Body of Knowledge* (PMBOK Guide).

Russell, L. 2015. *Project Management for Trainers.* Alexandria, VA: ATD Press.

Tarne, B. 2017. "Applying Agile Techniques to Change Management Projects." In *How Successful Organizations Implement Change*, edited by Emad Aziz and Wanda Curlee. Newtown Square, PA: Project Management Institute.

Involving the Right People in the Right Way

5

The JCo Acquisition Case

It was a done deal. Luis, director of learning and development at Wilab Holdings, mulled over the news that Sheila, the company's new head of business development, had relayed to him that morning. Wilab, a leader in the specialty foods market, was acquiring JCo. The deal fit with Wilab's strategy of growing through acquisitions, and it would help Wilab break into organics. Sheila had called the acquisition "opportunistic" and explained that the deal would proceed much faster than usual. JCo had been on the market for a while, and its expected buyer had just dropped out. So Wilab swooped in and made the purchase. The acquisition would be announced in a matter of weeks.

"I'm going to need your help with acquisition integration," Sheila had explained. "JCo is going to continue to operate as a separate company for a short while. But then it will probably begin using our business processes and technology—our financial tools, the sales management system, procurement processes, our HR system. And a few JCo executive assistants will face job eliminations. It will be a big change. So start by thinking about who at each company we need to get involved in planning and executing the integration."

Luis groaned. He imagined that JCo employees might feel resentment, sensing that their beloved little start-up was about to be devoured by the big, bad Wilab. And they likely would feel angry about the job cuts in the executive assistant ranks. But, he thought, many JCo employees might feel relief, knowing that they now had Wilab's substantial financial and operational resources to tap into. The change would be significant for Wilab too. Just last week, Luis had heard Wilab's head of IT complain that the company's financial and HR systems were stretched to their limits. The company had acquired three new businesses in the past two years, and the number of users accessing its systems had exceeded what they were designed to accommodate.

Luis also wondered what it would be like collaborating with Sheila. This would be their first time working together since Sheila had joined Wilab, and Luis wanted to make a good first impression. From his experience working on other acquisitions, Luis knew that the more people they could involve in the integration effort, the better. But he wasn't sure if Sheila held the same view. He prepared a document that summarized the best practices he'd used in the past. But Luis still felt uneasy as he emailed Sheila his recommendations later that afternoon. About an hour after hitting send, Luis called Sheila to walk her through the file.

"As I'm thinking about who to include in the acquisition integration," Luis explained, "I'm pretty confident we'll need four different teams."

Sheila cut him off before he could elaborate. "Four teams?" she challenged.

Luis sensed some agitation and skepticism in Sheila's voice, so he switched gears. "Let's focus on the core project team," Luis counseled. "We need employees from Wilab and JCo to plan the nuts and bolts of the integration."

"That's what I had in mind," Sheila concurred. "We need to get this right. We need the A team. So who are you thinking about?"

Luis proposed forming a project team that included some strong performers he knew in both companies—people who could represent the departments most affected by the integration and who had enough authority to make some of the key decisions the project team would be charged with. Sheila agreed to most of Luis's recommendations and suggested a few other employees. When they were done brainstorming, Luis decided to see if he could encourage Sheila to consider some additional names.

"What if we thought about the core project team from a leadership development perspective?" Luis proposed. "We absolutely need to include employees who already have technical expertise and who have the authority to make decisions. But what if we expanded the team just a bit to include a few folks we've got our eyes on for future leadership roles? This project could be just the leadership development experience some Wilab and JCo employees need."

"Maybe," Sheila replied. "But I'm not sure how they'll learn anything from this project. So, I'm not agreeing. But maybe."

Luis decided to take "maybe" as a win. He looked at his notes and pressed on. "We haven't spoken yet about the change management team. We need a team that plans communications and training," Luis continued.

"Yeah, I'm fine with that," Sheila quickly assented. "We definitely need people to create communications and training."

Luis actually thought the change management team could do much more than that, but he decided not to press his luck. Sheila had already agreed to two of the four teams he was proposing. True, they were the most obvious ones: They needed a project team to work on integration planning, and they needed someone to focus on communication and training. Still, Luis wondered if he could nudge Sheila a little further.

"You know, Sheila," Luis proposed, "I think we need a transition-monitoring team."

"Wait, aren't we already creating a change management team?" Sheila queried. "Isn't that the same thing? What's this other team for?"

"The transition-monitoring team is different," Luis explained. "The change management team has responsibility for actually planning communications and training. The transition-monitoring team will let us know how well these plans are working."

"You're asking a lot," Sheila responded. "I don't want a free-for-all. If we have too many people working on the integration, it's going to get unwieldy."

"Don't worry, I have a plan for that," Luis replied.

"Fine. What's this other team you want to propose?"

Luis moved on to explain the fourth team he had recommended in his email to Sheila. "I know this acquisition is a done deal," Luis explained. "But I think we need a red team."

Luis hoped this would get Sheila back into his corner. He knew that Sheila had used red teams in the acquisitions and divestitures department at her former workplace. Each time the company evaluated whether to purchase a company, they assembled a team whose sole purpose was to poke holes in the deal—to come up with all the reasons their company should stop and walk away. The goal was to ensure that in their excitement about the benefits an acquisition could bring, they didn't start ignoring warning signs that this was a bad deal.

"I love the red team concept," Sheila responded.

Luis wondered for a second if he had scored another win. But Sheila continued, "The JCo acquisition is already a done deal. It's a go. I don't think a red team would be useful here."

Luis wanted to explain his logic, but Sheila wasn't done speaking. "Let's say for a moment I agree with your idea to set up four teams," Sheila asserted. "And I'm not saying I do agree. But if we had the four teams, have we identified everyone who needs to be involved?"

"That's a great question," Luis responded. "Even with the four teams, I don't think we've got everybody."

For a second, Luis thought he heard Sheila groan.

"To answer your question, I think we need to conduct a stakeholder analysis," Luis explained. "You know, brainstorm all the people and groups who will be touched by the changes this acquisition will bring. And the people who can have an impact on whether the acquisition is successful or not. Then we can figure out how to involve each person or group in the right way."

"Four teams plus a stakeholder analysis?" Sheila queried. "You're recommending a lot, Luis. It's going to be a free-for-all."

"I agree there's a lot of people and moving parts," Luis responded. "But we can construct a RACI matrix that will help clarify—"

"Stop, Luis. Stop," Sheila interrupted. Luis could see he had lost Sheila again. "I want to involve the right people in the right way," she continued. "And I'm sure you do too. But with all these teams and processes, I think you may have lost sight of the problem we're trying to solve here."

Luis sat in silence as he tried to understand the pushback he was getting from Sheila. This conversation wasn't going well.

"Here's what I want you to do, Luis," Sheila continued. "Go back and think about the challenges we're trying to address. I'm not saying I disagree with what you're proposing. But you have to convince me that we're doing all of this for the right reason. What's the problem we're trying to solve here?"

Luis remained silent for another moment as he tried to absorb what Sheila was saying. "I'll do that, Sheila," Luis finally responded. "I agree we both want to involve the right people—and only the right people—in the right way. And I agree, we don't want a free-for-all. Let me do some thinking and I'll call you back."

Luis hung up the phone and let out a groan. Things were so much easier when Luis had worked with Wilab's prior head of business development. He didn't question Luis's recommendations. But here was Sheila, a newcomer, challenging everything he had to say.

Luis closed his eyes and inhaled deeply. He was trying to regroup. After a few deep breaths, he started to think that, just maybe, Sheila was right. Maybe, in his pitch, he hadn't been clear about the problems he was trying to address. Perhaps, he should have started off by outlining the challenges he thought Wilab would face during the acquisition integration. Then he could show how the teams and approaches he recommended could address those challenges.

Luis thought back to the acquisitions and other change initiatives he had worked on in the past. Why did some of them go off the rails anyway? And what were the issues they faced trying to involve the right people in the right way?

Luis started typing furiously on his laptop. A half hour later, he read back the notes he had organized into a table (Table 5-1).

Table 5-1. Luis's Notes for Tools to Solve Wilab's Problems

Problem We Encountered When We Didn't Involve the Right People in the Right Way	Tool or Approach to Address the Problem
• We made faulty decisions and experienced delays when we didn't assign people with the right knowledge, skills, authority, and credibility to work on the project. • We missed the opportunity to develop employees' leadership skills when we included only proven leaders in the change effort.	Core Project Team
• Employees were confused about what was happening within the organization, they didn't have the knowledge or skills needed to support what was changing, and they didn't buy into the change when we failed to allocate the right resources to focus on communication, training, and building support.	Change Management Team
• We didn't fully understand what was important to the people most affected by the change when we didn't gather enough input from employees "on the ground." • There was confusion, miscommunication, and gossip when employees filled the void in communications with speculation and rumors. • We failed to generate buy-in and support among employees when we didn't leverage those who were willing to advocate for the change.	Transition-Monitoring Team
• We failed to see the faults and mistaken assumptions in our plans when we didn't hear from the naysayers and people who were skeptical about the change effort.	Red Team
• We made misguided decisions because we didn't thoroughly understand the current state and how things would change when we didn't identify everyone who would be affected by the change, and how they would be affected. • Employees didn't buy into and support the change when we failed to identify influencers and other key people who could shape—in either a positive or a negative way—how others would view what was coming. • Employees affected by the change felt anxiety, resentment, and anger when they felt we didn't provide them with appropriate opportunities to participate in the change effort.	Stakeholder Analysis
• People felt confused and resentful, and we experienced delays when we failed to clarify the roles, responsibilities, and authority of each person involved with the change. • Employees resisted adopting the change when they perceived that they should have had more say in how the change was implemented.	RACI matrix

"OK, I know what to do," Luis thought to himself. He realized that his recommendations hadn't changed. He still thought Wilab needed to establish four teams, conduct a stakeholder analysis, and construct a RACI matrix.

But he recognized that he needed to alter the way he presented his ideas to Sheila. He would start by discussing the problems they needed to solve, then show how the team or approach he was recommending would help address the problem. "I can do this," Luis announced to himself with renewed confidence. He redialed Sheila.

"Hi, Sheila," Luis began. "You're right. Can we do this again?"

Let's explore what happened here. When Sheila called Luis and asked for ideas about whom to involve in the JCo acquisition integration, she likely was focused on all the work that had to get done to successfully complete the integration project. After all, business decisions needed to be made regarding how Wilab and JCo would operate after the purchase was complete. It's possible that Sheila wanted Luis's help to figure out who was going to implement these decisions once they were made.

But Luis interpreted Sheila's question about who to involve in the integration project from a much broader perspective. He thought about how the project team would make smarter, more informed decisions if it gathered input from the numerous parties affected by the acquisition. He thought that Wilab and JCo could help allay the anxiety employees were bound to feel regarding the acquisition and could head off unproductive rumors before they had a chance to circulate if they provided employees with opportunities to actively participate in the change effort. Luis understood that for the JCo acquisition to succeed, Wilab and JCo needed to plan and operate the project from both the hard side—making smart, informed decisions and getting all the work organized and done on time—and from the soft side; that is, ensuring that the employees affected by the change felt they had the appropriate say in how that work would be completed. He knew that whether he was working on an acquisition, an organizational restructure, a software implementation, a leadership change, or something else, the company needed to involve the right people in the right way for the change to succeed. That's probably why Luis wanted to set up so many teams and involve so many people.

And yet, Sheila was right to be concerned too. When embarking on a change initiative, you need to be clear about the challenges you're facing and the problems you're trying to solve. And you need to ensure that each action you take serves a purpose—that each tool or approach you deploy meets a real need and will help make things better. You need to be sure you're using scarce resources—especially people's time—wisely. And you want to be clear about how and why you're asking people to participate, so you avoid a free-for-all.

In the remaining chapters in this section, we'll look at the challenges your organization may face as you try to involve the right people in the right way in your change initiatives. And we'll look at the tools and approaches you can use to address these challenges. Just like Luis, you'll see that to involve the right people in the right way, you need to:

- Allocate resources with the right skills, authority, and credibility to guide project planning and execution. In chapter 6, you'll see how the core project team can help you do that.
- Assign and integrate resources focused on communication, training, and building support. In chapter 6, you'll learn how the change management team can help you tackle this challenge.
- Gather input and build advocacy for your change initiative from people "on the ground." In chapter 7, you'll see why you should consider establishing a transition-monitoring team to address this need.
- Hear from the skeptics and naysayers, so you can identify and address the flaws in your planning. In chapter 8, you'll see how the red team can help you here.
- Understand who's affected by the change and how. In chapter 9, we'll cover how you can conduct a stakeholder analysis to meet this need.
- Clarify roles, responsibilities, and authority. In chapter 10, you'll learn how to construct a RACI matrix to help you address this challenge.

As you read each chapter, you'll see that some tools will help you address the challenges presented by the hard side of change. And you'll see that to use these tools effectively, there are soft-side factors you need to consider. Likewise, for the tools designed to help you address the soft side of change, you'll need to consider some hard side factors.

Are you eager to find out how to involve the right people in the right way? Let's get started.

6

Leading and Managing the Change

I have to admit that as a learning and organization development profession-al, I knew next to nothing about how annual budgets were approved in my organization. Yet there I was, sitting in a project kickoff meeting, listening to a presentation about the company's plan to completely overhaul its budget approval process. The company's CFO had just wrapped up explaining why the current process wasn't working and how he needed all of us to design a new approach and implement it across the organization. I scanned the room and saw that most of the meeting participants had far more expertise in finance and accounting than I did. What could I add to this effort, I wondered?

But then Sunita, the company's director of financial systems, chimed in and described the various roles and responsibilities the meeting attendees would play to help guide the project. The company's CFO was our project sponsor, and Sunita would serve as project leader. The four division finance managers in attendance would provide input about how the current budget approval process worked and would help guide the design of a new process. Two representatives from the company's IT team would coordinate all the technology changes that needed to be made. And the company's head of change management and I would create and implement plans that addressed communications, training, and build-ing employee support for the initiative.

We were the "Reimaging Budgets Team!" How utterly unexciting, I laughed to myself. But it was what it was. I just hoped I could help.

In the months that followed, I learned more about the company's budget creation and approval process than I ever really wanted to know. And yet at the same time I also discovered that I absolutely could and would contribute a lot to the success of the change effort. Despite my lack of expertise in finance and accounting, I knew a lot about change management, and it turns out that, like most change initiatives, those skills were sorely needed on this project. I may not have had the same background as most of the other members of the Reimaging Budgets Team, but I still brought very valuable skills to the project. Each of us had a role to play to help make the project a success.

In this chapter, we will explore what those roles are. Specifically, we'll look at the responsibilities of the core project team and the change management team, and the steps you can take to staff these two teams to support change initiatives in your organization. You'll see that core project team members focus on creating and executing project plans, monitoring project implementation, and making adjustments as needed. They keep their eyes on the outcome that the organization is shooting for—the reason the organization embarked on the change initiative in the first place—and they make sure the organization keeps making progress toward that goal. To do its work, the core project team uses tools that address the hard side of change. You'll also see that the change management team ensures stakeholders understand the change and have the motivation and competence to adopt it. While also remaining dedicated to the ultimate outcome, it focuses on ensuring that the people affected by the change are willing to change their behavior to help the organization reach that goal. To do its work, the change management team uses tools that address the soft side of change.

We're covering the core project team and the change management team together because their work is so intertwined. The core project team can't perform its project management responsibilities effectively without considering the soft, people side of change, the expertise of the change management team. And the change management team can't perform its stakeholder engagement, communication, and training responsibilities effectively without considering the hard, project management side of change, the expertise of the core project team. Collaboration is key.

What Is a Core Project Team?

If you've seen your organization work on a major change initiative in the past, you probably saw it establish a core project team that focused on planning the change and ensuring that these plans were well executed. In the JCo acquisition case, the core project team, once it was assembled, was charged with making decisions like determining if, when, and how JCo employees would adopt Wilab's financial, HR, and procurement processes and systems. It also had responsibility for ensuring that these decisions were implemented successfully.

When an organization establishes a core project team to lead a change initiative, the team typically has responsibility for:

- Clarifying and defining the objective of the change and identifying expected business benefits and outcomes
- Developing and executing project plans for the change, including key decisions to be made and milestones to be achieved
- Engaging with the organization's leadership for needed decisions, resources, and communication
- Collaborating with the change management team to identify and engage with project stakeholders
- Monitoring project implementation and making adjustments as needed
- Partnering with the change management team to ensure that plans address both the hard side of the change, or achieving desired business results, and the soft side, or addressing the people side of the change

To do their work, core project team members use tools covered in this book that address the hard side of change, such as the project charter, project plan, red team, RACI matrix, and action review. They also collaborate with change management team members as those team members take the lead using tools that address the soft side of change.

On most core project teams, you'll probably see people fulfilling these roles:

- Project leader
- Project sponsor
- Project team members

Project Leader

The project leader oversees the project as it moves through its various phases. At the outset of the initiative, they work closely with the project sponsor to clarify the overall objectives and deliverables of the project. Ideally the sponsor and project leader work together to create the project charter (see chapter 3). The project leader also typically takes the lead in drafting the project plan, incorporating input from the sponsor, change management leader, team members, and key stakeholders (see chapter 4).

When the change initiative moves into the execution stage, the project leader manages day-to-day activities for the initiative, ensuring that deliverables are achieved on time and within budget. They manage the core project team, as team members perform activities that fall within the scope of the project, and they typically manage the financial resources allocated to the initiative. The project leader meets frequently with the project sponsor, key stakeholders, and other organizational leaders to keep them informed about the change initiative, often chairing periodic status-update meetings. They collaborate with the change management leader to ensure that there's an effective plan for engaging, communicating with, and training stakeholders.

And the project leader resolves issues that arise over the course of the project. To do that, they may facilitate action review meetings (see chapter 16) to help identify course corrections that are needed.

Usually, the project sponsor appoints the project leader. In selecting who will guide the project team, the sponsor considers individuals who have strong credibility across the organization and proven project management skills. Depending on the change and the structure of the organization, the sponsor may select a project leader from one of the functional areas that's most significantly affected by the change. That's what happened in the Reimaging Budgets initiative I described at the beginning of this chapter. Sunita, the company's director of financial systems, was assigned responsibility for leading the project team, in part because the department she managed played such a significant role in how the company created and approved annual budgets.

Project Sponsor

The project sponsor sets the overall vision for the initiative and ensures that the initiative aligns with the overall strategic objectives of the organization. They work closely with the project leader to define specific objectives and deliverables for the project. Ideally they take the lead, in collaboration with the project leader, in drafting the project charter (see chapter 3). Based on responsibilities and authorities outlined in the RACI matrix (see chapter 10), project team members usually need the project sponsor's approval on major decisions, especially those relating to the financial, human, and time and material resources allocated to the project.

The project sponsor plays a key role in communicating about the change, sharing what's happening and why with employees at all levels across the organization. Together with the project leader, the project sponsor keeps members of the organization's executive team up-to-date about the status of the change initiative. And they typically serve as the key champion for the project as they communicate with the rest of the organization about the goals and purpose of the change. See chapter 12 for more information about the key role the project sponsor plays in leading communications.

In their leadership capacity, the project sponsor may step in from time to time to help resolve an issue related to the project, especially when a member of the organization's leadership team isn't adequately demonstrating their support for the change. See chapter 14 for more about the role the sponsor may play to help address resistance.

Typically, the project sponsor is a member of the organization's senior leadership team who has a significant stake or interest in the outcome of the project. For example, in the Reimaging Budgets project I worked on, the company's CFO assumed the role of project sponsor. In the JCO acquisition case you read about in chapter 5, it's possible that Sheila, Wilab's head of business development, would serve as project sponsor. For very large-scale change initiatives, your organization may assign the project sponsor role to a steering committee comprising multiple senior leaders who have a stake in the project outcome.

Project Team Members

The project team is made up of the organizational members who have been assigned, on either a full- or part-time basis, to work on the project's various activities and deliverables. They're responsible for executing the tasks that are defined in the project plan.

Typically, the team includes representatives from different functional areas affected by the change. They usually bring a diverse set of skills, expertise, and insight to the project, and have the functional knowledge and soft skills required to complete the project-related tasks they have been assigned. For example, in the Reimagining Budgets project, the core project team included division finance managers, who understood the company's current budget approval process and had the creativity needed to imagine a new process. The team also included IT staff, who had the skills needed to plan and implement the technology changes that would occur.

To ensure that activities related to stakeholder engagement, communication, and training support the project's goals and deliverables, the change management leader assigned to the project should be in the core project team. That certainly was the case on the Reimagining Budgets project.

Usually, the project sponsor, project leader, and change management leader collaborate to decide who will serve on the core project team. For example, in the JCo acquisition case, Sheila, project sponsor for the initiative, asked for input from Luis, who likely would play the role of change management leader, regarding whom they should include on the project team. In practice, you may end up drawing team members entirely from your organization's in-house staff, or you may include vendors and outside contractors on the team, depending on how much time is needed to complete the project, the availability of resources with needed skills and talents within your organization, and your project's budget.

We will take a look at responsibilities for the change management team soon. For now, let's focus on steps you can take to help staff a core project team for a change initiative in your organization.

Identifying Competencies of the Core Project Team

When your organization launches a change initiative, you may find that senior leaders have already identified a project sponsor or project leader, and have begun recruiting members for the core project team. You can help them recruit team members by considering the different tasks to be completed during the project, and listing out the skills, knowledge, and kinds of experience team members will need to complete these tasks.

Start by creating a list that initially just identifies the functional and technical skills that are required for your project, such as:

- In-depth knowledge of current processes, technology, and situations that will be affected by the change
- Experience and expertise working in the functional areas or organizational units that are the target of the change
- Knowledge of the needs and interests of members of the targeted functional areas or organizational units
- Expertise in implementing or using the processes or technology represented by the future state that will exist after the change
- Functional and technical knowledge required to perform the tasks to be accomplished by the core project team

For example, in the JCo acquisition case, here are examples of the functional knowledge, skills, and experiences that Luis, the change management leader for the project, might list out:

- Understanding of JCo financial, sales, procurement, HR, and clerical systems and processes
- Understanding of Wilab financial, sales, procurement, HR, and clerical systems and processes
- Process mapping and process redesign skills
- Experience migrating users from one IT platform to another

- Experience managing acquisition integration
- Expertise managing a layoff
- Project management skills

For your own change initiative, take a look at the project charter (see chapter 3) and project plan (see chapter 4) if they exist at this point. They may be in very early draft form. Based on what you see in these documents, have you identified the functional and technical knowledge and experiences the team will need to complete work on the project?

But don't stop there. When change initiatives fail, it's often because the core project team didn't focus enough on understanding the people side of the change rather than because they lacked functional or technical expertise. You need people on the team who can establish relationships with stakeholders, speak with credibility, think creatively, and demonstrate enough personal discipline to stay focused on the work through good times and bad. When you're identifying the competencies you need on the core project team, be sure to include interpersonal, leadership, analytical, and self-management skills too. For example, in the JCo acquisition case, Luis might add some of the following to the list of competencies JCo should seek in its team members:

- Verbal and written communication
- Problem solving and decision making
- Business savvy and cultural awareness
- Organizational influence
- Customer focus orientation
- Flexibility, creativity, and a bias toward innovation
- The ability to inspire and motivate
- Personal discipline and organizational skills
- Empathy and listening skills
- Courage and advocacy

To do their work effectively, core project team members need skills for managing the hard side of change, including functional and technical competencies, and skills for managing the soft side of change, including leadership and interpersonal competencies. You can help your organization staff its core project team by reminding it to focus on both.

Recruiting Core Project Team Members

After you've identified the knowledge, skills, and experiences that core project team members need, start thinking about who within your organization has these skills and who has the availability to work on the project. Clearly no one person will have all of the competencies you've listed. That's why you need a team!

The project sponsor and project leader for your initiative may have already begun preparing a short list of prospective candidates. They may have spoken with peers and human resources executives to solicit possibilities. And if your organization's HR system provides the ability to search for employees by competency, they may have used the HR system to generate a list of potential team members.

You can help here by recommending employees to include on the core project team, and by offering to review the list of prospective team members drawn up by project sponsors and organizational leaders. As you evaluate each person who might potentially serve on the core project team, refer back to the list of functional, technical, leadership, and interpersonal skills and experiences required for this change initiative. Which competencies and backgrounds does each candidate bring to the project? Where are there gaps in knowledge and experience that you still need to fill by recruiting additional core project team members?

You may find it useful to organize your analysis into a team competency matrix, in which you list out the knowledge, skills, and experiences that team members need, the names of employees under consideration, and an assessment of each candidate's current level of competence. Table 6-1 shows a partially completed example that Luis, in the JCo acquisition case, might have created in preparation for his conversation with Sheila.

Notice that Luis highlighted the competency "Wilab procurement systems/ process" because he hadn't yet thought of any prospective candidates for the team who had experience in that area. Assuming they need someone with that competency on the project, Luis and Sheila need to work at recruiting candidates with that missing background. Notice also that Luis listed D. Currick as a possible candidate to include on the team, given his knowledge of JCo sales and procurement systems. But Luis highlighted that D. Currick currently lacks some of the interpersonal and organizational skills that team members need. Luis and Sheila might decide not to advance D. Currick as a candidate, and to include a different candidate who can bring both the requisite technical and interpersonal skills to the team. Finally, note that this is a partial example that lists only eight potential candidates that Luis might propose to Sheila. In practice, the company would likely consider many additional prospective candidates before making decisions about whom to recruit for the team.

Table 6-1. Partial JCo Acquisition Team Competency Matrix

Potential Candidate	M. Brogan	D. Currick	F. Devish	A. Patel	G. Grove	T. Tarnack	B. Smith	A. Jones	Other	Other	Other	Other	Other	Other
Competency														
JCo financial systems/process	P													
JCo sales systems/process		P	P											
JCo procurement systems/process		P	P											
JCo HR systems/ process	M			P										
JCo clerical systems/process				P										
Wilab financial systems/process					P									
Wilab sales systems/process						P								
Wilab procurement systems/process														
Wilab HR systems/process								P						
Wilab clerical systems/process			P				P							
Process mapping/ design	P	M	M	P	P		P	P						

Table 6-1. Partial JCo Acquisition Team Competency Matrix (cont.)

Potential Candidate	M. Brogan	D. Currick	E. Devish	A. Patel	G. Grove	T. Tarnack	B. Smith	A. Jones	Other	Other	Other	Other	Other	Other
IT migration					P		P							
Acquisition integration	P	M	M	P	P		P	P						
Layoff management	M			P				P						
Project management	P	M	M	P	M	M	P	M						
Verbal/written communication	P	M	P	P	M	P	M	P						
Organizational influence	M	M	P	P	M	P	M	P						
Personal discipline/organization	P	▓	P	P	M	P	P	P						
Customer focus	P	M	P	P	M	P	P	P						
Bias toward innovation	P	▓	P	P	M	P	P	P						
Empathy/listening	M	▓	P	P	M	P	M	P						
Tact	M	▓	P	P	M	P	M	P						

P= highly proficient
M = moderately proficient
Blank = not proficient

As you identify potential members for your core project team, consider their current workload, the amount of time you anticipate that team members will need to commit to the project, and the project schedule and timeline. Remember, employees are already busy with their regular jobs! Be sure to select team members who can allocate the time they'll need to attend team meetings and work on project-related tasks. Perhaps a team member will need to devote an hour per week during the initial planning stages of the project, but that time commitment is expected to balloon to 20 to 25 hours per week when implementation gets into full swing. Prepare a plan for how team members' regular work duties will be performed during times when they are more fully involved in the project. Some organizations hire temporary employees to cover the day-to-day work of team members, so team members can focus full time on implementing the change. As an alternative, you might recommend adjusting the project timeline, so the project proceeds at a slower pace, allowing team members more time to perform their regular jobs.

Beware of over-committing your team members. They may begin resisting the change they are supposed to be leading, simply because they feel so overworked by the hours required to perform their regular jobs plus their project-related tasks.

Addressing the Soft Side With the Core Project Team

Seek out core project team members who will bring diverse perspectives—in terms of age, gender, race, ethnicity, tenure with the organization, and so on to the project. For example, you may find that early career team members bring much-needed technical skills to the project team and have a real sense of ease in using social media, which is needed for engaging stakeholders. And employees with long tenure in the organization may bring a rich knowledge of why current processes are set up the way they are. They might provide information that's critically important to consider before process changes are introduced.

After you prepare a draft list of prospective team members, take a step back. Do team members reflect the diversity found across the rest of your organization?

And just like Luis proposed in the JCo acquisition case, consider how working on a change initiative can be a phenomenal leadership development opportunity. Over the course of a project, team members may be called upon to understand the needs and requirements of employees in job functions other than their own, research and evaluate alternative paths to achieving business objectives, propose and defend decisions, navigate conflict, negotiate agreements, deliver presentations, communicate at multiple levels within the organization, and manage complex tasks in a tight timeframe. Project team members may be afforded invaluable exposure to company executives during a change project. And executives may have a unique opportunity to observe and evaluate project team members as they perform challenging tasks and assess their potential for future leadership roles within the company.

When staffing the core project team, consider employees who already have the functional, technical, leadership, and interpersonal skills required to get the project work done. But also consider assigning a few employees who need to develop these skills. Make it clear to prospective team members that you anticipate the project will provide numerous opportunities for them to stretch beyond their current skill level, and that the organization expects them to take full advantage of these opportunities. This means they'll take on challenges and tasks they may not yet feel ready to perform. This also means they'll need to seek feedback on how well they performed these tasks and accept coaching and critical feedback when it is offered. Consider amending team members' development plans to explicitly state the skills you want them to focus on building through their participation on the core project team. And make sure organizational leaders are on board too. They need to recognize their role in providing coaching and developmental feedback to team members as they take on these challenges.

Questions to Ask When Assigning Responsibilities and Recruiting Members to the Core Project Team
- Have we identified the functional and technical knowledge, skills, and experiences that team members will need to complete the work of the project?
- Have we considered the interpersonal, leadership, analytical, and self-management skills that team members will need?
- As we evaluate prospective candidates, do we need to recruit additional members to fill gaps in the knowledge and experience we need on the team?
- What do we need to do to ensure that team members have enough time to work on this project while performing their day-to-day work responsibilities?
- Are we including team members who bring diverse perspectives—in terms of age, gender, race, ethnicity, tenure with the organization, and so on—to the project?
- Have we considered how we can use the project to help team members develop leadership expertise?

What Is a Change Management Team?

While the core project team focuses on project management activities needed to help the organization achieve the business objectives of the change, the change management team focuses on "the people side." In the JCo acquisition case, if Luis served as change management leader for the initiative, he'd probably oversee activities like:

- Partnering with the project leader to ensure they identified everyone at Wilab and JCo who would be affected by the acquisition and understand how the acquisition integration would affect each stakeholder group. Together they'd conduct a stakeholder analysis (see chapter 9) to do that.
- Providing opportunities for employees affected by the acquisition integration to share their ideas and concerns. He'd use lots of approaches to support two-way communication, including establishing a transition-monitoring team (see chapter 7).
- Creating and executing plans to ensure employees at Wilab and JCo understood what was happening and why, and how and when their own jobs would be affected. He'd create a communications plan (see chapter 12) to help guide and organize those efforts.
- Ensuring employees at Wilab and JCo developed the knowledge, skills, and attitudes they needed to succeed in their jobs during the acquisition integration and after it was complete. Assuming that JCo employees needed to begin using Wilab's finance, sales, procurement, and HR systems, Luis would make sure employees received the training they needed to successfully make the transition. He'd ensure that the overall project plan for the initiative included a detailed training plan (see chapter 13).
- Working with Wilab and JCo leaders to identify employees who were most likely to resist the changes that were coming and develop plans to help address that resistance. He'd coach leaders to help them understand why employees might be reluctant to support the change and what role they could play, as leaders, to help employees feel more comfortable with what was happening. Luis would create a resistance management plan (see chapter 14) to guide those efforts.

For most change initiatives, the change management team has responsibility for:

- Understanding the needs and concerns of stakeholders by ensuring that stakeholders have been identified, establishing appropriate mechanisms for engaging with each stakeholder group, and understanding the impact that the change will have on each stakeholder
- Developing and deploying communication strategies and tactics to help stakeholders understand the overall vision and purpose of the change and how the change will affect them
- Creating plans to ensure that stakeholders have the knowledge and skills they need to adopt and execute the change
- Identifying and creating mechanisms for building organizational support for the change and for addressing potential resistance
- Coaching and guiding organizational leaders, project sponsors, the core project team, and others supporting the project to help establish, protect, and maintain an environment of honest dialogue and trust as the change is implemented within the organization
- Collaborating with the core project team to ensure that change management efforts integrate with the overall project plan

To do their work, change management team members use tools covered in this book that address the soft side of change, such as the stakeholder analysis, transition-monitoring team, communications plan, training plan, and resistance management plan. They also collaborate with core project team members as those team members take the lead in using tools that address the hard side of change.

Competencies of the Change Management Team

When you're working on a change initiative, be sure a person or team has been assigned to focus on change management responsibilities. This person or team will need functional and technical skills like:

- An understanding of the change vision and the ability to communicate it
- Knowledge of change management principles, tools, processes, and best practices
- Knowledge of different mechanisms to support two-way and one-way communication
- Knowledge of learning and development tools and approaches
- Coaching, negotiation, and conflict management skills
- Team participation and facilitation skills

Change management team members also need the same leadership and interpersonal skills required of core project team members, including communication, problem solving and decision making, cultural awareness and business savvy, organizational influence, the ability to inspire and motivate, organizational skills, and courage and advocacy.

Staffing the Change Management Team

So who typically performs change management responsibilities during a change initiative? Well, it depends.

For very complex change initiatives that are long in duration or that affect many employees across the organization, you might need a full team of people assigned to perform different change management responsibilities. For example, the Reimagining Budgets project that I described at the beginning of this chapter ultimately would affect the work of almost 1,000 managers across many different divisions, locations, and departments in the company. I was just one member of a change management team assigned to the project. Over the course of the project, our team grew to include:

- A member of the company's internal communications staff, who was charged with preparing and executing the communications plan for the initiative.
- A technical trainer who worked in the company's finance department. He analyzed the training needs of employees who needed to learn about the new budget approval process and created online training to address those needs.
- The change management leader, a professional change management expert from our company's HR function. She would take the lead on engaging with the various stakeholders affected by the project and ensuring their needs were addressed. She would also oversee the work of the other change management team members and would partner closely with Sunita, the project leader, to ensure that change management efforts were aligned with the overall project.
- And me! I had years of experience working in learning and organizational development and led the company's training and development function. My role on the Reimaging Budgets team was to work with the change management leader on stakeholder analysis and engagement and to provide input on the communication and training plans.

For change initiatives that are less complex or shorter in duration, or that affect fewer people, change management responsibilities may be assigned to a single individual who serves as change management leader for the project. For a change that's really short and simple, the project leader might assume those duties.

Whatever the complexity, scope, and duration of your change initiative, make sure someone is assigned to the project who can ensure that change management is appropriately addressed. Like with the core project team, your organization may draw change management team members entirely from your organization's in-house staff, or may include vendors and outside contractors on the team, depending on the complexity of the project, the availability of resources with needed skills, and the budget. If you're drafting team members from in-house staff, consider employees in your organization's internal communications, HR, talent development or organizational development functions, because they often have the background and skills needed to perform change management activities. But beware of the tendency some organizations have to simply relegate change management to "the HR team" or "the T&D department." The person or team leading change management efforts for a project needs to be fully integrated with the core project team. This means that the change management leader or team should be present and should act as a full participant during core project team meetings. The change management leader's role during these meetings is to ensure that stakeholder concerns and needs are represented as project decisions are made, and that communications and training are fully incorporated into project plans. Likewise, change management team members need to be fully aware of the business issues and other concerns that contribute to project decisions, so they can appropriately represent the project as they work with stakeholders to build their support.

That's what happened on the Reimaging Budgets project I worked on. Our change management team functioned as a subteam within the core project team. We participated in most project team meetings so we could stay current on the details of the project and so we could update the rest of the project team on the needs and concerns of stakeholders as they evolved over the course of the initiative. And that's how I learned more than I ever really wanted to know about the company's budget approval process! For a very large and complex change initiative, it may be more efficient for the change management leader to serve as the only change management representative on the core project team. The change management leader can participate in all core project team meetings, and then coordinate separately with other members of the change management team.

Do you have the functional, technical, interpersonal, and leadership skills that change management team members need? If this is you, volunteer to take on the change management role for change initiatives occurring in your organization. You'll be amazed at how much you can help and how much you will learn.

Questions to Ask When Putting Together the Change Management Team
- Who will focus on understanding the needs and concerns of stakeholders, and engage with them and the core project team to ensure that stakeholder needs are addressed?
- Who will develop and deploy communications strategies and tactics so employees understand what's happening and why, and how the change will affect them?
- Who will create and execute plans to ensure that employees develop the knowledge, skills, and attitudes needed to support the change?
- Who will work with leaders to help them understand sources of resistance and steps they can take to build employee support for the change?
- Do we have people assigned to the project with the communications, training, organizational development, and change management expertise required to perform these responsibilities?
- What have we done to ensure that the change management team and core project team stay aligned, collaborate, and keep one another informed?

Collaboration Between the Core Project Team and the Change Management Team

Let's take a step back and look again at the key responsibilities of the core project team and the change management team and the tools they can use to perform these responsibilities (Table 6-2).

Table 6-2. Responsibilities and Tools for the Core Project Team and Change Management Team

Responsibility	Who Leads?	Tools Used	Chapter
Clarify and define the project objective, expected business benefits, and outcomes	Core Project Team	Project Charter	3
Develop and execute project plans for the change, including key decisions to be made and milestones to be achieved	Core Project Team	Project Plan Red Team	4 8

Table 6-2. Responsibilities and Tools for the Core Project Team and Change Management Team (cont.)

Responsibility	Who Leads?	Tools Used	Chapter
Engage with the organization's leadership for needed decisions, resources, and communication	Core Project Team	RACI Matrix	10
Understand the needs and concerns of stakeholders and establish mechanisms for engaging stakeholders	Change Management Team	Stakeholder Analysis Transition-Monitoring Team	9 7
Develop and deploy communication strategies and tactics	Change Management Team	Transition-Monitoring Team Communications Plan	7 12
Create plans to ensure stakeholders have the knowledge and competencies they need to adopt and execute the change	Change Management Team	Training Plan	13
Identify and create mechanisms to address potential resistance	Change Management Team	Resistance Management Plan	14
Monitor project implementation and make adjustments as needed	Core Project Team	Action Review	16

But remember, the core project team can't perform their responsibilities effectively without collaborating with the change management team. To develop well-informed project plans for changing things, the core project team needs to know who all the stakeholders are and what they currently do and care about. The change management team can help the core project team identify and engage with stakeholders before project plans are developed in final form. And to execute project plans, the core project team can rely on the change management team to help employees understand (or support) what's happening and what's expected of them, and ensure that employees have the knowledge and skills needed to adopt the change.

Likewise, the change management team needs the core project team. To understand who is affected by the change and how, the change management team needs the core project team to outline what's changing and when. And to help stakeholders support the change, the change management team needs to know the logic behind key decisions made and alternatives considered, which the core project team can provide.

Bottom line, the core project team and change management team need to work together to maintain focus on the soft side of change while engaging in their project management responsibilities—and on the hard side of change while engaging in their stakeholder engagement, communication, and training responsibilities. We'll see how that's done, as we look at each of the hard- and soft-side tools and practices in more depth in the chapters that follow.

About to Begin?

Think about a project you're already working on with a team. Try to map out the different roles people are playing. Who is your project sponsor—the person who has authorized the project or has asked the team to do the work? Who is your project leader, who's providing day-to-day oversight for the work your team is performing? Who else is on the team and what functional, technical, and interpersonal skills do they bring to the team? Assuming that your project will have an impact on others outside the team, who is handling change management responsibilities, like engaging with those who will be affected by your work, ensuring they understand how your project will affect them, and helping them develop the knowledge and skills needed for your project to be a success?

Then think about a change initiative your organization is about to begin, maybe one that you've already been asked to play a role in. Speak with the project leader and see if you can help them as they staff the core project team and change management team. In your discussion with your project leader, refer back to the "Questions to Ask When Assigning Responsibilities and Recruiting Members to the Core Project Team" and "Questions to Ask When Putting Together the Change Management Team." Review these questions with your project leader and see if you can help them find the answers. Your project leader may appreciate your help ensuring that the project involves the right people in the right way.

Of course, like Luis in the JCo acquisition case, you probably will find that you need to involve lots of other people, beyond the core project team and change management team, to ensure that your change initiative succeeds. In the next chapter, we'll look at the transition-monitoring team that Luis recommended forming. Who are they? What do they do? And how can they help make your change initiative a success?

Learn more. Check out:

Aziz, E.E., and W. Curlee. 2017. *How Successful Organizations Implement Change: Integrating Organizational Change Management and Project Management to Deliver Strategic Value.* Newton Square, PA: Project Management Institute.

Crawford, L., and A.H. Nahmias. 2010. "Competencies for Managing Change." *International Journal of Project Management* 28:405–12.

Purohit, S. 2018. "6 Essential Roles in Project Management." *Elearning Industry*, September 22. elearningindustry.com/roles-in-project -management-6-essential.

7

Generating Advocacy on the Ground

Many organizations struggle to establish an effective performance management process, but I beam with pride when I think back to how we revamped and revitalized the process at one global company I worked with. I served as change management leader for the project, and after a year of pretty intense work, I was pleased to see managers and employees holding productive discussions that focused on setting goals, building accountability, and developing new skills. But before I get too cocky about my contribution to this effort, we need to discuss the people who really made this project a success. There was a cadre of ordinary employees on the ground who, in addition to performing their day-to-day jobs, served as key advocates for the changes we were introducing. They were the members of our project's transition-monitoring team.

Who were they? Well, there was a plant manager from one location, a finance supervisor in another, a safety engineer, a member of the IT team from our corporate office, an R&D scientist from one of our labs, and a smattering of other employees who held different roles across the company. We recruited one employee from each of the company's locations and divisions, about 25 people in all. These were employees we knew already supported the transition. We leveraged their existing interest and support and asked them to help us advocate with their peers for the change that was coming.

What did they really do that helped make our project a success? They provided us with input about what they thought would and wouldn't work in their location as our team designed the new performance management process. They reviewed drafts of what we had designed and told us what they did and didn't like. We shared draft communications with them, and they were candid— really candid—about where we were hitting the right note and where we were about to step into a mess unless we made changes. They talked up the new performance management process with their co-workers. They encouraged their peers to attend training and helped answer their questions and challenges about why the company needed to make changes in the first place. And they told us what was working and what wasn't and where we needed to intervene to address resistance.

Our transition-monitoring-team members didn't have any formal decision-making authority on the project—they weren't members of the core project team or change management team—but they sure helped those of us who were on those teams make better, more informed decisions.

Some organizations refer to their transition-monitoring-team members as change champions. When I think back to how these ordinary employees really stuck their necks out for us on this project—and helped save our necks too—I see that they were in fact our project's champions. They weren't shy about telling us that the rating system we designed would confuse employees, and so we made changes that incorporated their feedback before the system launched. And transition-monitoring team members alerted us when communications we had sent out via email were being ignored. They helped us realize that additional steps were required to get employees to pay attention to our messages about the new process. I salute our transition-monitoring team for all the help they provided.

In this chapter, we take a closer look at the transition-monitoring team. You'll see that a transition-monitoring team can be an invaluable tool for establishing the two-way communication you need for your change initiative to succeed. You can use the practice to help build involvement among stakeholders and ensure that those most affected by the change have opportunities to be heard. You'll see that the transition-monitoring team can help you address the soft side of change by providing a structured way for you to listen to, communicate with, and involve stakeholders. But the tool can also help you address the hard side of change by ensuring you gather input and ideas you can use to make more informed decisions and improve your project plans.

That's certainly what happened when I worked with the transition-monitoring team as my company revised its performance management process. And it might be why Luis, in the JCo acquisition case you read in chapter 5, recommended establishing a transition-monitoring team for his project. Let's see how the team works and how you can use a transition-monitoring team to support a change in your organization.

What Is a Transition-Monitoring Team?

In his seminal book *Managing Transitions,* change guru William Bridges (2003) defines a transition-monitoring team as a group of people chosen from across the organization who don't have responsibility for planning the change, or authority to make decisions related to it, but who serve as a two-way channel to support rapid and accurate communications. Transition-monitoring-team members act as advocates for the change that is occurring within their part of the organization. They supplement traditional communication vehicles like emails and supervisor presentations with peer-to-peer communication.

In championing the change, the transition-monitoring-team members help their co-workers understand how the change affects them and encourage them to adopt what's coming. But transition-monitoring-team members also listen to their co-workers' views about the change, communicate issues and concerns to the core project team and change management team, and advocate for the needs of their peers. Their role extends beyond mere promotion of the change to one of representing the needs and interests of their co-workers.

Whatever it is called, the goal of the transition-monitoring team is to support two-way communication throughout the change initiative. As Bridges explains, a transition-monitoring team can help you:

- Convey to employees that your organization cares how employees are responding to the change.
- Provide a sounding board and point of review for plans and decisions made by the core project team.
- Expand participation in the change, and provide more employees with a sense of accountability and ownership of the change.
- Enhance speed of communication by allowing information to be quickly disseminated throughout your organization and misinformation to be corrected.
- Provide an additional formal mechanism for upward communication.
- Support face-to-face communication.
- Help tailor communications about "what's in it for me" to each specific part of your organization affected by the change.

As I found when my company was changing its performance management process, a transition-monitoring team can serve as an internal focus group for the core project team and change management team. On my project, the transition-monitoring team reviewed project plans and decisions before we rolled them out and provided us with feedback about how well those plans were working, in real time, as we implemented them. Our transition-monitoring team helped us communicate updates about the change throughout the company. And from time to time, it helped us dispel misplaced rumors about the overall intent of our project.

To set up a transition-monitoring team for a change initiative that's occurring in your organization:

- Choose your transition-monitoring-team members and charge them with their responsibilities.
- Communicate the team's purpose to the rest of your organization.
- Meet regularly with the team members to solicit their input and convey messages you need them to share with their peers.

Let's look at each of these steps in more depth.

Choose Transition-Monitoring-Team Members

To staff your transition-monitoring team, start by thinking about each part of your organization that will be affected by the change. Your goal is to enlist at least one team member in each part of your organization that's affected. This may be one team member for each department or each organizational subunit, depending on the size of your organization and how it is structured.

Look at an early draft of your stakeholder analysis if you have one (see chapter 9), and think about all the various groups of stakeholders you've identified. For each stakeholder group, ask yourself:

- Who isn't serving on the core project team but might have a real interest in this project and might already support what this project is designed to accomplish?
- Who is known for their innovative thinking, and may not be satisfied with how things currently are done?
- Who is well respected by their peers as being competent and trustworthy?
- Whom do employees listen to? Who are employees comfortable sharing their concerns with?

To identify transition-monitoring-team members, you can ask project leaders or department supervisors to nominate prospective candidates, or ask for volunteers. Be sure to choose employees at different organizational levels. And ensure that transition-monitoring-team members reflect the diversity of your organization members.

As you're recruiting transition-monitoring-team members, explain that their responsibilities will include:

- Reviewing plans and decisions before they're implemented to provide the core project team and change management team with input about how their co-workers may respond
- Checking in with their peers to see how they're interpreting and responding to the change, and updating the core project team and the change management team on how the change is being accepted in the part of the organization they represent
- Conveying information to their co-workers about the change, helping to supplement and fill gaps that may exist in other forms of communication
- Advocating with their peers regarding the overall purpose of the change and encouraging them to take necessary steps, such as attending training or trying out new procedures, to adopt the change
- Helping to dispel rumors and misinformation that may be circulating regarding the change

Let your transition-monitoring-team members know how much your organization values the review and communication role they will play during the change project, but make it clear that they won't have decision-making authority. Their role will be to make recommendations based on what they see in their part of the organization. But when decisions are made, your organization will consider many factors, in addition to input that transition-monitoring-team members will provide.

So why would someone want to participate on a transition-monitoring team if they don't get to make decisions about what's happening? Well, this is an opportunity for an employee to provide input and to help contribute to the success of an initiative without having to assume the day-to-day work that core project team members are charged with. They can help shape how the change will be introduced in their area. They can demonstrate peer leadership by helping to guide and influence the perceptions and actions of their co-workers. And in purely practical terms, in most change initiatives there just isn't room for everyone who wants to, or thinks they should, serve on the core project team. The transition-monitoring team provides an opportunity for people to still play a critically important role when they want to be included on the core project team, but can't for any number of reasons.

On the performance management project I described earlier, eight employees served on our core project team, and most of them had functional expertise related to the project, such as knowledge of our HR information system or significant managerial experience preparing and delivering employee reviews.

On the other hand, 25 employees served on our transition-monitoring team, and most of them had little to no background developing or deploying performance management systems. They were just interested managers and employees, each representing a different part of our company, who wanted a hand in shaping how the new process would be introduced.

Communicate the Purpose of the Transition-Monitoring Team

For the transition-monitoring team to do their job effectively, the rest of your organization needs to understand the role that the team will play. When your organization begins communicating information about the project, let employees know who is working on the initiative and the role each person will play. Share who's sponsoring the project, who's serving as project leader, and who is working on the core project team and change management team. At the same time, explain that your organization has established a transition-monitoring team that will help support the dissemination of information to employees affected by the change, that will listen, and that will ensure that project leaders hear about concerns. Reiterate that the purpose of the transition-monitoring team is to support two-way communication and will help the project team make more informed decisions.

Let department supervisors know that transition-monitoring-team members supplement—but do not replace—the critically important communications role they play on the project. Reassure supervisors that the project team will always share key information with them first before it's shared with the transition-monitoring-team members who report to them.

Ask department supervisors to announce to their employees the name of the person serving on the transition-monitoring team from their area. This helps legitimize the role that transition-monitoring team members will play on the project and conveys that supervisors and transition-monitoring-team members are working together to help employees stayed informed about what's happening related to the change.

Be aware that some employees may view the transition-monitoring team as "management stooges," moles, or spies. To combat that risk, ask transition-monitoring team members to reassure the employees they represent that they'll protect their anonymity whenever they share information with the core project team and change management team.

And reiterate to transition-monitoring-team members that some of the information they're receiving regarding the change initiative is confidential. You're sharing plans and draft documents with them and asking for their input and feedback, and you're trusting they won't share information with their peers unless and until you've expressly asked them to do that.

> **Tips for Communicating the Purpose of the Transition-Monitoring Team**
> - Share the purpose of the transition-monitoring team at the same time you announce the project and who is working on it.
> - Let employees know that the transition-monitoring team is there to help support two-way communication: to listen to the concerns of co-workers and convey ideas to the project team—and to share information about the project with their co-workers to help them stay up-to-date.
> - Reassure department supervisors that the transition-monitoring team supplements—but does not replace —the role they play in leading communications within their area.
> - Ask department supervisors to announce to employees the name of the transition-monitoring-team member who is representing their area on the project.
> - Remind transition-monitoring-team members that you're trusting them to protect their co-workers' anonymity when they share ideas and concerns with the project team. Likewise, you're trusting transition-monitoring-team members to protect confidential information the project team shares with them.

Conduct Periodic Transition-Monitoring-Team Meetings

To gather input from transition-monitoring-team members and provide them with information they need to convey to their peers, schedule regular meetings with the transition-monitoring team—perhaps once every two to four weeks over the course of your project. Your project leader should attend, accompanied by some or all of the core project team and change management team, depending on the specific topics you plan to address during the meeting.

In most organizations, the change management leader convenes and facilitates these meetings as part of their communications and stakeholder engagement responsibilities. They make sure that transition-monitoring-team members are given appropriate time to share what they are seeing and hearing. They establish and maintain an environment where project team members listen to feedback, which may feel critical at times. And they remind transition-monitoring-team members that although their role is to provide input and to advocate among their peers for the change, many factors—in addition to their input—will be weighed as decisions are made. Through their skillful facilitation, the change management leader ensures that no one participant or viewpoint dominates or hijacks the discussion.

Here's how a typical meeting may go.

Before the Meeting

- Send transition-monitoring-team members the agenda highlighting the specific topics they need to be prepared to discuss, including any documents you need them to provide feedback on when you meet. For example, if the meeting will focus on communications that are planned, email draft documents to team members so they're prepared to discuss them at the meeting.

During the Meeting

- Kick off each meeting by asking transition-monitoring-team members for an update on how the change is being received in their portion of the organization. Provide them with an opportunity to ask questions and raise concerns that they are hearing from their co-workers. To protect confidentiality, insist that transition-monitoring-team members consolidate feedback from multiple co-workers and eliminate the identities of specific individuals from all information they share during their update.
- Have the change management leader, project leader, or core project team members respond to questions and concerns raised by the transition-monitoring team by providing needed information or clarity, and committing to address issues and concerns that were raised.
- Ask a representative from the change management and/or core project team to review updates on what has changed since the last transition-monitoring-team meeting. Be sure they highlight any actions that were taken as a result of feedback that transition-monitoring-team members previously shared.
- Have the change management and/or core project team present any new project plans or decisions, and ask the transition-monitoring team for feedback on how they anticipate that these new plans will be accepted in the area they represent. For example, you may review draft communications you asked team members to read prior to the meeting and ask for ideas about how these communications are likely to be understood or misunderstood.

- Let attendees know that the core project team and change management team will address issues and concerns they raised during the meeting.
- Wrap up the meeting by reviewing any key messages you need transition-monitoring-team members to convey to their co-workers back on the job and any feedback or input you need them to gather and present at the next transition-monitoring-team meeting. For example, if training is about to begin, you may ask transition-monitoring-team members to encourage their co-workers to enroll. Or if the project team is weighing whether to include a particular feature in an app they're developing related to the change, you may ask transition-monitoring-team members to solicit input from their co-workers about how likely they are to need and use that feature.

After the Meeting:

- Depending on the type of input that transition-monitoring-team members need to gather from their co-workers, they may conduct a formal meeting, ask their supervisor to allocate a few minutes to the topic during an upcoming department meeting, solicit feedback via email, or have a quick, informal chat with their peers. Usually, transition-monitoring-team members report the feedback they're hearing at the next, regularly scheduled transition-monitoring-team meeting. But if the project team needs input before the next meeting, or if a team member becomes aware of a concern that needs to be addressed immediately, there may be some back-and-forth communication between the change management leader, project leader, and transition-monitoring-team members between meetings.

Addressing the Hard Side With the Transition-Monitoring Team

Although the transition-monitoring team is a tool that focuses on the soft, "people side" of change by prioritizing two-way communication, use the practice to improve the quality of your project plans and decisions (that is, the hard side of change). Transition-monitoring-team members don't have decision-making authority, but they do have vital, on-the-ground insight to share about how well the change may work in the part of the organization they represent.

Core project team members may just want to plow ahead to complete something that the transition-monitoring team wants changed. Be sure to listen—really listen—to the information that transition-monitoring-team members share. Ask everyone to demonstrate patience, maturity, and emotional intelligence during their interactions. Build into your project plans enough time for the transition-monitoring team to solicit input from their peers, and for the core project team to respond to this feedback. There will be times when it won't make sense to modify plans or decisions to incorporate ideas and feedback shared by transition-monitoring-team members. But there also will be times when you realize, like I did on my performance management project, that the transition-monitoring team has provided feedback that will save you from making a critical mistake.

About to Begin?

To introduce the transition-monitoring-team concept to your organization, consider starting small and building gradually over time. Assemble representatives from each area affected by a change and ask them to participate in a one-time focus group. In this internal focus group meeting, ask participants to review and provide feedback on project plans, draft communications, and tentative decisions. Participants might welcome the opportunity to share their input and ideas. After your organization feels comfortable using the one-time focus group approach to support change initiatives, expand the idea to include more frequent update and review meetings with participants. Then expand on the idea again, and assign participants with responsibility for peer-to-peer communication. By then, congratulations are due! You've implemented the full transition-monitoring-team practice in your organization.

The transition-monitoring team provides you with an opportunity to involve employees who may be positively inclined to support what's changing. But is there a role you can provide to the naysayers—those who may be inclined to view what's changing from a more skeptical perspective? In the next chapter, we'll look at the red team, whose members are specifically charged with posing objections and pointing out all the flaws in your plans. You'll see that, just like the transition-monitoring team, the red team can provide you with critically important input that can help make your project a success. So yes, there's a role for your beloved skeptics too! Read on to learn more.

Learn more. Check out:

Bridges, W. 2003. *Managing Transitions: Making the Most of Change.* Cambridge, MA: Perseus.

University of Georgia. 2017. "Change Champions." onesource.uga.edu /_resources/files/documents/uga_change_champions_responsibilities.pdf.

8

Listening to Opposing Views

Have you ever been in a situation at work that could be described as "a slow-moving train wreck"? You could see disaster coming as a result of some misguided decision, but didn't feel like you had the opportunity to voice your concern or the authority to stop the decision from being implemented. Perhaps your co-workers saw the calamity coming too, and they also said nothing. And, when it was all over, and the damage was done, perhaps you said to yourself, "I knew this was going to be a disaster. Why didn't anyone stop it?"

I've experienced this scenario, and I bet you have too. But I've also worked with an organization that deliberately took steps to avoid this kind of mishap. I was in a room where the project leader presented a plan for implementing a key decision they'd just made, and I was asked, "What's wrong with our thinking here? Tell me what we have missed. Why isn't this going to work? Be brutal with us. Tell us everything. We need your help. Please."

I was on a red team, a group that was assembled for the express purpose of poking holes in an action the organization was about to take. Amid all the pressure to go-go-go, my role during the meeting was to tell the project leader all the reasons they should stop. My job was to tell the project team why their plan just wasn't going to work.

The project team had just decided to ditch a well-established technology vendor and replace the vendor with a relative newcomer to the market. During the red team meeting, I shared my concerns about the new vendor's unproven technology, the fact that their suite of offerings was incomplete, and that they lacked experience working with our industry. My fellow red team members and I shared our views about steps the organization would need to take to supplement the new vendor's offerings, if the project team decided to proceed with their plan. As we presented our thoughts, project team members noted our concerns. They didn't defend their decision to us. The project team truly seemed eager to hear our views about the risks and costs we thought their plan would pose to our organization.

They'd move ahead anyway. But not without first making a change or two or three that addressed the problems my fellow red teammates and I had surfaced. I like to think that our input made a difference and helped our organization score a real win with the project.

In this chapter, we'll take a look at the red team and explore how you can apply the practice in your organization. You'll see that the red team is a tool that focuses on the hard side of change, because its main function is to help your project teams make better decisions and improve your chances of achieving planned results. But you'll see that the tool also helps you focus on the soft side of change. When you implement the red team concept correctly, you create an environment in which it's safe to voice opposition and dissent. And that questioning and critical thinking may be just what's needed to keep your project safely on the rails.

What Is a Red Team?

Marko Kovic, principal at the consulting firm Ars Cognitionis, describes a red team as "an independent group or team that is tasked with critically challenging decisions, procedures, or strategies in order to detect and eliminate cognitive blind spots" (Kovic 2019). Separate from your core project team, change management team, and transition-monitoring team, the red team meets periodically—perhaps just before your team completes a key milestone—to review plans and decisions you're about to implement. The team's goal during these meetings is to point out all the reasons your plans and decisions may not work. That way, you can make adjustments, if needed, before you move forward with a plan that might otherwise contain hidden flaws and weaknesses.

Strategist Micah Zenko explains that the idea can be traced back to the Middle Ages, when the Roman Catholic Church established the role of "devil's advocate" to identify potential character flaws in candidates under consideration for sainthood (Zenko 2015). Today, businesses, government institutions, and not-for-profits around the globe establish red teams to perform that same function. They ask their red team members to play the role of devil's advocate by actively challenging decisions and critically evaluating whether their plans really make sense.

Why set up a team that's specifically charged with pointing out flaws and potential mistakes? Won't people just tell you if they think you're about to do something that could go wrong? Well, maybe . . . or maybe not.

Sometimes employees stay silent when they know their organization is about to do something that isn't going to work. They may feel like their ideas just don't matter, or they sense that they'll experience retaliation or suffer other negative consequences if they express disagreement. They don't want to be told to "Get with the program," or that "You're either on the bus or under the bus." So they keep their concerns to themselves. The red team combats this tendency by providing an environment in which employees feel safe to voice objections and disagreement, because that's exactly what you've asked them to do.

And even if you've established a psychologically healthy environment, your team can make errors when you ignore, or just fail to see, the risks in your plans. As Joel Neeb (2020), from the consulting firm Afterburner, states, it's easy for teams to sit "so close to the problem, so close to the plan that they don't see the forest for the trees. And there are glaring omissions that if anybody else were to put eyes on this plan they'd be able to help them out." Sometimes a team just becomes overconfident or falls victim to "groupthink." Or a leader becomes wedded to a decision, perhaps sensing that their own reputation is on the line if a decision needs to be reversed. So they start ignoring contrarian evidence when the flaws in their ideas start to surface. A red team provides an independent, second pair of eyes that can help your team navigate past these blind spots.

Perhaps that's why Luis, in the JCo acquisition case you read in chapter 5, recommended establishing a red team for his project. He may have recognized that JCo employees would feel pressured to acquiesce to whatever plans the acquisition integration team set forth, even if they knew these plans were flawed. After all, Wilab had just acquired their company and their jobs might be at stake. Perhaps it really was better to just stay quiet and go along with things. Luis might have realized that he needed to establish an opportunity for JCo employees to safely ask questions and poke holes in the plans the core project team had prepared. And Luis also might have recognized that in their haste to move forward and quickly integrate JCo into Wilab, the project team might make some misguided assumptions that, if left unchecked, could create major problems. He probably saw how helpful it would be to have an independent set of eyes critically evaluate their plans before they proceeded to implement them. That's why he recommended establishing a red team.

But why did Luis feel compelled to set up the red team as a separate, independent body? Couldn't he just ask core project team members or members of the transition-monitoring team to do double duty? Couldn't these other teams just take a step back and critically evaluate whatever was planned "from a red team perspective?"

Luis was wise to resist this temptation. Your core project team is responsible for moving your change project forward and for meeting deadlines. Once they get cooking, it may be hard for them to stop their go-go-go momentum and take a critical look back. And yes, your transition-monitoring team does serve as an internal focus group–the group you run plans and communications by before they are finalized and launched. But remember that they also serve as internal champions of the change within their respective organizations. So once they get started, their natural bias may be to support the change as well. Establish the red team as a separate group of individuals who you specifically charge with finding flaws and for putting on the brakes. You need a group who's biased toward thinking "Here's why this isn't going to work."

Are you convinced? Let's see how you, like Luis, can establish a red team for your change initiative. You'll need to:

- Choose your red team members and charge them with their responsibilities.
- Communicate the team's purpose to the other project teams.
- Meet with red team members to solicit their input, and respond to their feedback and ideas by adjusting your plans and decisions when appropriate.

Let's look at each of these steps in more depth.

Choose Red Team Members

To staff your red team, start by thinking about the people you haven't already selected for another team who have the functional knowledge and experience needed to understand—and evaluate—the plans or decisions you're reviewing. Who knows enough, or has seen enough, in the area covered in your plan that they can detect misguided assumptions and errors in your thinking? This might be a seasoned staff person with years of functional experience in an area that's related to your project. Perhaps it's someone who has lived through similar change projects in the past and has the battle scars to show for it. They're someone who has done lots of things right, but also who has made mistakes that they've learned from. Who has the functional or technical expertise needed to determine if your plan makes sense?

For example, in the JCo acquisition case, when Luis recruits red team members to evaluate plans for migrating JCo employees to Wilab's finance, sales, procurement, and HR systems, he might seek team members who already have significant experience using these systems at JCo. He might also recruit someone who has worked on system integrations in the past.

But think beyond the functional and technical skills needed to critically evaluate your plan. As you recruit members for your red team, include employees who have distinguished themselves by their analytical thinking skills. Who are the fearless critical thinkers in your organization? Who are the creative nonconformists? Who's known for questioning decisions and for challenging the status quo? Who might lack functional expertise or experience in the area addressed by your plan, but who can spot a problem from a mile away—and they're not afraid to call your attention to it? This might be a promising up-and-comer who's participating in your company's high-potential leadership development program, a staffer in your organization's compliance or risk management function, a smart new hire, or just someone you know can really think three steps ahead. Make sure you include on your red team individuals who are skilled at critically evaluating assumptions and questioning decisions, regardless of their functional background.

And finally, think about who might be most inclined to doubt the wisdom of the change you are embarking on. As you staff your red team, consider including a few individuals who are known to be critical of the project or decision that is under review. Who are your naysayers? They likely have a valid perspective that's important for your core project team and change management team to hear. For example, in the JCo acquisition case, Luis noted that Wilab's head of IT had complained about Wilab proceeding with another acquisition at this time. Luis might ask Wilab's head of IT to join the red team to ensure that the core project team appropriately heard, and potentially addressed, this person's reservations. And don't be surprised if you see one or two naysayers convert into project champions after they participate on a red team. Some red team members may become strong advocates for a change once they realize that they have had an official opportunity to critically evaluate plans and present their concerns.

After you compile a list of prospective red team candidates, take a step back. Are you seeing the same names on this red team that you've used in the past on other projects? Resist the urge to ask the same employees to join red teams over and over again. Even when your organization completely accepts the value of the red team concept, red team members may get labeled as organizational naysayers if they're seen participating on red teams too frequently. Instead, consider rotating membership. This way, you'll provide more employees throughout your organization with experience voicing critical perspectives. And you'll help strengthen the critical thinking skills across your entire organization when red team members return to their regular jobs equipped with a bias toward challenging assumptions and asking probing questions.

Educate red team members about the distinct role they will play in the meetings they're invited to join. Explain that their role will be to ask clarifying questions, probe for assumptions, and offer critical feedback about why the plan or decision might not work. Their job is to be critical, yet thoughtful, objective, and respectful. Make it clear that they may raise objections or surface risks that organizational leaders may end up deciding not to address. Their feedback is highly valued, but many factors, in addition to their input, influence how the project team will proceed. And reiterate to red team members that the information they receive is confidential. Your organization is trusting that red team members won't share what they see with their peers and won't disparage the project based on the discussion that occurs. This definitely is a situation where what happens in a red team meeting stays in the red team meeting!

Questions to Ask When Recruiting Members of the Red Team

- Do team members have the functional and technical knowledge, skills, and experience needed to determine if our plan makes sense?
- Have we included team members with strong analytical thinking skills who can challenge our assumptions and identify risks?
- Have we included the doubters and naysayers—those who may be naturally inclined to question the wisdom of our plan, given how the change will affect them?
- Will team members be candid but respectful during the red team meeting? Will they show good judgment and respect the confidential nature of the information we share with them?
- Are we being inclusive and exposing enough new people to the red team process? Are we sure we're not relying too heavily on the same team members over and over again?

Communicate the Purpose of the Red Team

For the red team to serve its purpose, core project team and change management team members need to understand the role they'll play when they meet with red team members. Their job during a red team meeting will be to present their plan with the understanding that it will be reviewed to expose flaws and weaknesses. They need to share information, answer questions, and provide needed clarification. But most important, they need to listen—not to debate or defend their plans and decisions. They're there to hopefully learn. They need to accept that there are risks and vulnerabilities they may not have adequately accounted for, and they must be willing to hear contrarian perspectives.

During their meeting with the red team, core project team and change management team members may hear objections that they've already accounted for. That's okay. They can describe the actions they had planned to address the risk, and ask the red team if these plans are sufficient. Or they can nod, say "Thank you," and ask for additional feedback. But they need to avoid critiquing the critique. That's the purpose of the red team—to criticize, object, and find faults.

Although red team members need to demonstrate objectivity, respect, and good judgment, core project team and change management team members do too. They can't disparage red team members for their analysis after the red team meeting has concluded. What's said in the red team meeting needs to stay there.

Conduct Red Team Meetings

Plan to meet with your red team whenever you're approaching a key milestone on your project or whenever you've reached a key decision point, where it would be helpful to hear an independent review. You may meet with your red team only a few times throughout the course of your change initiative—perhaps once after your team has created its project plan, again right before you pull the trigger on a major action contained in your plans, and then anytime you're about to make a significant change to what you had planned. For example, in the JCo acquisition case, Luis might schedule a red team meeting after the core project team had developed its plans for when and how JCo employees will migrate to Wilab's systems. The focus of that meeting would be to hear from JCo and Wilab employees serving on the red team about the possible gaps and mistaken assumptions contained in that portion of the acquisition integration project plan.

I've seen a red team convene immediately before an organization announced a major restructuring they had planned. Another organization conducted a red team meeting before proceeding with their decision to terminate a massive project that had been under way for years.

You don't need your red team to review every aspect of your project plan and every decision your team makes. That would be overkill. Just ask it to assemble whenever you've reached a major juncture in your project plan or need a critical review of a decision.

Here's how you can conduct a red team meeting in your organization.

Before the Meeting

- Identify the portion of the plan or the decision you need the red team to review. Ideally, select a portion of the plan or decision that is still in draft form, that isn't ready yet to be executed. You and your team need to be open to making changes based on the ideas you hear in the red team meeting, and you need to have time to make these changes before moving forward with implementing your plan or decision.

- Decide who will attend and who will lead the meeting. Invite members of the red team and members of the core project team or change management team whose plan or decision will be reviewed. Usually, your project leader will attend and facilitate the meeting, unless the discussion will focus on communications, training, or stakeholder engagement, in which case the change management leader should lead. Regardless of the topic, be sure to include at least one member of the change management team. They should listen carefully as the red team surfaces objections and concerns, because they may need to address these issues as they create communications plans, resistance management plans, and other plans for building stakeholder buy-in and support. And, of course, sometimes it will make sense for the red team to review and evaluate decisions and plans created by the change management team! If that's the case, the change management team needs to be open to this critique and willing to adjust their plans and decisions based on what they have heard.

- Schedule the red team meeting and send any documents you want red team members to review in advance. In your invitation, remind participants about the overall purpose of the red team and the upcoming meeting, including the area the meeting will focus on. For example, you may say, "During this meeting, we're asking the red team to review and critique the training plan we've created for this project. We're eager to hear ideas about how we can make the plan even better." As you're setting the timeframe for the meeting, build in time at the end for core project team and change management team members to review and discuss what they have heard.

During the Meeting

- Open the meeting by having the project leader (or change management leader, if the discussion will focus on communications, training, or stakeholder engagement) state the purpose of the gathering. Ask the project leader to kick off the meeting by saying something like, "We are eager to review our plan with you. It isn't complete yet and we know it has holes in it. We need your guidance and ideas so we can make this better. We specifically want to hear from you about what's wrong with our thinking. Tell us what we have missed. Why isn't this going to work? Be brutal with us. Tell us everything." You want to signal to the red team members that you're eager to hear their feedback, need them to focus on gaps and omissions, and appreciate the role they will play in helping to make your project a success.

- Review and agree on meeting ground rules. Consider establishing ground rules like:
  - Leave titles at the door. Everyone has a valid perspective to share.
  - Red team members will offer criticism and objections respectfully and thoughtfully.
  - Core project team members will listen to the feedback provided, and will not debate the feedback or defend their plans.
  - Core project team members will thank red team members for their feedback and ideas.
  - The plans and discussion are confidential. Nothing discussed in the meeting will be shared outside the meeting.
  - There will be no retribution or repercussions for anything discussed in the meeting.

- The facilitator then presents the plan or proposed decision to the red team.

- Encourage red team members to ask clarifying questions so they can fully understand the plan or decision and the factors the team considered when creating it. To maintain an environment of respect, urge red team members to ask questions such as "Have you considered . . .?" as opposed to "Why didn't you . . .?"

- Ask red team members to offer their criticism of the plan, proceeding in round-robin fashion as they identify all the risks, flaws, errors, and omissions they have detected. While red team members state their concerns and objections, core project team and change management team members should listen quietly, ask for clarification as needed, and take notes.
- Keep the conversation going by asking questions like:
  ○ "What else have we missed?"
  ○ "Why isn't this going to work?"
  ○ "What problems do you think we'll run into?"
  ○ "What could go wrong and what do you think we should do about it?"
  ○ "Where are we making the wrong assumptions?"
  ○ "What are we risking by doing this, and how likely are we to encounter that risk?"
- After red team members have provided all of their criticism, close this portion of the meeting by thanking them for their time and input. Say something like, "Thanks for sharing all your insight and feedback. We are going to take a step back and review everything you've just shared with us, and decide how to proceed."

After the Meeting

- Immediately after the red team exits the meeting, review and discuss what you have heard and decide how to adjust your plans or decisions if that's needed. The red team may have surfaced risks or objections that you've already adequately considered and accounted for in your plan. You might note that feedback and decide not to act on it. Of course, the red team probably also identified real gaps and omissions that you hadn't considered. Where possible, amend the plan or decision to incorporate and address this feedback.
- Recognize that the red team may present bad news about the viability of some portion of your project or decision. Be willing to act on that news. Nothing can shut down trust more than when employees know that leaders had access to information that would have helped them make a sound decision, but that they chose to ignore. This doesn't mean that the red team can reverse decisions. But make sure there's a sound reason for why you are proceeding with a decision given the risks that the red team has surfaced.

- If appropriate, notify red team members of the changes you made to the plan or decision. Thank them again for the vital insight they provided.

Addressing the Soft Side With the Red Team

The red team concept focuses on the hard side of change—after all, it's used to produce more informed decisions and better business outcomes. But for the practice to pay off, you need to carefully attend to the soft side of change too. As you implement the tool, you need to create and maintain an environment in which it's safe for employees to raise objections and express dissenting views. This is a habit you can build in your organization over time. There are active steps you can take to promote and protect that habit.

Train employees and leaders on how to engage in productive and respectful dialogue. Some organizations require anyone attending a red team meeting—including organizational leaders and red team, core project team, and change management team members—to attend training prior to participating.

Encourage meeting participants to respond to criticism with statements like, "This is great feedback. Thanks for sharing that," "I hadn't thought of that. Tell me more," wor "That's interesting. Why do you say that?"

Ask leaders to model appropriate behavior during red team meetings. Encourage them to demonstrate humility, curiosity, appreciation, and respect. Ask them to say things like, "I clearly don't have all the information you do from your experience working in xyz, so I need your help," or "I'm confident I've missed things—maybe many things—and would love to hear your thoughts."

During and after the meeting, strictly monitor compliance with the ground rules, and actively enforce them.

Acknowledge that hearing critical feedback can be hard. After the red team exits the meeting, encourage core project team and change management team members to take some deep breaths before deciding how to respond. This may be a situation where it's best to "sleep on things" for a short while. Team members may need to pause, take a step back, and let the sting of criticism fade a bit before deciding how to proceed.

About to Begin?

Do you want to try out the red team concept in your organization, but are you concerned your colleagues just won't want to get on board? Start by inviting your co-workers and internal clients to conduct a critical review of a project you are leading. Let them know that you want to explore the red team concept by having them participate in a red team meeting where the focus is on your plans and decisions. You may find that your co-workers welcome—and even respect you for providing—an opportunity to evaluate your project. After all, it's not their work that is being critiqued! As you present your plan or decision to your co-workers for their review, ask:

- What am I missing?
- Why isn't this going to work?
- What problems do you think we'll run into?
- What could go wrong and what do you think I should do about it?

Don't defend your plan or explain your thinking. Just listen and thank your co-workers for their honest review. Then let your co-workers know about changes you plan to make to your plan or decision, based on the input they provided. (Come on, there must be something you can change!) Once your co-workers have seen the value of the red team meeting they participated in, they may be more willing to apply the same concept to their plans and decisions.

When you begin meeting with your red team, don't be surprised if they tell you that your plan contains a glaring omission—you've left out a key stakeholder whose input you need for your project to succeed. In chapter 9, we'll look at the steps you can take to try to avoid making that error. We'll look at the stakeholder analysis—the process you can use to make sure you have identified everyone you need to involve as you move forward with your project. And yes, we'll also look at what you can do if a red team member, or someone else, lets you know that despite your best planning, you've made that mistake anyway.

Learn more. Check out:

Kovic, M. 2019. "What Is Red Teaming, and Why Do You Need It?" *Medium*, March 15. medium.com/arscognitionis/what-is-red-teaming-and-why-do-you-need-it-31a6d4087d2e.

Murphy, J.D. 2011. "The Red Team: A Simple But Effective Method to Improve Mission Planning." *Toolbox HR*, October 27. hr.toolbox.com/blogs/james-d-murphy/the-red-team-a-simple-but-effective-method-to-improve-mission-planning-102711.

Zenko, M. 2018. "Leaders Can Make Really Dumb Decisions: This Exercise Can Fix That." *Fortune*, October 19.

9

Accounting for Key Stakeholders

For a moment, let's think back to the JCo acquisition case you read in chapter 5. In that case, Luis recommended that his company establish four teams to work on an acquisition integration project—the core project team, change management team, transition-monitoring team, and red team. Assuming his company agrees to set up these teams, have they appropriately identified and included everyone they need to get involved with this change initiative? It's natural to say "Yes, that's enough people," but the reality is probably not. And Luis appeared to know this too.

Luis seemed to understand that despite creating these four teams, his organization still hadn't accounted for—or appropriately involved—all of the stakeholders who would be affected by the acquisition. There were employees in JCo's finance, sales, procurement, and HR departments who might need to switch the processes and systems they used to perform their work each day. Wilab employees in these same departments might also find that their jobs were changing. And JCo executive assistants were targeted for job elimination. Clearly these targeted employees faced a significant impact, and their immediate managers and co-workers would be affected too. Wilab and JCo customers might hold very different impressions about the acquisition. And the leaders in each company likely differed in their views too.

Luis probably knew that each of these stakeholder groups had the ability to influence the ultimate success of the acquisition, each in a different way and each with a different level of influence. And Luis may have thought that if each stakeholder group was properly engaged—if each person or group affected by the acquisition felt that their unique concerns and needs were considered, or at least known—then they might be more willing to make the changes needed for the acquisition to succeed. But if key stakeholders felt ignored and weren't properly engaged, Luis knew that they would resist adopting the changes and the acquisition could fail.

That's probably why Luis suggested conducting a stakeholder analysis—a tool that could help him and his project team identify everyone who was affected by the acquisition integration and understand how they were affected. In this chapter, we'll look at the stakeholder analysis that Luis recommended. We'll see that the tool can help Luis and his team—and help you—identify stakeholders' needs and concerns, and make more informed decisions as you create project plans. And in the chapters that follow, you'll see how the stakeholder analysis provides the foundation for communication, training, and other stakeholder engagement plans you need for your change initiative to succeed.

What Is a Stakeholder Analysis?

A colleague of mine with decades of experience leading successful change projects says that the most vital tool you can use during a change project is a stakeholder analysis. My co-worker explains it is essential to understand who will be affected by the change, what they are doing today, and how they will be affected by the change. Then you can use it to involve these stakeholders in the right way, which will be different for each stakeholder group. The stakeholder analysis is your anchor. You need this for your change to succeed.

Why is my colleague so adamant about conducting stakeholder analysis? Why does she think it's such a vital tool—the anchor in your change management toolkit?

Well, change initiatives often fall short of delivering expected results when organizations fail to:
- Identify key stakeholders and understand how the change will affect them.
- Understand each stakeholder group's concerns, needs, expectations, and willingness to adopt the change.
- Develop training and communication tailored to the unique requirements of each stakeholder group.

The stakeholder analysis helps you address these gaps. It's a tool that helps you clarify:
- Who is affected by the change and how
- The level of impact each stakeholder group will experience

- The degree to which each stakeholder group can influence successful adoption of the change
- Stakeholder concerns and points of resistance
- Preferred methods for involving and communicating with each stakeholder group

Armed with the information the stakeholder analysis provides, you can tailor your project plans, communication, training, and other actions to ensure that you're addressing the unique needs and concerns of each stakeholder group. This will help you build buy-in and support for your change initiative as you convey to each stakeholder that you understand how they are affected by the change and that the actions you've planned address their unique circumstances. It's worth the time you invest here.

Let's take a look at the stakeholder analysis document Luis might prepare for the JCo acquisition project, and see how you can conduct a stakeholder analysis for a change project you are supporting (Table 9-1).

Identify Each Stakeholder or Stakeholder Group

In the stakeholder analysis Luis might prepare for the JCo acquisition, he'll start by compiling a list of all the various people and groups that will be affected by Wilab's acquisition of JCo. It doesn't matter if the impact is expected to be significant or relatively minor. At this point Luis just needs to identify each and every party who might be touched by the acquisition integration. For example, Luis understands that members of JCo's finance department might need to perform their jobs in an entirely different way after the acquisition is complete. The impact on this stakeholder group will be significant, so he lists them on the stakeholder analysis. But Luis also may know that the only change likely to happen to JCo manufacturing staff is that a different company name will now appear on their paystub. The impact of the acquisition on this stakeholder group is extremely small, but he lists them on the stakeholder analysis anyway. The list presented in Table 9-1 is only a partial inventory of all the stakeholders Luis and his team need to identify. It is sure to expand as Luis's project team performs their stakeholder analysis in earnest and as their project unfolds.

As you prepare a stakeholder analysis for your change project, start by identifying all the stakeholders who will be affected by the change. The impact the stakeholder experiences may be substantial. Or the impact on a stakeholder group may be extremely minor. At this point, it doesn't matter

Table 9-1. JCo Acquisition Stakeholder Analysis

Stakeholder Group	What Will Change?	Level of Impact	Level of Influence	Key Concerns	Current Commitment	Ideal Commitment	Preferred Method of Communicating	Planned Action
JCo finance department staff	Will adopt Wilab finance processes and systems May restructure department	High	High	JCo finance systems and processes may be highly flexible and tailored for use in a small organization; may lose that flexibility moving to more standardized Wilab systems Loss of job status and authority	Neutral	Supportive	Department meetings	Representative on core project team Representative on transition monitoring team Representative on red team
JCo manufacturing department staff	Company name on paystub will change from JCo to Wilab	Low	Low		Neutral	Neutral	Department meetings Email	Announce change at regularly scheduled department meeting Emails regarding name change
JCo executive assistants	Role elimination	High	Low	Job loss	Hostile	Neutral	Department meetings	1:1 meeting with immediate supervisor
Wilab executive assistants	Absorb work previously performed by JCo executive assistants	High	Moderate	Extra work volume	Against	Supportive		
...								
....								
...								
JCo customers								
Wilab customers								

what the expected level of impact is. Just assemble a list of every person or group. Capture the identities of each stakeholder and stakeholder group on a spreadsheet. Depending on the change initiative, the number of stakeholders affected, and the varying impact on each stakeholder, you may want to identify stakeholders by their individual name or title (for example, Sunita Evans or JCo CFO) or you may represent them by the group to which they belong (for example, JCo sales department staff).

To identify a comprehensive list of stakeholders, gather input from members of your core project team and change management team, project sponsors and organization leaders, members of the transition-monitoring team, and the stakeholders themselves. You can:

- Ask the core project team and change management team to brainstorm and prepare a draft list of every person and group they believe will be affected by the change. During this brainstorming session you can also begin to capture initial ideas about what will change for each stakeholder.
- Review the draft list with your project sponsors and with organization leaders to determine if the list is complete. Amend the list of stakeholders based on their input.
- Review the list with members of your transition-monitoring team, and update the list to include any additional stakeholders they have identified.
- During project status meetings with stakeholders, share the list of stakeholders that you and your team have identified. Ask if they can think of others who will be affected by the change, and amend the stakeholder list accordingly.

Think of your stakeholder analysis as an evolving document. If you learn about new stakeholders—even well after the change has begun—update the stakeholder analysis to include them. You may need to put the project on pause for a moment so you can get these newly identified stakeholders caught up, and so you can update project plans to reflect their needs and interests. It is worth it. Projects often fail when people forget key stakeholders and don't appropriately engage them in the change process. It is better to amend your analysis to include stakeholders whom you've inadvertently omitted than to ignore the mistake.

As you identify additional stakeholders, you may need to modify the composition of the teams working on your project. It's absolutely fine to expand your core project team or the transition-monitoring team or the red team to include a newly identified stakeholder. You want to ensure that your project plans consider and address the needs of everyone who's affected by the change.

Summarize What Will Change

As you compile a list of stakeholders, identify what will be changing for each and capture this information in a column on the stakeholder analysis spreadsheet. For example, in the JCo acquisition case, JCo finance staff likely will begin using Wilab's financial systems and processes, so that's what's listed for them on the sample stakeholder analysis. JCo executive assistants might face job eliminations, so that's what is captured on the spreadsheet for them.

Use a few phrases or a short bulleted list to summarize what is changing for each stakeholder. Over the course of your project, your core project team and change management team will need to develop a detailed and fully comprehensive understanding of what will change for each stakeholder group. For the purposes of the stakeholder analysis, just present this information in summary form.

- Gather information about the expected impact during meetings and conversations with members of your core project team and change management team, as well as project sponsors and organization leaders.
- Review the expected impact with your transition-monitoring team and ask if they believe the analysis appropriately captures how the change will affect the stakeholder group they represent. Modify the stakeholder analysis document to reflect their input as needed.
- During project status meetings with stakeholders, share how you anticipate they will be affected by the change. Ask for their input to determine if anything is missing, and update the stakeholder analysis document accordingly.

When communicating with stakeholders about what will change, be as specific and as honest as you can be, tailoring your message about what will change to the particular stakeholder group you are meeting with. Where possible, frame what will change in terms of who will be affected, what specifically will change, when the change will happen, and how the change will be implemented—including the role the stakeholder will play in implementing the change. But also be clear about why the change is happening. What are the organizational benefits—and what is in it for the particular stakeholder you are speaking with?

Of course, when you are just beginning the stakeholder analysis, the information you share with stakeholders may be a bit vague, because you haven't yet performed a comprehensive assessment of how each stakeholder group will be affected by and involved in the change initiative. It's OK to let stakeholders know that at this stage you are just sharing what you anticipate will change for them, that you are asking for their input to be sure the analysis is complete, and that you will update them frequently with specific details as the project unfolds. For example, in the JCo acquisition case, JCo finance employees may be told that, as a result of the acquisition, they probably will begin using Wilab's financial systems at some point in the future. They also will be told that leaders haven't yet decided if, how, or when that will occur. For now, the project team just needs their help gathering information that Wilab and JCo leaders will use to determine how best to proceed. As they speak with employees whose input is needed, organizational leaders will reassure them that they'll be kept in the loop as they make decisions that affect them.

When you need to inform stakeholders about how a change may or may not affect them, thank them for being patient and flexible while your organization figures things out. Apologize for being tentative. State that you don't want them to worry needlessly about events that may or may not occur, and say that you're erring on the side of communicating too much. Hopefully stakeholders will appreciate your efforts to involve them in the decision-making process and to keep them informed. For more details about communicating change, see chapter 12.

Identify the Level of Impact

Identify the extent to which each stakeholder will be affected by the change—whether it is high, medium, low, or none—and summarize this information in a column on the spreadsheet. You can determine level of impact during meetings and conversations with members of the core project team, change management team, project sponsors, and organization leaders, and you can validate your assessment in meetings with the transition-monitoring team. For example, in the JCo acquisition, Luis knew that if and when JCo finance employees start using Wilab's financial systems and processes, their day-to-day work will change considerably. The extent of impact for these stakeholders is high. Likewise, the impact on JCo executive assistants who face job eliminations is high. On the other hand, Luis knew that the impact on JCo manufacturing employees will be low, because the only change they will experience is that a different company name will appear on their paystub.

As you determine level of impact, consider:

- To what extent will this person's day-to-day work change because of this initiative? Will all, some, or none of their work processes and systems change?

- To what extent will the change affect the employee's stated job responsibilities? Will a substantial portion of their job description change, or will the change have a more moderate impact?
- How much does the person need to learn or relearn to remain proficient in their job after the change is implemented?
- To what extent will changes in your organization's structure affect this person? Will the person report to someone new after the change is implemented? Will they have new co-workers?
- Is the stakeholder losing something important as a result of the change? Are they losing their job? Beloved co-workers? A short commute? A prestigious job title?

Identifying the extent to which each stakeholder will be affected by the change can help you determine the most appropriate way to involve them in the change initiative. In most cases, you should provide highly affected stakeholders significant opportunities to get involved, such as having a designated representative on the core project team, membership on the transition-monitoring team or red team, or frequent opportunities to receive project updates and provide feedback.

Identify the Level of Influence

Identify the extent to which each stakeholder can influence whether the change is successfully adopted. That is, to what extent can the stakeholder's decisions and actions influence whether the organization can achieve the ultimate objectives of the change. Summarize this information—whether it is high, medium, low, or none—in a column on the spreadsheet. Again, you can determine level of influence during meetings and conversations with members of the core project team and change management team, as well as project sponsors and organization leaders, and validate your assessment in meetings with the transition-monitoring team.

For example, in the stakeholder analysis Luis might prepare for the JCo acquisition case (see Table 9-1), he indicates that JCo finance employees have a relatively high level of influence. That's because JCo finance employees will need to learn and begin using Wilab's financial processes and systems in order for the project goals to be realized. However, Luis indicates that JCo executive assistants will have a lower level of influence on the project outcome, because they are expected to depart the organization as their jobs are eliminated.

In most cases, high-influence stakeholders should receive priority consideration as you and your team make project-related decisions. Depending on their role in the organization, highly influential stakeholders may serve as project sponsors for the initiative or may have a designated representative on the core project team, the transition-monitoring team, and/or the red team. Provide them with frequent project updates and opportunities to give input and feedback.

Once you've identified the extent to which each stakeholder is affected by the change and their level of influence, map out your analysis in a two-by-two grid. Table 9-2 gives an example that Luis might prepare.

Table 9-2. JCo Acquisition Stakeholder Impact Influence Grid

		Influence	
		Low	High
	High	JCo Executive Assistants	JCo Finance Staff
			Wilab Executive Assistants
Impact	Low	JCo Manufacturing Staff	Wilab Executive Team

Use the grid to tailor a change strategy for each stakeholder group based on the quadrant in which they fall. As you craft your project, communication, training, and stakeholder engagement plans, provide high-impact, high-influence stakeholders with lots of opportunities to get involved. For example, you may provide these stakeholders with opportunities to participate, or have a co-worker represent their needs, on your core project team, transition-monitoring team, or red team. Provide them with numerous opportunities for two-way communication. You need their input and support! On the other hand, you can focus less time and resources communicating with stakeholders who are minimally affected by and have minimal influence over the change.

Here's how Luis might use information in the stakeholder influence impact grid in Table 9-2 to guide change strategies for the JCo acquisition:

- If the only change JCo manufacturing staff will experience is that the company name appearing on their paystub will be different, they likely will experience a very low level of impact and will have low influence over whether the project will be a success. Communication to this group may be more one-directional and delivered via their regularly scheduled department meetings, emails, and the company website.

- JCo executive assistants, whose jobs will be eliminated, will experience a high level of impact, but their level of influence over the ultimate success of the acquisition will be relatively modest, because they will be exiting the organization. Communication with this group of employees should be handled via one-on-one, in-person conversations occurring between each affected employee and their immediate supervisor. The goal of this communication won't necessarily be to have the affected employees buy into or support the change—after all, they are unfortunately losing their jobs—but to help them understand what's happening and feel like they are being treated with respect.

- Some Wilab executive team members may experience little change in their day-to-day work or oversight responsibilities because of the acquisition. But they may have significant influence over the resources that will be allocated to the acquisition integration and to strategic decisions that will be made. They should receive frequent, in-person updates regarding the status of the acquisition integration project, and may play a key role making or approving various project-related decisions.

- It's possible that work volume for Wilab's executive assistants will increase significantly, if they are expected to complete the work previously performed by JCo staff whose jobs are being eliminated. The ability—and willingness—of Wilab executive assistants to absorb this additional work could influence in a moderate way the success of the acquisition. Wilab executive assistants likely will need to be involved in acquisition integration planning in some way, so they understand what is expected of them and why, they feel involved in determining how to take on the additional challenge, and they feel invested in ensuring that the change is executed successfully.

Gather Other Needed Information

Depending on your change initiative, there are other columns of information you may want to include in your stakeholder analysis. Gather this information during conversations and meetings with each stakeholder group, and capture it in summary form on the stakeholder analysis document. Then use this information to determine how to best involve each stakeholder group in the change project.

Consider gathering information such as:

Key concerns: What might the stakeholder group lose as a result of the change? Are they at risk of losing their sense of competence as current systems and processes are replaced? Might they lose a sense of status because of job title changes? Will they have a longer commute? Lose beloved co-workers? Identifying and documenting these concerns can help you plan how best to address the specific sense of loss stakeholders might experience as the initiative unfolds.

Current commitment level: To what extent does the stakeholder currently support the initiative? Are they hostile, openly opposing the change? Against the change, but not openly hostile? Neutral, neither supporting nor opposing the change? Supportive, even willing to assist if asked? An advocate, openly prompting others to adopt the change? Tailor your change plans and tactics based on each stakeholder's current commitment level.

Ideal commitment level: For the change to be successful, what level of support do you need from the stakeholder? A low-impact, low-influence stakeholder who is currently openly hostile about the change may only need to be moved into the neutral zone, where they will neither oppose nor support the change. Tailor your strategies to do that. Likewise, for the change to be a success, you may need high-impact, high-influence supervisors, who currently are supportive of the change, to be converted into advocates. You'll need to use a different approach to make that move.

Preferred method of communicating: How does the stakeholder group want to receive updates and information about the change? Do they prefer one-to-one conversations? Do they have biweekly department meetings that can be used to provide updates? Are they heavy social media users? Is there a culture of providing updates and information via email? Tailor how you share information, depending on the stakeholder's preferred method of communication.

Feedback channel: How does the stakeholder prefer to provide input and feedback? Is there a culture of providing input via anonymous survey? An online "suggestion box"? Or is feedback typically provided in person during one-on-one meetings or in group settings? You likely will need to establish multiple methods for receiving input and feedback regarding the change initiative, tailored to the different types of feedback channels each stakeholder group prefers.

Planned action: Based on all the information you have captured in your stakeholder analysis, what actions will you take to ensure that the stakeholder is appropriately engaged with the change initiative? What will you do to involve the stakeholder in the change? Will you ask them to fully participate in the core project team, or will you send them a few simple emails updating them about the project status? Will you meet one-on-one with them to solicit their active endorsement of and advocacy for the change, or is that not needed for this particular stakeholder group? Will you develop and deliver a comprehensive classroom-based training program to help the stakeholder group develop the knowledge and skills they need to adopt the change, or can the stakeholder group complete a brief online tutorial to help them build the skills they need? Your action plan will evolve over the course of the initiative, as you learn more about each stakeholder and as your plans for the project advance. Use this column on the stakeholder analysis to capture a concise summary of what you have planned.

For the information presented in the stakeholder analysis to be complete and accurate, plan on having conversations with people, and lots of them. You can begin crafting the stakeholder analysis by conducting brainstorming sessions with the core project team and the change management team. But also plan on conducting one-on-one discussions with organization leaders, managers of each stakeholder group, project sponsors, and other key stakeholders. Present the information you collect to members of the transition-monitoring team or the red team to validate the information you have already collected, correct misinformation, and flesh out and add missing details. Likewise, consider presenting appropriate portions of the stakeholder analysis during project update meetings with stakeholder groups.

But be sure to use good judgment when sharing the stakeholder analysis. You don't want a group of stakeholders to see that they—or their co-workers—have been labeled as hostile. Likewise, it likely doesn't make sense to share information about possible job eliminations via a presentation of your stakeholder analysis. The appropriate leader needs to share that information one-on-one with the affected parties. As you share the stakeholder analysis with members of the transition-monitoring team, red team, and stakeholder groups for their validation and feedback, consider which portions of the analysis make sense for these individuals to see. Be sensitive. Protect confidentiality.

And remember, the stakeholder analysis has value only if you use it to create action plans targeted to the unique characteristics of each stakeholder and stakeholder group. Use the information you have gathered in your stakeholder analysis to create your communication plans, training plans, and resistance management plans. These plans are addressed in section 3 of this book.

Addressing the Hard Side With the Stakeholder Analysis

By focusing your attention on the people who are affected by the change as well as their needs and concerns, the stakeholder analysis helps you manage the soft side of change. But the tool can also help you avoid mistakes that could affect your project plans (that is, the hard side of change). When compiling a list of stakeholders who will be affected by the change, err on the side of being over-inclusive. It is better to learn that a group you have included won't be affected after all, than to discover late in the game that you have omitted a stakeholder who has a real vested interest in what's happening. You can avoid resentment and project delays by thinking very broadly as you identify stakeholders.

What Do You Do When You Identify a New Stakeholder Late in the Project?

Even if you and your project team are meticulous as you conduct your stakeholder analysis—even if you check and recheck with stakeholders, transition-monitoring-team members, red team members, project sponsors, and organizational leaders to verify that you've identified all the right stakeholders—sometimes a new stakeholder will emerge late in the game. Maybe it was an oversight. Maybe the new stakeholder just joined your organization and is figuring out which initiatives to get involved with. However it happened, what do you do? How do you appropriately involve a new stakeholder when project decisions have already been made and acted upon?

Certainly meet with the stakeholder to get them up to speed. Apologize for not including them sooner. Share the rationale for the project, the outcomes you're working toward, and the key deliverables. Review the project charter and project plan (see section 1) and update the stakeholder on the current status of the project. Ask the stakeholder how they see the project affecting them. Ask what role they see themselves playing in the project. Which decisions do they need to be consulted about? Which decisions do they just want to be informed about? Which decisions do they believe they have the authority to make?

As a project team, discuss how involving the new stakeholder will affect your change initiative.

- If their impact on project decisions will be substantial, does the new stakeholder need to be included on the core project team? If their role will be less substantial, should they participate in the transition-monitoring team? Should they join the red team?
- How do the stakeholder analysis and RACI matrix (see chapter 10) need to be updated to reflect the new stakeholder?
- How is your project plan affected? Are there key project decisions that need to be revisited? Does the project timeline change? Is your project rolling out in phases? Perhaps it makes sense to include the new stakeholder in a later phase of the launch. Or perhaps there's substantial rework to do and the timeline and budget need to be adjusted.
- Do plans related to communication and training need to change?

Check back with your project sponsor, and other key stakeholders if necessary, to ensure they concur with the changes needed to accommodate the new stakeholder. And be sensitive about how you frame the reason for the changes. The new stakeholder may already question why they were overlooked when project planning began. You don't want them thinking that they're now being blamed for project changes and delays. Let stakeholders know that new information emerged and that project plans need to be updated accordingly.

About to Begin?

While it might seem daunting to perform a comprehensive stakeholder analysis, it's almost always worth it! If the process is new to your organization, consider starting by simply compiling a list of the stakeholders affected by your change initiative and summarizing what is changing for each. Use that list to determine how best to involve and communicate with each stakeholder group. As you and your organization become more comfortable using the tool, add level of impact and influence to your analysis. Prepare a two-by-two grid that maps out impact and influence for each stakeholder, and refine your action plans based on this additional information.

Over time, as you perform stakeholder analyses on multiple change initiatives, consider which additional fields of information add value to your planning and decision making. Does capturing the key concerns of stakeholders help guide your planning (it probably does!)? If so, add that field in to your stakeholder analysis. Is gathering information about stakeholders' preferred feedback channels useful? If so, add that field in too. Play with the stakeholder analysis until you have a format that works best for the change initiatives you help lead in your organization. And tailor the structure to fit the unique requirements of each change project you work on.

At this point, you might wonder if there's a downside to knowing too much about all the people who will be affected by your change initiative. Once you've identified everyone who needs to—or wants to—get involved with your project, isn't it difficult making sure everyone stays on the same page about the role they're supposed to play? Can't you get bogged down as everyone starts to weigh in and provide their opinion about how things should go? How do you help people understand who gets to make each decision, who can influence them, and who just needs to be kept informed?

In the next chapter, we'll look at the RACI matrix, a tool that can be invaluable for helping you establish and maintain order—and avoid ruffled feathers—as your stakeholders start to weigh in on the change they're experiencing. Let's see how the RACI matrix can help you keep your project moving forward amid all the input that's swirling around you.

Learn more. Check out:

Rittenhouse, J. 2015. "Improving Stakeholder Management Using Change Management Tools." Paper presented at PMI Global Congress 2015, Orlando, FL. Newtown Square, PA: Project Management Institute.

Smith, L.W. 2000. "Stakeholder Analysis: A Pivotal Practice of Successful Projects." Paper presented at Project Management Institute Annual Seminars & Symposium, Houston, TX. Newtown Square, PA: Project Management Institute.

10

Designating Roles, Responsibilities, and Authority

When you're working on a major change initiative, it can feel really daunting to involve all the right people in all the right ways. You want to give everyone who's affected by the change an opportunity to provide input. And your stakeholders may be eager—really eager—to have their say. But how do you make sure that in your effort to be inclusive, you don't end up with a free-for-all? Now that you've conducted your stakeholder analysis and have identified everyone who will be affected by the change, how do you make sure you don't get stuck in "analysis paralysis," where you keep receiving input and never make a decision about how to proceed? How can you make it clear who—among all the stakeholders you've identified—can provide input, and who actually has the responsibility and authority to decide what to do?

In this chapter, we'll look at one final tool for involving the right people in the right way: the RACI matrix. We'll see how the RACI matrix can help you and your organization clearly designate and communicate the roles, responsibilities, and decision-making authority of different people who are working on and affected by your change initiative. It is a hard-side tool because it helps you define and clarify who is assigned to perform the actual work of the change project. But the tool also helps you address the soft, people side of change, because it helps you communicate to everyone touched by the change that you are thinking about them and that they have a role to play as the project unfolds.

Think back to the JCo acquisition case you read in chapter 5. In that case, Luis was wise to recommend taking a broad and inclusive approach as organizational leaders decided whom to involve in the company's acquisition integration efforts. But Sheila, the company's head of business development, was also right to be concerned about including so many people in the project. After all, the change involved multiple decisions and tasks that needed to occur simultaneously. The more people the two companies involved, the more difficult it would be to coordinate all those moving parts, and the longer it would take to make decisions about things that had to happen fast. Sheila probably imagined that things would become unwieldy, and she wanted to avoid that at all costs. Luis recognized this too. Most likely that's why he recommended that they construct a RACI matrix.

What Is a RACI Matrix?

According to Bob Kantor, founder of Kantor Consulting Group, "A RACI matrix is the simplest, most effective means for defining and documenting project roles and responsibilities" (Kantor 2018). It's a tool that helps you clearly convey who is responsible, who is accountable, who needs to be consulted, and who needs to be kept informed for each major task and decision that needs to be completed. Kantor explains that a RACI matrix can help you build wide participation in your project, and simultaneously provide clarity about decision making. The tool can also help you avoid miscommunication about who is working on what. It can even help you identify potential stakeholders who are at risk of overwork.

At its core, a RACI matrix identifies who is responsible, accountable, consulted, and informed for each major task or key decision.

Responsible

Who is actually going to complete the task? Who gets to make the decision? For each task or decision, at least one party must be responsible for completing the work—otherwise, it won't get done! Likewise, you can't have too many stakeholders assigned responsibility for completing a task or making a decision, or things will become unwieldy.

Accountable

Who gets to approve the work that has been completed? Who gets to say yes or no to a decision that's been made? Think of the accountable party as the place where the buck stops. For most tasks and decisions, there should be only one person who is ultimately accountable.

Consulted

Who should provide input on how the task is performed or the decision is made? Those who are consulted may have specific knowledge or expertise that you need to tap into before completing the work. Or they may have a significant vested interest in the change and may have considerable influence over whether the change is successfully adopted. These are people who expect to have a say, and who should be consulted.

Informed

Who can you just keep abreast of what is happening? Who needs to be in the know, but doesn't expect to be involved in planning the task or making the decision? These are the people you can inform about the task or decision.

Use a RACI Matrix to Help You . . .

- Build broad participation in your project without making things unwieldy.
- Avoid missteps by making it clear whom you need to consult with and whose authority you need to receive before proceeding with a decision.
- Prevent logjams and analysis paralysis by designating who has decision-making authority.
- Ensure that everyone working on the project understands their role and responsibilities.
- Identify when too many tasks or too much authority has been assigned to any one stakeholder.
- Build effective communications by making it clear whom you need to keep informed.

How to Use a RACI Matrix

To construct a RACI matrix for a change initiative you are supporting, you can follow these easy steps:

- Create a spreadsheet with a row for each major task or decision and a column for each stakeholder or stakeholder group. Use your project plan (see chapter 4) and stakeholder analysis (see chapter 9) as input to this spreadsheet.
- Fill in the spreadsheet cells, indicating R for stakeholders who are responsible for the task or decision, A for those who are accountable, C for those who need to be consulted, and I for those who need to be informed.
- Review the spreadsheet to ensure you've assigned at least one stakeholder responsibility for completing each task, and that no single stakeholder has been assigned too many responsibilities or too much

Table 10-1. JCo Acquisition RACI Matrix

	Sponsors		Integration Project Team						External Parties	
	Wilab CEO	JCo CEO	Wilab CFO	JCo CFO	Wilab IT Leader	JCo IT Leader	JCo Finance Staff	Change Management Subteam	Wilab Clients	JCo Clients
Governance Decisions										
Task 1	R A	C	C	I	I	I		I		
Task 2	C	R A	I	C	I	I		I		
Task ...										
Phase ...										
Systems Analysis										
Analyze JCo Financial Systems Requirements			C	A	R	R		I		
Systems Training										
Develop Financial Systems Training			C	A	C	C	I	R		
Deliver Financial Systems Training			C	A	C	C	I	R		
Internal Communications										
Task 1	A	C	C	C	C	C	I	R		
Task 2	A	C	C	C	C	C		R		
Task ...										
External Communications										
Task 1	A	C	C	C	C	C		C	I	I
Task 2	A	C	C	C	C	C		C	I	I
Task ...										

decision-making authority. Likewise, make sure you've assigned an accountable party for each task.

- Share your draft RACI matrix, resolve any conflicts, and revise and make updates as needed.

Let's take a look at a RACI matrix that Luis, in the JCo acquisition case, might create as his project proceeds (Table 10-1).

Luis starts by creating a spreadsheet that includes a row for each major task and decision the two companies need to complete during the acquisition integration project. In this partial example, we've just listed a few tasks, like "Analyze JCo financial system requirements" and "Deliver financial systems training." Luis and the core project team will document all the major tasks and decisions on the spreadsheet as their planning evolves.

Next, Luis adds a column on the spreadsheet for each stakeholder involved in the project, such as the project sponsors, including Wilab's and JCo's CEOs; members of the core project team, like JCo's IT leader; and external parties such as Wilab's and JCo's clients. The example shown in Table 10-1 isn't complete by any means. As Luis and his team conduct their stakeholder analysis, they will be sure to add a column in the RACI matrix for each stakeholder they identify.

Luis then fills in the spreadsheet cells, indicating R in each cell where the listed stakeholder is responsible for completing the task or making the decision, A in the cells where a stakeholder is accountable for the task or decision, C to indicate when a stakeholder will be consulted or provide input on the task or decision, and I in places where stakeholders will simply be informed of the task or decision. For example, in Table 10-1, we see that the change management team will be responsible for delivering financial systems training, JCo's IT leader will be consulted on that delivery, and JCo's CFO will ultimately be accountable for ensuring that the training is delivered to her staff. Again, the RACI matrix presented in Table 10-1 is incomplete. Luis's core project team and change management team, with lots of input from Wilab and JCo leadership and stakeholders, will ultimately create a draft RACI matrix that conveys their thoughts about who will play what role and have what kind of responsibility on the project.

Involving Stakeholders

Once you have created your RACI matrix, use it, along with your stakeholder analysis, to plan how you will involve each stakeholder at the appropriate level.

- For each stakeholder you've identified as having responsibility for a task or decision, make sure you communicate with them about what you expect them to deliver and by when. Before finalizing project plans, secure their agreement on the role you need them to play. Use the RACI matrix to remind those who are responsible about the work they need to perform (that hopefully they have agreed to!) for your project to proceed.
- Secure authorization from those assigned the accountable role before committing resources to a task or widely communicating a decision. Refer to the RACI matrix and make sure the accountable party associated with a task or decision agrees with the planned action before you proceed.
- For each stakeholder identified as having a consulting role, think about the methods you will use to gather their input and feedback. For some stakeholders, it will make sense to gather their input via one-on-one meetings. For others, you may want to invite them to participate, or have a co-worker represent them, on the core project team, transition-monitoring team, or red team. As project plans and decisions are made, refer to the RACI matrix to make sure you have gathered input from everyone who needs to be consulted before your plan or decision is finalized.
- As you develop communication plans, review your RACI matrix to make sure you create plans for each stakeholder group you need to keep informed. Use the RACI matrix to remind you about whom you need to keep up-to-date about what. We'll explore this again in chapter 12, when we'll talk in depth about creating communication plans.

Use Your RACI Matrix to Help Address These Common Events and Challenges

- Are you ready to move forward with a key action in your project plan, commit a major resource, or broadly communicate your plan? Check your RACI matrix to make sure you've obtained input from everyone you need to consult with. Verify you've obtained authorization to proceed from the person who's accountable for the decision. And make sure you communicate what's happening with everyone whom you've identified needs to be kept informed.
- Are you getting pushback about who is supposed to be working on some portion of your project plan? Review the RACI matrix and remind people about who has responsibility for completing the task.

- Do stakeholders disagree with one another about how the project should proceed? Have they reached a stalemate? Check your RACI matrix to make sure you've consulted with everyone who needs to weigh in on the decision. Then look at who has responsibility for making the decision and who needs to approve it. Rely on these parties to break the logjam.
- Do you need to change course on your project and reverse a major decision? Make sure you've consulted with everyone who needs to provide input. And make sure you have approval from the person who's ultimately accountable for the decision before you proceed.

Addressing the Soft Side With the RACI Matrix

The RACI matrix is a well-proven project management tool that can help you manage the hard side of change. It helps you make sure that someone is assigned to work on each project-related task and that someone is charged with making each key project decision. But when the tool is used most effectively, it also can help you convey to those affected by a change that you are thinking about them, that their involvement matters, and that you want and need them to play a role in the change initiative.

Here are some tips for maintaining focus on the soft, people side of change as you create a RACI matrix for your change initiative.

- When assigning consulting responsibility to stakeholders, think broadly. Where possible, assign consulting responsibility to stakeholder groups who could lose the most because of the change—those whose jobs are changing considerably who will need to work hard to rebuild their level of job competency; employees who will experience a marked increase in work volume, either on a temporary or permanent basis; and stakeholders who might lose their job status because of the change. Sometimes employees will resist a change, not because they disagree with what's planned, but because they resent not having the opportunity to provide input. Refer back to your stakeholder analysis. Which stakeholders have you determined will be most significantly affected by the change? Should you and your team consult with them and gather their input before project decisions are made?
- Be clear with stakeholders who are assigned consulting responsibility that you are asking for their input, but that they don't have decision-making authority. Be honest with those who are assigned consulting

responsibility that you will provide them with numerous opportunities to share their ideas, and that you will consider their input when making decisions. But let them know that other stakeholder views and other business needs will be factored into the decision as well, and that someone else has ultimate authority to make the decision. Let consulting parties know that you will share decisions with them as soon as is reasonably possible.

- Review your draft RACI matrix with stakeholders who have been assigned responsible, accountable, and consulting roles. To avoid ruffling feathers, be sure to let them know that the initial RACI matrix is just a draft, that it likely contains mistakes, and that you absolutely need their input before final roles and responsibilities are assigned. You may need to engage in multiple conversations to resolve disagreements, but it's worth it to hammer out issues up front until you reach agreement. Negotiating and relitigating roles and responsibilities while a project is ongoing can lead to delays and hard feelings. Work on resolving conflicts and gaining agreement on the major roles and responsibilities represented in the RACI matrix before officially launching and widely communicating the news about your project.

About to Begin?

To introduce the RACI matrix to your organization, start by creating one for a project you are working on. It doesn't matter if the initiative is already under way; just practice creating the tool. Share your draft RACI matrix with the stakeholders you have identified and ask for their feedback. Did you accurately capture the role, responsibilities, and decision-making authority they expect to have on your project? And review your draft RACI matrix to identify any gaps. Are there tasks or decisions for which no one is assigned responsibility? You can fix that now, even though your project in already in progress. Are there stakeholders whom you should have assigned a consulting role? Is it too late now to ask for their input? Once you have gained practice creating a RACI matrix for your projects, volunteer to help create them for other change initiatives that are getting under way in your organization. The project team may welcome your effort.

Before we move on to the next section, let's reflect for a moment on the tools we've addressed in section 2. We explored the core project team, change management team, transition-monitoring team, red team, stakeholder analysis, and RACI matrix—six approaches and tools you can use to involve the right people in the right way as your change initiative proceeds. At this point, you may wonder if setting up those four teams plus preparing a stakeholder analysis and RACI matrix are worth all the effort. You've got a lot of work to do. Can't you skip a few steps? Well, let's consider.

Do you need to establish a formal core project team for every change initiative? Maybe not, but you do need to make sure that some person or group is responsible for planning the initiative and providing oversight as your project moves through its various phases. A core project team can help you do that. And do you always need to create a change management team? Again, no, but someone needs to perform the change management function. For your change to succeed, someone needs to identify all the stakeholders who will be affected by the change and make sure their needs and concerns are considered as decisions are made. And someone needs to make sure employees understand, support, and have the skills needed to implement the change.

How about the transition-monitoring team? Well, depending on the complexity and scope of the change you're working on, you may or may not need to set them up as a formal team. But you do need some vehicle for gathering feedback from stakeholder groups affected by your change, for testing out draft plans and communications before you finalize them, and for reinforcing communications on the ground. And the red team? We already said that it's overkill to obtain an independent critique of each and every action and decision you make. But it's still an excellent discipline to pause and take a step back every now and then to critically evaluate decisions before you execute them. And it's even better to have an independent pair of eyes, like you'll find on the red team, to provide that critical assessment.

Do you need to perform a stakeholder analysis on every change initiative? Yes, you do! For your change initiative to succeed, you really do need to think about who will be affected by the change and how, and you do need to find ways to appropriately engage them. Stakeholder analysis, whether it's represented in a formal chart or spreadsheet, or just captured in handwritten notes on a piece of scrap paper, can make the difference between project success and failure. And finally, do you need to create a formal RACI matrix? No, but you do need to clarify roles, responsibilities, and decision-making authority before your project launches. A RACI matrix provides just the tool you might need to make things clear so you can avoid costly delays and misunderstandings.

The bottom line: You may decide to fully implement the core project team, change management team, transition-monitoring team, red team, stakeholder analysis, and RACI matrix. Or you may decide to use these tools in a more abbreviated form. Just remember that for your change to succeed, you need to involve the right people in the right way. These tools and approaches, however you choose to deploy them, can help you achieve that goal.

Of course, you also need to make sure the people affected by your change initiative understand what's changing, feel motivated to adopt the change, and have the knowledge and skills needed to adopt it. In section 3, we'll see how that's done.

Learn more. Check out:

For a template and an instructional video, take a look at raci.com.

Kantor, B. 2018. "The RACI Matrix: Your Blueprint for Project Success." *CIO*, January 30.

Building Awareness, Understanding, and Support

11

The PCo Business Transformation Case

Sharon had a hunch that joining PCo as the company's new director of learning and organizational development would be an opportunity of a lifetime. PCo was a midsize, privately held developer and manufacturer of chemical additives, with research facilities and manufacturing plants in the northern half of the US. After the sudden resignation of its long-time CEO, the company's board promoted Petrina Kovac, PCo's young chief operating officer, to the company's top leadership position. Petrina had just joined the company six months earlier, and had already impressed the board with ideas for strengthening the company's rather tepid market position. With the departure of the prior CEO, the company could now move into high gear with changes needed to produce much-needed market and financial improvements.

During her job interview with Petrina, Sharon learned that the company's product development, production, and sales processes were seriously outdated. If PCo was going to survive into the next decade, radical transformation was needed. This meant introducing rigorous business practices at the company's R&D labs and manufacturing facilities and completely overhauling PCo's approach to sales. And the company's culture needed transformation too. PCo was widely known to be a nice, low-pressure company to work for. The work was steady and predictable, albeit not all that exciting, and employees felt like family. It was a place where good news—whether it was business-related or personal—was openly shared. And bad news? Well, no one really ever brought that up. Petrina knew that for the company to change, employees needed to hear the truth about PCo's weak market and financial position. New performance goals needed to be set that stretched people beyond their current comfort zones. Everyone needed to be held accountable for producing results. Petrina hoped the company could retain its family feel and culture of niceness. But it also needed to run more like a business. That meant that some hard work—and some unpleasant news—was in store.

When Petrina called and offered Sharon the job, Sharon wondered how wise it would be to join PCo at this moment in its history, because the company's financial viability was a real question. But Sharon was intrigued by the chance to apply her change management skills to a full-scale organizational transformation. She had created training and communication programs to support other companies as they implemented change, but PCo's change appeared massive in comparison. And Sharon looked forward to working with Petrina. From what she could see, PCo's new CEO really seemed to get it. She understood the need for change, wasn't afraid to make big moves, and respected the role that learning and organizational development could play in helping employees embrace the changes that were about to occur. After all, it was Petrina who had recognized the need for the lead L&OD position that Sharon had been offered. And it was Petrina who convinced Sharon to take the role.

Sharon had barely begun to settle into her new job when Petrina invited her to join one of her regularly scheduled CEO staff meetings. "We'll be discussing some of the changes planned for R&D, sales, and operations," Petrina relayed during a quick phone call with Sharon. "We'd love to bounce some ideas off of you. We'll send you the WebEx info."

A few days later, when Sharon called into the meeting, she was early. She surveyed her screen, and saw that most of Petrina's direct reports had already logged in and were exchanging pleasantries. There was Ivan, PCo's vice president of R&D. Sharon had met him during one of the meet-and-greet sessions that had been arranged during her first week on the job. Ivan had joined PCo just a year earlier, and he seemed as eager as Petrina to shake things up. Sharon also recognized Phil, the company's CFO, and Lupe, PCo's vice president of sales. Lupe was a relative newcomer to the company too. Sharon's manager, Evelyn, who led HR and internal communications, had the day off, and had promised to check in with Sharon when she returned.

Right on time, Petrina pinged in. And a moment later, another face appeared. Sharon assumed it was Ed, PCo's acting vice president of operations. Ed managed PCo's largest plant and had stepped into the acting VP role following Petrina's promotion to CEO. Ed wasn't available during Sharon's meet-and-greet sessions, so she was eager to connect with him. Perhaps they could arrange a videochat after today's meeting ended.

"Good, we're all here," Petrina announced as she kicked off the meeting. "Thanks, Sharon, for joining us today. I think you all know our brightest new addition to the PCo team. Sharon has a wealth of experience helping companies manage change. I know you'll all enjoy partnering with her as we take some big steps forward."

Sharon nodded and smiled. It felt good to be recognized as a partner to the executive team. Petrina really did get it.

"OK," Petrina continued. "So we have some ideas we want to share with you, Sharon. You're the expert, so let us know what you think."

"I'm eager to hear and I'm here to help," Sharon responded. This meeting really was opportune. From what Sharon could tell, all PCo employees knew at this point was that there were leadership changes at the top. It would be Sharon's job to create a communications plan. The plan would summarize the steps PCo would take to help employees understand what was changing at the company and why, and how their own work would be affected. She needed to create a training plan, too, that described how employees would build the knowledge, skills, and attitudes they needed as their jobs and work environment changed. And she'd create a resistance management plan, because not everyone would see the changes at PCo as a good thing. There could be some foot dragging and even outright opposition. Sharon wanted to make sure employees felt like they were part of the transformation—that they were participating in creating the change, and that it wasn't just something happening to them. Today's meeting could really help Sharon start developing these plans. She was excited to hear everyone's ideas and to have the opportunity to share some of her own thoughts.

"Ivan, why don't you kick us off with your thoughts about R&D?" Petrina proposed.

"Hi, Sharon. It was great talking with you last week," Ivan began. "As I mentioned, we're in a bit of a pickle at the labs. Our lab managers are brilliant researchers. They're creative geniuses. The ideas they have in the pipeline will be phenomenal for PCo when they finally hit the market." For a moment Sharon thought she saw Phil rolling his eyes as Ivan gushed about his team. "But we're facing significant cost overruns," Ivan continued. "These guys aren't business people. They're chemists. And despite all their brilliance, they're making really stupid decisions when it comes to buying equipment for the labs and managing people. They just want to run their labs and focus on the science. But we have to pay attention to the business side too."

Sharon nodded. Ivan was repeating what he had shared during their quick meet and greet.

"So here's what I've decided to do," *Ivan continued.* "I'm going to hire a business manager for each lab, someone who can handle day-to-day lab operations so each lab manager can focus exclusively on science and innovation. The business manager and lab manager will be partners in running the lab—co-equals of sorts."

Phil, PCo's CFO, interrupted. "Ivan, they will never go for that! The R&D managers are going to see it as a whopping demotion. They're used to being kings and now they need to consult with someone when they want to buy supplies for their own labs? We need these guys, and they're going to be heading for the hills!"

"I think I can convince a few of them," *Ivan responded.* "They really do just want to focus on the science. Everything else is just a big distraction. I can help them see that the business manager will be there to remove distractions."

"And the R&D managers who don't agree?" *Phil countered sharply.*

Sharon was about to speak when she saw Petrina frantically waving her hands. "Stop, guys. Stop!" *Petrina cut in.* "I think Sharon can help us out here. Sharon can join the meeting when Ivan lets the lab managers know about the plan. And then she can circle back to the ones who seemed to have the most issues with the idea. I agree with Phil that some of the lab managers won't want to get on board. But Sharon's an expert here. She'll turn them around."

That wasn't at all what Sharon was about to propose. She'd hadn't even met the lab managers yet. Why would they listen to her? Sharon was about to unmute herself so she could suggest a different approach, but Petrina wasn't done speaking.

"So, Lupe, how about sales?" *Petrina asked, switching gears.*

Lupe was quick to respond. "Our sales staff and sales managers have been really complacent. They spend most of their time calling their regular customers for reorders. They figure, why seek out new customers when the regulars are sure things? That worked in the past when we were really the only game in town, but there's tough new competition now. I need sales staff out there hustling. And they need to view themselves as consultants to prospective customers, instead of just order takers."

Sharon nodded. Lupe had shared this assessment when they had met too.

"So I want the entire sales team to take a consultative selling course," *Lupe continued.* "There are lots of good vendors out there. I need the sales team to learn what consultative selling is and then they need to just do it."

Petrina interjected again. "You got that, Sharon? When we're done today, why don't you and Lupe look at a few vendors and decide which one we can use."

Sharon was about to ask a question, but Petrina pressed on. "Phil and I have been talking about PCo's culture. Employees are clueless about our financial situation because we don't share the numbers with them."

"Sharon, our P&L is confidential," Phil explained. "We can't have any leaks."

Petrina cut in. "Phil, you and I both keep talking about accountability. But how can we hold employees accountable for results they know nothing about? We need to figure out which financials make sense to share. And we need to let employees know we're trusting them to use these financials wisely."

Sharon jumped in. "Will employees understand what the financials mean? Will they know how their work affects the financials?" she asked. She had to admit, interpreting P&L statements wasn't her forte. And although she thought she knew how her work affected PCo's P&L, she wasn't 100 percent sure. Sharon assumed most PCo employees would struggle to see the connection for their own work too.

"Great question," Petrina responded. "Phil and I have been talking about that. Tell her, Phil."

Phil sighed as he explained. "We think everyone should complete an online tutorial. You know, Finance 101. I can show you some examples of what we have in mind. And maybe we can do a tutorial on ethics and confidentiality too."

Sharon sensed Phil wasn't completely on board with the approach. "OK, I'd love to talk with you about that," Sharon assured Phil. "A tutorial could address a piece of what's needed."

"Great," Phil responded. "I'm willing to give it a try. But the finance managers are going to go nuts over this. You know, they consider themselves to be the keepers of the secrets. What will they think when every last employee knows those secrets too?"

"The numbers can't be secret, Phil," Petrina reiterated. "Nothing is going to change if people don't know what's going on."

Phil smiled. "Yup. Sharon and I are going to work up a plan."

Petrina nodded and pressed on. "So I'm going to start holding town hall meetings during my visits to the labs and plants. I'll share the financials during these meetings, let employees know what's happening in the business. And I'm going to use those meetings to talk about accountability: what it means, what it looks like."

Sharon thought back to her interview with Petrina. She found Petrina to be an engaging storyteller. Maybe they could tap into Petrina's storytelling skills during the town hall meetings. But she'd need to rein Petrina in and make sure employees had a chance to speak too. She didn't want the town hall meeting to be a repeat of what this meeting felt like. She had come prepared with ideas but found she couldn't get more than a word or two in.

Right on cue, as Sharon was about to share a thought, Petrina plowed forward. "And speaking of needing more accountability, there's operations." Sharon thought she saw Phil and Lupe wince.

"Present!" Ed chimed in.

"We have some real work to do there," Petrina continued. "The plant managers know how to make stuff. But they're ignorant about financials and marketing, and they're making some really bad decisions because of that. They don't act like they're running a business. I need them to act more like entrepreneurs."

Ed was silent so Petrina pressed on. "During her interview, Sharon told me about an MBA boot camp she created at another company. We need something like that for the plant managers—PCo executives and faculty from a university working together to teach the plant managers how to act like businesspeople." Now Sharon was wincing. Maybe that's what the plant managers needed and maybe not.

"Sounds great," Ed responded, a bit too quickly. "I'm all in. Just let me know when and where and my folks will be there."

"Well, let's talk first," Sharon jumped in. Was she finally going to have a chance to speak? "If you all have time now, I have some questions. And I have some ideas I'd love to bounce off of you."

"That would be great, Sharon," Petrina responded. "Right now, we have some other agenda items we need to cover. But I think you're clear on what we need. So, it was so great having you join us. Thanks so much for your time today."

Wait, Sharon thought. Was she being dismissed? She had barely scratched the surface of what she hoped to discuss.

"Bye, Sharon!" Petrina announced.

Yup, Sharon realized. She had just been dismissed.

Sharon clicked "Leave Meeting" and watched the images of the executive team members disappear from her screen. She sighed as she chastised herself for not pushing back on some of the ideas Petrina and her team had proposed. She vowed to do better when she circled back to each executive later this week.

Sharon had so many questions for the team, and real doubts that the ideas they wanted her to move forward with would have any impact.

Did Petrina and Ivan really think she could convince R&D managers to share their labs with a business manager? They'd never even met her. Sharon didn't want to engage in arm-twisting anyway. Perhaps there was a better way.

Did the sales staff need consultative selling skills training? True, Sharon thought, the sales staff were just operating like order takers today. But was that because they didn't know how to engage in consultative selling? Or was something else going on?

What was up with Phil, PCo's CFO? Sharon wondered if the financial tutorial Phil proposed was just a throwaway—something Phil agreed to work on to appease Petrina. He certainly seemed to have reservations about sharing financial documents with employees, and his finance staff did too. Their concerns about confidentiality seemed valid. Or maybe they didn't like losing their status as "the keepers of the secrets."

How about Ed, PCo's acting head of operations? He seemed almost too agreeable, but in a passive sort of way. Was he just "checking the box" on the whole MBA boot camp idea? Sharon had seen behavior like this at her last company—leaders outwardly complying but not really changing anything in the way they ran their business.

And what did Petrina really want when she talked about culture change and accountability at PCo? Sharon was happy that Petrina wanted to conduct town hall meetings. They could provide a good opportunity for PCo employees to meet Petrina and hear her ideas and perspectives about the company. But from what she'd just witnessed, Petrina could be a bit of a bulldozer. Would she be open to hearing what PCo employees had to say? And who else besides Petrina should be talking about accountability, anyway?

Sharon shook her head as she realized that only 10 minutes had elapsed since she first joined the meeting. "So much for being a partner," she muttered out loud, glad that no one could hear her in her home office. So where to begin?

Sharon mused for a moment, then clicked to open a blank spreadsheet on her laptop. "Just get down everything you just heard." Sharon chuckled as she realized she was still speaking to herself. But it seemed like good advice. "Then you'll figure out what to do."

A half hour later, Sharon had created three separate spreadsheets: PCo Communications Plan, PCo Training Plan, and PCo Resistance Management Plan (Tables 11-1, 11-2, and 11-3).

Table 11-1. PCo Communications Plan

Communication Event	Key Messages	Audience	Sender/ Leader	Start Date/ End Date	Frequency	Owner/ Creator
R&D Department Meeting	To help manage costs and labor issues, a business manager will be hired for each lab; lab managers will partner with their business manager as co-equals in running the lab	Lab Managers	Ivan and Sharon		Once	Ivan
Town Hall Meetings With CEO	Update on current market status and financials—here's why we need to change and how we're doing To change, we need everyone to be accountable for the results they contribute to	All Employees	Petrina			Petrina

Table 11-2. PCo Training Plan

Audience	Objective	Training Program	Method	Start Date/ End Date	Frequency	Owner/ Creator
Sales Staff	Understanding of and ability to engage in consultative selling process	Consultative Selling Skills	Classroom instruction led by vendor			Sharon and Ed
All Employees	Ability to read and interpret simple financial document	Finance 101	Online tutorial			Sharon and Phil
All Employees	Understanding of what information is confidential and why; ability to treat confidential information appropriately	Ethics 101	Online tutorial			Sharon and Phil
Plant Managers	Ability to make marketing and finance decisions	MBA Boot Camp	Classroom instruction co-led by university faculty and PCo business leaders			Sharon

She skimmed the documents and shook her head. "Not good," Sharon announced aloud. "Not good at all. But it's a start. I have my work cut out for me."

Table 11-3. PCo Resistance Management Plan

Stakeholder Group	What Will Change?	Level of Impact	Level of Influence	Key Concerns/ Source of Resistance	Current Commitment	Ideal Commitment	Planned action
Lab Managers	Need to manage costs and labor issues more tightly May need to work closely with new business manager	High	High	Used to working completely independently; don't want oversight Loss of prestige and authority	Against	Supportive	One-on-one meetings with Sharon
CFO	Need to begin sharing financial data more broadly	High	High	Need to protect confidential information	Against	Supportive	
Finance Managers	Need to begin sharing financial data more broadly	Moderate	Moderate	Need to protect confidential information Loss of prestige when they no longer have exclusive access to financials?	Against	Moderate	
Acting Vice President of Operations	Needs to hold plant managers accountable for financial and marketing decisions	High	High	Unknown	Unknown	Supportive	

What work was Sharon thinking about? Was she wondering about the communications plan she needed to flesh out? In chapter 12, we'll look at the many factors to consider as you develop plans to help employees understand what is changing, why, and how their own work is affected. You'll see that Sharon was right to think about who—besides Petrina—should be talking about the changes planned for PCo. And you'll see that there are lots of other approaches to communication that Sharon and the PCo executive team need to employ.

Was Sharon wondering about the items she had included in PCo's training plan? In chapter 13, we'll review steps you can take to help employees build the knowledge, skills, and attitudes they need to succeed as their jobs and work environment change. You'll understand why Sharon was uncomfortable proceeding with the training plan she had drafted. And you'll see why she felt like she had so many questions to ask about training that PCo employees may or may not need.

Or was Sharon thinking about resistance to the change? In chapter 14, we'll look at steps you can take to create a resistance management plan. A well-crafted plan can help your organization anticipate and address resistance and use that resistance to improve how your organization's change process unfolds. You'll see that Sharon has lots of opportunities to intervene and address resistance as it emerges at PCo.

As you read on, you'll see that Sharon does indeed have her work cut out for her. Building awareness, understanding, and support for organizational change isn't easy. The position Sharon accepted at PCo is in fact challenging. But it also can be, as Sharon thought, the opportunity of a lifetime. Let's look at the steps Sharon—and you—can take to meet that challenge.

12

Communicating About Change

"As you know . . ."

How often have you heard those words when someone is talking about change? "As you know, we are outsourcing . . ." "As you know, our implementation will go live . . ." "As you know, we will be relocating operations . . ." "As you know, we are changing . . ."

Perhaps you've said those words yourself as you updated employees about a change initiative that was happening in your organization. I've certainly said "As you know" many times when I've talked with people about change. That's a mistake. We need to change our mindset around communicating about change.

In fact, Caroline Langer, director of corporate communications at a global manufacturing company, and a leader with more than 30 years of experience communicating about change, has banned "as you know" from all change-related communications at her company. "I never assume I know what someone else has heard or understands about a change that's forthcoming," Langer explains. "Even if we've said something a hundred times, it might be the first time someone has finally tuned in to what's going on." Langer elaborates further, "We can't climb inside someone's head, and it would be really presumptuous of me to pretend to know what someone else is thinking. People can feel really offended when they hear 'As you know.' It can sound belittling and dismissive. Instead, we keep reiterating the messages in a variety of ways and through various forms of communications—memos, stories, videos, meetings, even posters—as we seek to have employees understand and accept what we're trying to convey."

That's wise advice, a pitfall to avoid as we communicate about changes that are happening in our organizations. We certainly don't want to insult anyone.

It's funny how many traps we can fall into as we attempt to communicate about change. Just about everyone recognizes how important it is to focus on communication for our change initiatives to succeed. And yet so many organizations struggle to communicate effectively. Maybe it's easy to see why. If three little words, like "As you know," can offend, what other dangers lurk out there?

In this chapter, we'll look at steps you can take to avoid the most common mistakes organizations make when they communicate about change. We'll look at who should communicate, so stakeholders feel involved and pay attention. We'll look at what to communicate, so employees understand what's changing and why it matters for them. And we'll look at how to communicate, so the messages you send have an impact and are remembered.

You'll see that communicating effectively requires a real commitment to addressing the soft side of change. You need to communicate honestly to build trust. You need to provide lots of opportunities for employees to share their ideas and concerns so they feel like they are full participants in the change. And you'll see that to communicate effectively, you also need to focus on the hard side of change. You need to make sure employees are clear about how their jobs are changing and what they specifically need to do to keep the project moving forward. You need to really listen to the ideas and concerns employees share so you and your project team can make better, more informed decisions.

Although the change management team oversees communications during a change initiative, many other people need to get involved to ensure that employees understand what's happening, why, and how they're affected. There are lots of people and moving parts you need to keep track of and coordinate. We'll cover the steps you and your colleagues can take to create a communications plan that helps you plot out and organize the who, what, when, and how related to all that activity. Depending on where you work and your role, you might be the person who creates and executes the communications plan, or someone in your organization's internal communications function might hold that responsibility, with oversight from the change management leader. Whether you create the plan, provide input for it, or just review it, you'll see that communicating effectively about change requires many, many interrelated actions. It can be challenging, but you and your organization can communicate about change effectively. You may need to avoid three little words, but you still have many others at your disposal.

Who Should Communicate?

Let's review who should communicate during a change, from leaders to managers to the project team. But first, let's think more broadly.

Everyone

When you're in the midst of change, who in your organization communicates? The answer is simple: everyone. A project team meets to discuss next steps. A senior leader shares impressions with a peer about how things are going. Employees gather at the coffee station and whisper about what they've been told and what it "really" means. A group of managers lingers after a video status-update meeting concludes to compare notes about what they should do next. When there's change, just about everyone will talk with someone about it. There will be buzz. You can count on it.

And yet, far too often, when organizations plan communications related to change, they act like that buzz doesn't exist. They focus efforts on crafting formal announcements and deciding when announcements should be made. They plan for "the tell" and ignore the buzz. They spend far too much time focused on what they will say, and far too little time listening.

Listening to the buzz can really matter. Organizations experience greater success with their change initiatives when they provide opportunities for two-way communication. Set up ways for employees to formally share what they're thinking and feeling about a change initiative—whether it's through one-on-one discussions, town hall meetings, surveys, or some other means—and you'll find out how people are interpreting the messages you've sent, or misinterpreting them. You'll learn about how things currently work, so your project team can make more informed decisions about how to change things for the future. You'll hear concerns that, if addressed, might help generate employee support for the initiative. And you'll help employees feel more involved with the change—as if they are active contributors to the change, rather than passive recipients—and that will help generate buy-in and support too.

Remember that, in its most basic form, all communication involves someone sending a message, the message itself, and the receiver. When thinking about who communicates change, recognize that sometimes you—and project leaders and organizational leaders—need to be the senders of a message, and sometimes you and your fellow leaders need to be the receivers.

Leaders

When an organizational consultant I know describes the worst project she ever worked on, she shudders. "The company was restructuring," my friend explains. "Some locations were shutting down, and employees at these sites would be terminated. Other locations would absorb the work from plants and offices that had closed." She was brought in as an external consultant to help the company's leaders figure out how to share this news with all the affected employees. It was a tough job, no doubt. "So I met with the CEO and we scripted everything he needed to say as he met with employees at each site," my friend says. "This is what is changing at the company. This is why. And the bottom line. So this is what will happen at this location, and this is what it means for you. The CEO practiced the script and I gave him pointers. And then the night before he was supposed to leave for his first meeting, the CEO called me and said he couldn't do it. You have to do it." She explains, "So there I was, flying from location to location, introducing myself to people, saying you don't know me but here's what's going to happen to you. It was awful. People kept looking at me, stunned, asking, 'And who are you?' I never should have agreed to do it."

My friend is right. If she could have found a way to convince the CEO, or some other senior leader within the organization, to deliver the news themselves, she should have done so. She understood that, without any personal connection to the company making the changes or to its employees, she lacked credibility. Why would people believe and accept the news she shared? Why should they do anything differently based on what they'd just heard? My friend was a stranger who just arrived on a plane and then would be gone. And yet, so often when organizations communicate about change, they make the same mistake this CEO— and my friend—did. Rather than talking about the change themselves, some senior leaders "outsource" delivery of the message. They ask the project leader to take the lead in communications. After all, they're the expert on what's happening each step of the way, aren't they? Or they ask the head of human resources or the change management leader to deliver the news. People really connect with them, right? Sometimes a leader just doesn't want to be the bearer of bad news. They don't want people to associate the downside of a change with them. Or a leader may feel ambivalent about the initiative's chances of success. They don't want to risk being connected with a failure.

But for employees to actually do anything differently after a change is announced, they have to believe that their organization's leaders support the change. For employees to alter their behavior—to attend the training, try the new procedure, commit to their new job responsibilities—they need to see and hear that message from their leaders. They can't just be told that the company's executives support the change. Employees need to witness it personally. They need to see that leaders have skin in the game. Employees need to see their organization's leaders out front, willing to take the blame and hear the criticism, rather than hiding behind someone who takes the darts for them. If leaders want employees to commit to a change, they need to demonstrate commitment themselves.

Your change management role may be to coach your organization's leaders on how they can communicate most effectively about a change. Help them plan messages, and figure out whom they need to speak with and when. Help them anticipate objections, and prepare appropriate responses. Help them "manage the crowd" during Q&A sessions. Debrief with them after town hall events. But don't fall into the trap that my consultant friend stepped into. Let the leaders lead.

In the PCo business transformation case you read in chapter 11, Sharon, PCo's head of learning and organizational development, recognized the role she could play in helping PCo leaders communicate effectively about change. Sharon knew she needed to help Petrina, PCo's CEO, structure the town hall meetings that Petrina wanted to conduct so that the events provided employees with ample opportunity to ask questions and share ideas. Sharon recognized that Petrina tended to dominate discussions. She saw that she'd need to coach Petrina to speak less and listen more as she shared her messages about PCo's business transformation. And Sharon saw that she'd need to encourage other leaders at PCo to get involved too. Petrina wasn't the only leader who should be out there speaking about the changes that needed to happen. Sharon recognized that she'd need to coach the rest of PCo's leadership team, too, so they'd understand the crucial role they needed to play to help employees understand and hopefully support what was changing.

Tips for Preparing Senior Leaders to Communicate About Change

- Provide talking points that summarize, in bulleted form, the key messages they need to convey. The bullet points should address what's changing, the rationale for the change, and what that means for the audience they're addressing.
- Help leaders practice delivering key messages. Coach them to avoid using jargon and to explain the change using stories, concrete examples, and clear terminology. Encourage leaders to convey empathy as they speak. Remind them to refrain from saying "As you know."
- Let leaders know who may raise objections, what those objections will likely be, and appropriate responses. Encourage them to speak honestly, and with empathy, as they hear concerns.

- Keep leaders informed about problems the project team has encountered or issues that are occurring related to the change. Don't let leaders get blindsided by hearing news about the project from others, when you and your team should have done a better job keeping them up-to-date about troubles that are brewing.
- Structure events so that leaders provide audience members with ample opportunity to ask questions and share ideas and concerns. During large-scale events, help moderate the Q&A process so leaders can focus on listening to ideas that are raised and on responding to questions while you manage the crowd.
- Ask leaders to convey their interest in and commitment to the change initiative by mentioning it frequently during formal and informal conversations with employees. Encourage them to view each business meeting as an opportunity to speak for a few minutes about, or to ask for an update on, the change. Encourage them to use chance interactions with employees to ask them how the change is going.

Frontline Supervisors and Managers

For employees to truly understand how a change will affect them, they also need to hear about it from the person they report directly to. Frontline supervisors and managers should be deeply involved in any change-related communication. They convey day-to-day expectations to employees. They provide rewards when employees comply and mete out consequences when they do not. They're the ones whom employees typically trust most to share news about how a change will affect them. And through their support or opposition, they signal to employees the extent to which they need—or don't need—to get on board themselves. Frontline supervisors and managers can be a powerful force to leverage during any change initiative. And yet, far too often, organizations fail to equip them for the crucially important role they need to play.

What is that role? What does your organization need frontline supervisors and managers to do to support a change? For most change initiatives, frontline supervisors and managers need to:

- Provide details to the core project team about how work is currently performed and about needed changes, so the project team can make informed decisions as they flesh out project plans. They need to share ideas, concerns, and expected hiccups that the project team can address in advance.
- Explain changes to their direct reports, so employees understand how a change will affect them personally. Often the broad goals and purpose

associated with a change are announced first by a senior leader. The frontline supervisor or manager needs to "translate" these more general plans into specifics. Supervisors need to explain what this means for the department: "Here's why this will help. Here's what the challenges will be for us. Here's when this will happen. Here are the decisions we need to make as a department about how to implement the change. Here's how you can help. Here's how I will help you." For example, in the PCo business transformation case, we saw that PCo wanted to completely overhaul the way its sales staff interacted with prospective customers. To make that happen, supervisors and managers in PCo's sales organization would need to translate the broad goal of "consultative selling" into specific behaviors they expected sales staff to engage in. Sales supervisors would need to convey, "Here's what I expect you to do to generate prospective sales," and "Here's how I expect you to interact with prospective customers." And PCo supervisors also needed to ask their employees, "What do you need so you can successfully engage in these new behaviors?" and "How can I help you succeed here, given these new expectations?"

- Respond to questions from direct reports about why the change is occurring, and how and when it will affect them. Supervisors and managers need to listen with empathy as employees express concerns about the change. And they need to encourage direct reports to share ideas for making the change work most effectively in their department.

- Establish expectations and consequences as they relate to the change. Frontline supervisors need to ensure that employees participate in training, follow new procedures, or pack their desks in preparation for the company's move to an all-virtual environment. They need to make sure that employees understand what they're supposed to do, and they need to check in with employees to ensure that these expectations are met.

- Share information with the core project team about what's working and what isn't related to the change. Supervisors and managers need to collaborate with the team to help diagnose and address the inevitable problems that will occur.

- Model the change themselves. Frontline supervisors and managers need to demonstrate their support for the change by ensuring that their own speech and actions conform with what's expected. They need to show employees that the change applies to everyone in the

department, including themselves. Supervisors and managers need
to demonstrate that they are willing to try out new behaviors and to
learn—just like they need their employees to try things out and learn.

Everything a frontline supervisor says and does related to a change communicates volumes to their employees. So what can you do to help prepare supervisors and managers for the role your organization needs them to play?

First of all, make sure supervisors and managers are in the know. Don't let them get blindsided by announcements that they hear at the same time as their employees. Nothing can undercut a supervisor's support more than putting them in a position where they have to admit to employees that they don't know what's going on. Communicate changes to them first, before news is shared with their employees, even if it's just 24 hours in advance. This requires trust. Your organization needs to trust that supervisors won't share news about the change until the appropriate time. And supervisors need to trust that their organization is preparing them adequately to carry out their supervisory responsibilities. You may not be able to share with supervisors all the details about the change. You may need to let them know that things will be ambiguous for some period. You may even need to provide coaching or training to help frontline supervisors and managers lead during this time of ambiguity. But try to share as much information with them as you can.

Provide supervisors and managers with details, if known, about how the change is expected to affect the area they lead. Let them know when and how the employees who report to them will be informed about the change. Ask for feedback on that plan. Give them plenty of opportunities to ask questions and to map out, at a more granular level, how to implement the change in the department they oversee.

Clearly convey to supervisors and managers what you need them to do. Make sure they understand the role your organization needs them to play as leader of an area. And provide supervisors and managers with resources to meet these expectations. Prepare scripts they can use to communicate details about the change to employees. Create Q&A sheets, specifically tailored to help supervisors respond to questions employees are likely to pose. Coach supervisors on their communications role, and if appropriate, offer to join them during discussions they lead with employees about the change. Meet with supervisors and managers frequently to hear from them about what's working and what's presenting a challenge.

For example, in the PCo case, Sharon may have recognized the opportunity to involve supervisors and managers in the company's efforts to build employee accountability. After all, PCo's frontline supervisors were responsible for conveying to employees the results they were expected to produce. And supervisors were the ones who needed to hold employees accountable for generating those results. Perhaps Sharon could meet with frontline supervisors to hear their ideas for building greater accountability across the company. She could provide supervisors with discussion guides and other resources to use during their regularly scheduled department meetings to help them talk about accountability with their employees.

Support from frontline supervisors and managers can be key to the success of your organization's change initiative. Help them lead. Share information with them early and often. Be clear about what you need them to communicate to their employees. Provide them with resources to help them perform their communication role effectively.

Peers

Who else do employees trust to be honest and candid with them? Their peers. Organizations often forget about the power that peer-to-peer communication can play in building awareness and support for a change initiative. Smart companies recognize that employees typically communicate most throughout the day with their immediate co-workers. They harness that power by establishing mechanisms that rely on peer-to-peer communication to send and receive messages about a change.

Possibly the best way to do that is by establishing a transition-monitoring team. From chapter 7, you'll recall that it's a group of employees, chosen from across the organization, who meet periodically with the project team for updates about an impending change. Back on the job, transition-monitoring-team members convey to their peers the information that was shared with them, listen for concerns, and respond to questions posed by their co-workers. Transition-monitoring-team members help correct misinformation and dispel rumors that may be floating about. They share with the project team concerns they're hearing from their peers, to ensure these issues are addressed.

The transition-monitoring team is designed to supplement formal communications like emails and supervisor presentations. The approach helps enhance the speed and accuracy of communication about a change, and provides another vehicle to support upward communication. But even if you don't establish a transition-monitoring team, think about the steps you and your organization can take to leverage the communication that occurs naturally among co-workers.

Consider asking employees who are strong advocates for the change to talk it up with their peers. If an employee shares with you misinformation she's heard about the change, ask her to let others know the real facts. During formal and informal meetings, ask employees about their own concerns about the change, and ask what the word is "on the street" too. Co-workers are going to talk about your organization's change initiative anyway. Use that communication to benefit your project.

The Change Management Team

Over the course of a typical change initiative, you and your fellow change management teammates will probably find that you're communicating with just about everyone involved with the project. You'll meet with stakeholders to hear their needs and concerns, and you'll convey this information to members of the core project team to ensure they consider this feedback as project plans develop. You'll coach senior executives, managers, and frontline supervisors so they understand and successfully execute the role that they, as leaders, play to help employees comprehend what's changing, why, and how. You'll interact frequently with members of the transition-monitoring team. You'll plan and facilitate meetings with transition-monitoring-team members, to help them stay up-to-date about project-related activities and to gather their input and feedback. You'll participate in meetings with the red team to hear their ideas and concerns. You'll communicate continually with the project leader and other colleagues on the core project team, sharing information regarding the status of project plans and plans related to communications, training, and stakeholder engagement. As you fulfill your change management responsibilities, you may feel like you're communicating nonstop!

But as you do your job, make sure you don't assume communications responsibilities that really belong to someone else. Resist falling into the trap that my consultant friend found herself in when she agreed to deliver presentations that rightfully should have been delivered by the company's CEO. Use your communications plan and the RACI matrix (see chapter 10) to clarify responsibilities related to communications. Although the change management team is responsible for overseeing the creation and execution of the communications plan, you're not responsible for delivering every message and presentation described in it. Your role is to plan, coach, prepare, provide support, and advise. Help leaders, managers, and supervisors to perform their communications responsibilities, but don't do their job for them.

The Core Project Team

Of course, on any change initiative, core project team members will do a lot of communicating too. As they work on project deliverables, members of the core project team may feel like they're constantly meeting with one another. They need to. But project teams need to avoid the trap of too much togetherness. They need to avoid becoming insular, and instead need to focus their communications outward. To ensure leadership buy-in, core project team members need to meet frequently with senior leaders to provide updates and receive authorization on decisions needed to keep the project moving forward. To make informed decisions and build stakeholder support, they need to meet regularly with project stakeholders—sometimes one-on-one and sometimes in group settings—to gather input and share information about what's happening. They need to meet early and often with supervisors and managers, to ensure they're leveraging the power these frontline leaders can sway. And to harness peer-to-peer communications, they need to share information with transition-monitoring-team members and other organizational "influencers," and they need to make sure they're listening to them too.

Who Communicates About Change?
- Leaders share the overall vision for the change. They articulate what the desired future state will look like and why it's important for the organization—and they listen to employees' ideas and concerns.
- Frontline supervisors and managers translate the general plan into specifics for the area they lead, helping employees understand what the change will mean for them, when it will happen, and what they need to do to make it happen. And they solicit input and guidance from employees about how to implement the change most effectively in their area.
- Transition-monitoring-team members keep their peers updated about the change. They reinforce messages sent by their supervisor and other parties, correct misinformation, and help dispel rumors. They listen to their co-workers' ideas and concerns and share this information with the core project team and change management team.
- Change management team members oversee development and execution of the communications plan. They meet with stakeholders to ensure their needs are addressed in the project plan; coach and prepare senior leaders, managers, and supervisors to help them perform their communications

responsibilities; facilitate information-sharing sessions with transition-monitoring-team members; and meet regularly with project teammates to ensure that everyone stays informed.

- Core project team members update organizational leaders about the status of the project and ensure that the project stays aligned with the goals and needs leaders have articulated. They meet regularly with stakeholders, frontline managers and supervisors, transition-monitoring-team members, and members of the change management team to gather input they need to make more informed project decisions and to share information about the status of the project.

What to Communicate

Years ago, I worked with a company that—like most other organizations—struggled to find ways to control skyrocketing health-plan costs. To limit expenses, the company implemented a new policy that required employees to receive preauthorization from the company's insurance carrier for many routine medical visits and procedures. If an employee received care without preauthorization, the insurance carrier could refuse to pay the claim. The company informed employees about the change during a series of town hall meetings. "We know that it can be stressful when you need to make decisions about medical care," the company's vice president of human resources explained. "So we have implemented a new approach to help you relieve your stress. You no longer need to make that decision alone. You can talk things over with the insurance company before deciding if you need care."

Upon hearing the news, the audience erupted. "I'll manage my own stress!" one employee yelled. "Who do you think you are to think you should do this for me?" Employees raised objection after objection about the reason the company provided for the change, often shouting down the vice president of HR as she attempted to respond. And finally, one employee raised his hand and calmly summarized what he sensed everyone in the room was really thinking. "We know that healthcare costs are rising," the employee stated. "We understand you need to do something. Why don't you just tell us the truth? Just let us know you're making the change to control costs. We can accept that." The room quieted and the vice president of HR paused to assess her next move. "Benefit costs are skyrocketing," she affirmed. "We're making this change to control benefit costs." Employees in the room nodded. They asked a few clarifying questions. And the meeting ended.

Reflecting on the meeting, the VP of HR acknowledged that she had underestimated employees' willingness to hear and accept the truth. She hadn't intended to lie to employees. After all, it was possible some employees would welcome the chance to discuss medical care options with their insurance provider. It's conceivable the new requirement would help reduce stress for some employees. But that was only a possible side benefit. It wasn't the real reason the company was changing its health insurance plan. The VP of HR assumed employees wouldn't understand or accept the real reason. But by circumventing the truth, she undermined her credibility. She misjudged, and the company's employees called her on it.

Here's what needs to be communicated for any change to succeed.

The Truth

We can start with the obvious. People want to know that they can trust what they are hearing. They want to know that the information they are being told is the truth. And yet, when organizations think about what to communicate—when they decide what to tell employees about changes that are happening and the reasons for these changes—they sometimes find themselves veering away from the truth. They make the same misstep the VP of HR did in the story I just shared.

Why does this happen? Often it's because organizations think their employees can't understand or won't accept the truth. They think they need to come up with another reason for why they're making the change, because the actual reason is too difficult to comprehend or is objectionable on some level. If a company is making changes to cut costs, they may assume employees won't grasp the business fundamentals driving the change. Or they may fear that employees will argue for cuts to the executive ranks in place of the cuts the leaders had planned.

The problem, of course, is that at least some employees will see through what is being said. They will understand, or think they understand, the real rationale, and they will share that with their peers. Leadership credibility will be damaged, and employees will resist getting on board with the change. Employees will conclude that leaders cannot be trusted to be honest with them. They won't believe what is being said about the current change. And they won't believe what is being said about changes that will come in the future.

But what do you do if what is happening, or the rationale for the change, really is complex? One approach is to explain it three times whenever you talk about the change. Once, very briefly, provide the so-called technical explanation, or provide resources employees can review if they want to see the technical side for themselves. Acknowledge that it's complex, but don't be surprised if the technical explanation resonates with some people in your audience. Next, elaborate by explaining, in plain terms, what's happening and why. Some people call this the "grandmother test": Ask yourself if your grandmother would understand the explanation as you've described it. If not, perhaps you haven't really gotten down to the fundamentals yet. Keep working at it. And finally, provide an example or two specifically tailored to the audience who is hearing the message. By hearing the complex version, the basic version, and some examples, employees will appreciate that you're making the effort to share the truth with them.

If what's happening is truly objectionable, you might want to take a step back and consider if your organization really should be doing it in the first place. Perhaps this is one of those situations where you need to ask your organization's leaders for guidance about how the change fits with your company's stated values. Of course, it's possible your organization is in a situation where it's forced to choose from multiple bad options. If that's the case, say it. Let employees know that there weren't any good alternatives available, and so leaders chose the option that seemed the least bad. Employees may object to the alternative that was selected, but they'll probably appreciate the predicament company leaders faced. They likely have been there before too.

If you can't share the truth about what's happening or the reason behind it, let employees know that too. Organizations sometimes face this situation when a major restructuring is about to occur, or senior leadership changes are planned, or an acquisition or a divestiture is in the wings. This is when your organization's leaders will need to rely on the trust they hopefully have established with employees. Let employees know that you can't share everything with them, that they need to trust the company to do the right thing, and that the company will let employees know what's happening, why, and how it affects them as soon as it can. Sometimes that's the best and the most that can be done—and that's the truth.

The Whole Truth

Sometimes organizations make the mistake of sharing only a part of the truth with employees. During a major change, they inform employees about what's happening in the short term, but they withhold longer-term plans. They announce that a restructure is occurring within one part of the company, but fail to let employees know that it's only the first action to occur in what is in reality a multistep plan. They deny that more change is coming, perhaps because they perceive that employees won't be able to absorb, or will reject, the magnitude of what's planned. The problem with this approach is that as soon as the company proceeds with the next step, trust is undermined. Employees will view each announcement coming from their leaders with well-founded skepticism. Employee commitment to the organization will falter as they keep waiting for "the other shoe to drop."

Don't downplay the extent of a change that is planned. Share as much of it as you can. If the next step isn't known, it's OK to say that. Let employees know that the organization is making the current change, will evaluate how it goes, and then decide how to proceed next. For example, you might say, "Right now, we're restructuring the finance department to implement a service center model. We can't say for sure whether we'll implement that model in any other departments after the finance restructure is complete. Right now, we're focusing on finance and will see how well the model works there. We don't want to make any false promises about what might happen next."

If the next step is known, it's usually better to announce it and take steps to address the consequences. This may mean offering "stay bonuses" to high-value employees your organization doesn't want to lose. This may mean letting employees know that the next few years will be particularly challenging. Or this may mean informing employees that the organization is entering a period of change, and that leaders will let them know what's happening and why whenever they are able. Don't let employees get blindsided by the magnitude of a change that is about to occur. Let them know what's happening so they can prepare themselves adequately.

The Good and the Bad

It's good to keep things positive, but sometimes organizations make the mistake of focusing their change-related communications only on the upside. They think they need to "sell the benefits" associated with a change, so they emphasize "the spin" and downplay the reality. The problem with this approach is that when employees encounter the inevitable downside, they'll feel like they've been deceived. They'll feel like you have manipulated them so they would get on board, and realize now that they have been duped.

Yes, be clear about the benefits associated with a change. Hopefully there will be many, and you can explain that that's why your organization is pursuing the change in the first place. Where possible, describe the benefits the overall organization will receive, as well as the benefits the change will bring to the specific audience the message is targeted to.

But be honest about the challenges too. If it's a software implementation, say things like, "This means you'll now be able to do. . ." and then list the benefits. And "It also means that we have new procedures for doing . . ." and then explain the functionality that was lost. Or you can just list out the changes the new software will bring, and let employees decide for themselves what's a benefit and what's not. If it's a relocation, say something like, "In our new facility, we'll be able to . . . We recognize this will mean a longer commute for some people. We hope you'll find things you enjoy at our new location that will make up for that, at least in part."

Make sure the message is balanced. Any change has a cost associated with it. Acknowledge it. Say, "When these changes are fully implemented, you'll be able to. . . . And yes, that means there's going to be a lot of late nights and extra work over the next six months." Avoid "happy talk" that employees can see right through. And if there's more downside than upside for a particular group, acknowledge that too. Be frank about what's changing, the benefits the organization will accrue, and the impact that will have on the specific audience the message addresses. Let employees know that as organizational members, sometimes they have to absorb a change that provides little benefit to them. If it's the truth, let employees know that other changes may occur in the future where the scales will tip more in their favor.

What You Need People to Do and Achieve

Sometimes organizations communicate messages about a change that are so vague and grandiose that employees fail to understand that they play a role in bringing the change about. Leaders expound on their strategic vision for the future and the broad goals and outcomes they want their organization to pursue, without letting employees know specifically what the change entails for them. But when employees don't understand what they're personally expected to do or achieve to support the change, they keep doing things exactly the same old way.

Smart organizations recognize that they need to tailor specific messages to each group of employees affected by a change. They need to be clear about the "WIIFM," or describing "What's in it for me" so employees understand:

- Here's what's happening and why. In other words, here are the outcomes your organization is shooting for and the actions the organization is taking to get there.

- Here's what you will experience and when you will experience it. The message needs to describe what the employee who is receiving the message will see, hear, use, or otherwise experience that's different because of the change.
- Here are the benefits and challenges the change will bring for your area. Describe what is "in it" for them.
- Here's what you need to do and when you need to do it. Describe the concrete steps and actions you need employees to take to bring the change about. If possible, describe the specific outcomes, and associated measures, employees are expected to produce.

Where possible, provide employees with choices so they don't feel controlled. If it's feasible, let employees know the results they need to achieve, and the expected timeframe, and ask them to plot out the specific steps they'll take to get there. Whether you can provide options or not, be sure employees understand what they specifically are accountable for doing and achieving to support the change. Or as consultant Dawn Cocco explains, make sure each change-related message answers the questions "Why this?" "Why now?" and, perhaps most important, "Why you?" Make sure each message your organization sends clearly explains the role that members of the target audience need to play in bringing the change about.

Something for the Heart, the Head, and the Hands

What leaders say when they talk about a change reveals much about how they think. Some leaders share a lot about how a change supports the organization's values. They emphasize benefits and how good it will feel to work at the company when the change goes into effect. Or they focus on the losses employees may suffer as a result of the change, expressing care and compassion. They describe the change in terms of emotion. Other leaders lean more toward strategy and analytics. They present charts and figures and trend lines. They discuss options the organization weighed before deciding how to proceed with the change. They emphasize the reasoning behind the change, and focus on the rational. And finally, some leaders clearly prefer to talk about action. Their messages crisply delineate what's happening and when. They make sure employees know precisely what they're expected to do. They describe change in terms of the tasks to be completed.

The challenge with each of these approaches is that they paint an incomplete picture about change, and by doing so they fail to address the diverse needs employees might have as they hear the message. Some employees might be focused on processing the emotions they're experiencing related to the change, while others might want to hear about the organization's strategy and decision making. And some might just want to get on with things. They're ready for action. When a message focuses on a single aspect of the change—the emotional, the rational, or the tactical—it's going to miss the mark for someone. The leader will speak, and someone will say, "I don't know. It's just not resonating for me."

To avoid this trap, make sure each message you send addresses the change from both a soft, emotional perspective, and a hard, rational, and tactical perspective. Or as some professional communicators say, make sure each message includes something for the heart, the head, and the hands. Talk about how exciting the change is, or how employees may be frustrated by it. Convey care and compassion. Remind employees about the rationale for the change, and why the organization is pursuing it. Let employees know why it's smart for the organization to make the change now. And include a call to action. Describe what employees need to do, by when, to achieve what result.

By addressing the heart, the head, and the hands in each and every message, you're more likely to connect with the needs your audience members are facing at the moment. Those needs may change, moment to moment, for any given employee. They likely will change. But by including something for everyone, chances are you'll hit the mark and address at least some of their needs.

Stories

Often times, people need to see and hear a change explained in concrete, tangible terms before they'll buy into it. They need help envisioning what the change will really look and feel like before they're willing to offer their support. This is especially true for changes that relate to abstract concepts, such as organizational values, such as "accountability for results," or decision-making models, such as "centralized versus decentralized." But it holds true for simpler kinds of changes too, like "We're streamlining how to order supplies." When organizations communicate about things that are abstract, without providing any clarifying examples, the message often falls flat for people. Smart organizations recognize they need to provide employees with a concrete picture of what is changing and why so employees can visualize how they themselves can get involved. And one of the best ways they do this is through storytelling.

Think about the last movie you saw. If it told a good story, you paid attention. The movie grabbed you emotionally. You may have left feeling inspired to do something, even if it was just telling someone else about what you saw. You remembered the characters and plot. Wouldn't it be great if your change-related communications could do the same thing? Wouldn't it be wonderful if employees listened with attention as they heard about your change initiative, and felt motivated to really do something to make the change a reality?

Perhaps that goal isn't so far-fetched. In his 2020 book *Instructional Story Design: Developing Stories That Train,* Rance Greene describes how each of us can create compelling stories, in a business setting, that can help employees learn. Greene explains how a persuasive story presents a relatable character who takes action to address some issue, challenge, or conflict. Can you apply those same basic concepts and construct a story about some aspect of your change initiative? For example, perhaps your organization is implementing new software. Create a scenario that describes how a typical user wrestled with a business challenge and then used one of the software features to resolve the problem. Or perhaps your organization wants employees to demonstrate more initiative and risk taking to better address customer needs. Prepare a story that describes how an employee struggled with various options before choosing, perhaps wisely and perhaps not, which steps to take to satisfy a customer's demands. Find ways to incorporate the examples you prepare into your change communications.

Of course, true stories are often more compelling than made-up ones. As your change initiative progresses, ask employees for examples about how they are experiencing the change. With their permission, share the stories you're hearing in formal and informal communications. These stories will help employees see that the change is real. A company I worked with took this idea even further. They asked employees to submit stories about how they, or their co-workers, were demonstrating the company's values. Each month, a selection of these stories was published in the company's online employee newsletter. The organization wanted to help employees understand how abstract concepts like "continuous learning" and "environmental stewardship" applied in the day-to-day work they performed. They used examples that employees submitted to provide that explanation.

In the PCo case, Sharon seemed to appreciate the power of storytelling. She recognized that the company's CEO, Petrina, was an engaging storyteller. She saw that she had an opportunity to encourage Petrina to use those skills to help employees understand, in concrete ways, what was changing and why, and what they could do to support the change. And Sharon had an opportunity to extend the power of storytelling even further. Perhaps she could ask employees to share brief examples of what the transformation looked like in their day-to-day work life. Then, with the employees' permission, Sharon could publish these stories in the company's newsletter.

Successes

As your change initiative proceeds, you'll face many challenges, but you'll have successes along the way too. Your project will reach a milestone. Some early results will look promising. Someone on your team will solve a truly nagging issue. Don't forget to announce and celebrate these successes along the way. Leaders need to hear that they've made a smart choice in advocating for your project. Employees want to know that their hard work and sacrifices are paying off. Organizations sometimes hold back because they don't want to appear overconfident. They say they'll celebrate when the change initiative is finally complete. But when employees don't hear anything for a while about a change initiative, they start to wonder if the change is working. Don't fall into that trap. People need to hear that the change is in fact working, even if it's not yet complete. Something is going well. Be sure to acknowledge it.

As You Decide What to Communicate, Consider . . .

- How can you build trust by sharing the truth about what's changing and why? If you can't share details right now, can you assure employees you'll let them know what's changing as soon as possible?
- How can you help employees prepare themselves by sharing your organization's short-term and longer-term plans? Can you help employees understand what's changing now, as well as what may change in the future?
- What will you do to ensure that messages are balanced—that you're clearly conveying the benefits the change will produce, as well as the challenges employees may experience?
- How can you tailor messages to each group of employees affected by the change, so they understand "What's in it for me?" How can you help each stakeholder group understand how the change will affect them, what they need to do and when, the choices they can make to help bring the change about, and the benefits (if any) they'll receive from the change?
- How can you connect with the differing needs of your stakeholders by sharing messages that address what people might feel about the change (the heart),

the reasons your organization is pursuing the change (the head), and the actions people need to take to bring the change about (the hands)?

- Can you use storytelling to translate abstract and complex concepts into concrete, tangible terms? Can you explain the change so your grandmother understands it?
- What successes can you announce and celebrate so stakeholders see that the change is working?

How to Communicate

So far we've discussed who should communicate about a change (everyone!) and what we should communicate (the truth!). Now let's look at how we should communicate when our organizations embark on a change. Let's explore the different communication vehicles that are available to us and when we should use them.

Change guru John Kotter (1996) explains it simply: However well we think we've communicated about a change, we've probably under communicated by a factor of 10 or 100 or 1,000. If you think the email your team sent was sufficient, it's probably not. For some portion of your target audience, that email was lost among a sea of other memos. Is the town hall meeting your project sponsor led enough? Don't count on it. Despite being physically present, not everyone really tuned in to what the project sponsor said. And even if they did pay attention, not every employee fully grasped the nuances of the sponsor's message. Did department meetings do the trick? Probably not. Someone missed them and someone else was preoccupied by other items on the agenda.

Even if you've delivered a message multiple times, recognize that employees have been bombarded with lots of other communications that compete for their attention. You don't know when, amid all this noise, employees will finally tune in to the message about your change initiative. So the message needs to be repeated often, using every communication vehicle that's available. Here are some options to consider.

Formal Meetings

Face-to-face and virtual meetings are a great way to share information about a change, gather input that's needed to make project-related decisions, hear feedback, and respond to questions. When they're used effectively, formal meetings support two-way communications. Information is shared—ideally briefly—and then sufficient time is allocated for discussion.

Senior leaders often expect to receive updates via one-on-one meetings with the project sponsor, project leader, or change management leader. One-on-one and small group meetings are also an effective way to communicate with highly influential stakeholders and with stakeholders who are significantly affected by the change. Look back at your stakeholder analysis from chapter 9 and your RACI matrix from chapter 10. Who are your high-influence and high-impact stakeholders? Whom are you required to receive input or authorization from before proceeding with a decision? You want to provide these stakeholders with plenty of opportunities to share input, ask questions, and voice concerns. Arrange for announcements and status-update meetings to be conducted with them one-on-one, or with only a few other stakeholders, so robust discussion can occur.

One-on-one meetings also are usually the best way to address stakeholders who have voiced significant objections about the change, or who have expressed resistance in some other way. Chapter 14 features a structure you can follow to conduct one-on-one meetings with resisters to ensure you hear and address their concerns.

Department meetings can be used to provide announcements and updates, discuss how best to tailor the change to department needs, and address questions. As we mentioned earlier, employees often trust communications they receive from their frontline supervisor more than messages received from leaders further up the reporting chain. In the best circumstances, employees view their supervisor as a person who understands and appreciates how the change directly affects them. They believe that their supervisor recognizes the challenges department employees face as they try to implement the change. And they trust that their supervisor will represent their interests and needs during discussions with project leaders.

Here's what you can do: Brief supervisors in advance about changes that are forthcoming. If possible, provide them with resources, such as scripts and FAQs, to announce the change to their direct reports themselves. Arrange for a core project team member to attend the department meeting with the supervisor to address more detailed questions employees may ask about the initiative. Even if employees will be hearing about the change through other sources, prepare supervisors in advance so they can meet with their direct reports immediately following the announcement to discuss implications. As the change initiative proceeds, use department meetings to provide status updates and to hear feedback about what's working and where problems are arising. Continue to brief supervisors and equip them with resources to communicate with their teams about the change.

In-person and virtual town hall meetings send a consistent message quickly to many employees, though their impact can vary depending on the credibility and skill of the presenter. An announcement to a crowd may be well received when it's delivered by a highly trusted senior leader who speaks to the head, the heart, and the hands. Or the message can fall flat and meet with stony silence when it comes from a leader whose credibility is questioned and whose message is packed with technical jargon and double-speak. Choose your presenters wisely. Of course, with even the most trusted and skillful presenter, it can be difficult to make these types of meetings interactive due to the size of the audience. Arrange for the formal presentation to be brief, with more time allocated for comments from participants and for Q&A. Depending on the size of audience, use a moderator to manage the flow of comments and questions.

Whether you're meeting in person or virtually, consider using interactive polling software that allows participants to respond to inquiries and provide feedback in real time. Or arrange for in-person or virtual breakout rooms where employees can discuss in small groups different aspects of the change before reconvening and sharing their feedback with the larger group. Plan for ways to follow up on these large-scale events with more personalized and interactive forms of communication, such as department meetings, informal conversations with transition-monitoring-team members, and feedback surveys.

Informal Conversations

Most of the communicating that happens throughout each workday is conducted through informal conversations. A supervisor checks in with her direct report to see how things are going. A senior leader and a junior analyst chat during a shared elevator ride. Peers make small talk when they meet up at a coffee station. Teammates chat on a videoconference before the call officially begins. Take advantage of the frequency with which these conversations occur and use them to communicate about your change initiative. Ask supervisors and senior leaders to mention the change initiative during any and all discussions they hold with employees.

I used to work with a CEO who amazed me with his skill at working some mention of the company's transformation efforts into just about every conversation he had with employees, whether they occurred in a formal meeting or during chance encounters in the hallway. He really personified the counsel John Kotter (1996) provides: "A sentence here, a paragraph there, two minutes in the middle of a meeting, five minutes at the end of a conversation, three quick references in a speech." I clearly understood that the change initiative was important to the CEO because he talked and asked about it all the time. How often do the leaders in your organization mention the change initiative you're working on? The frequency of their comments and questions communicates volumes. Ask leaders to weave references about the change initiative into all of their conversations.

If you've set up a transition-monitoring team, ask them to use their informal conversations to check in with co-workers too. Suggest that they use chance meetings with peers to remind them about actions they need to take or to gather feedback about how the change initiative is working for them. Let transition-monitoring-team members know they don't need to plan formal meetings with co-workers to provide updates. While waiting for a videoconference to begin, they can check in with their co-workers to see if they've signed up yet for training or to ask what they thought about the training they recently completed.

Core project team members can follow this advice too. Let them know that part of their responsibilities is to communicate about the project. Sure, they're having formal meetings with stakeholders and conducting official status-update sessions. But remind them to briefly reference the change initiative or ask for feedback as they interact with co-workers throughout each day.

Emails

Emails are an effective vehicle for reaching a large number of employees quickly with a consistent message. But they can be fraught with issues. They don't allow for two-way communication, unless senders of the message are prepared to respond to each reply they receive. It can be challenging to convey the right tone in an email. Email messages can easily be misunderstood. People read them and can get offended. Or they don't read them, because the email gets lost in a sea of other messages. Employees complain they weren't told about a change, and then bristle when they hear a curt reply, "You were told. There was an email."

But email can summarize and document messages delivered through other vehicles, like in-person meetings. You can embed links in them that direct employees to other resources, such as websites and shared collaboration spaces including Google Docs, Google Drive, or Microsoft One Drive, where project-related documents are stored. Emails can be used to send out reminders and quick one-on-one follow-ups. And emails can be used to inform employees about a change that only tangentially affects them, such as an organizational restructure occurring in a department that the email recipients rarely interact with.

If you've established a transition-monitoring team, ask them to review email drafts and provide feedback so you're sure your message is clear and hits the right tone. If you haven't set up a transition-monitoring team, review email drafts with a few stakeholders anyway to ensure that your email is understandable and inoffensive.

Consider using email as a supplemental form of communication, paired with other vehicles that support two-way communication. If you need to announce a change via email, let the recipients know when and how they will have the opportunity to discuss it further. For example, arrange for informational meetings between supervisors and their direct reports, to be held immediately after the email is sent. Just be sure to prepare supervisors for these discussions, by updating them in advance and providing them with resources, such as a discussion guide or an FAQ document.

Shared Collaboration Spaces

Cloud-based spaces designed to support collaboration, like Google Drive, Google Docs, and Microsoft One Drive, are terrific tools you and the project team can use to store and maintain documents related to the change initiative. When you save project plans, meeting notes, and presentations on these sites, you and your fellow teammates can feel confident you're always accessing the most up-to-date version of these resources. You can also use these sites to collaborate as you prepare, review, and revise document drafts.

Some organizations use these sites to support communication beyond the core project team and change management team. They post documents, in read-only mode, that all employees affected by the change can access, such as the project charter, project plans, training plans, and presentations. Providing all affected employees with easy access to these documents lets employees know your organization's leaders have nothing to hide—they're happy to disclose details about the project. Just be sure to scrub confidential or sensitive information from the documents you share more broadly. You don't want employees stumbling upon a resistance management plan or a section of the shareholder analysis where they see that they, or their co-workers, have been labeled as resisters.

Note, however, that organizations typically don't use these sites as the primary way they're communicating with employees. The sites just serve as an extra resource employees can access if they want to see more details or review a presentation they might have missed.

Websites and Social Media

You can use internal websites to share details about a change initiative. If your organization is migrating to a "work from anywhere" environment, set up a site that employees can access to learn more about policies governing the change, tips for staying in touch with co-workers and supervisors, facts about the technology they need to use to conduct meetings, and best practices for managing a virtual workforce. If you're implementing new software, create a website that shares tips and tricks, links to online learning, and instructions for transitioning from the old software to the new. Refresh the website with new content frequently so the site doesn't become stale. Most websites are set up to support only one-way communication, so use them in combination with other approaches, such as in-person or virtual meetings, that allow for more interactivity.

If appropriate for your organization, consider communicating with employees on whatever forms of social media they use most, such as Twitter, Facebook, Slack, Instagram, or blogs. These tools can be useful for sending out reminders, celebrating successes, and sharing news about the change initiative. Some employees disconnect periodically from social media, and some never connect at all. So consider social media as a supplement to other forms of communication, like face-to-face and virtual meetings. And before using any form of social media, be sure the tool fits with your organization's culture. Some people find social media to be frivolous or intrusive, while other people live by it. Consider what fits best for your organization.

Visual Reminders

Use posters, video screens, and online banners to remind employees about the change and the action they need to take, whether it's to purge outdated files before the company installs new document management software, enroll in a training program, or complete a survey. Place visual reminders in locations where employees congregate and linger, such as in lobbies, at coffee stations and break areas, outside elevators, and inside elevator cabs. I know of some organizations that post simple fliers inside bathroom stalls. They refer to these fliers as "potty lines" and change them up frequently so employees will check them out to see what's new. Another organization writes short reminders in chalk on sidewalks between its buildings. "People look down when they walk, and they assume anything written in chalk must be new," the organization's change management leader advises. "We don't know why it works, but it does." Some organizations use banners on login screens and home screens to send reminders to employees.

Just think about any physical or virtual place that employees visit on a regular basis. How can you use it to remind employees about the change? Refresh what they're seeing frequently so the message doesn't become stale or fade into the background. Change visual displays often so employees keep checking in to see what's new.

T-shirts, coffee mugs, and other forms of marketing swag have their place. They're static, visual reminders that can be used to promote the change to employees and create a feeling of camaraderie. Who doesn't like getting something for free? But spend wisely. You don't want employees to think you're wasting money on frivolous giveaways that should have been directed to securing resources the organization really needs.

Videos

Prerecorded videos can reach a large number of people quickly, and they help ensure you're presenting a consistent message too. But they only allow for one-way communication. With video alone, you won't know how people are receiving your message. You won't know what they understand, object to, or have questions about. When you announce a change using a prerecorded video, employees may conclude that leaders aren't open to hearing questions or feedback. They may perceive that leaders are "hiding."

If you need to reach a large number of employees quickly, consider if other mechanisms that support two-way communication, such as in-person or virtual town hall meetings, will work. If you do use a prerecorded video, see if you can pair it with another mechanism that supports two-way communication. For example, perhaps employees can watch a video followed immediately by a discussion that's scheduled with their frontline supervisor or another leader. Just be sure to prepare supervisors for this discussion by updating them in advance and providing them with resources, such as a discussion guide or an FAQ document. Or pair a prerecorded video with a short survey, where employees can react to what they've seen, rate the extent to which they understand it, and submit questions and feedback.

Avoid investing in prerecorded videos that appear expensive and overproduced. Well-crafted videos can help reinforce messages you send via other channels. But you don't want employees questioning how you're spending what everyone knows is a limited budget.

Surveys

Surveys and polling software provide employees with formal opportunities to give feedback. If you design the survey or poll to allow employees to respond anonymously, employees may feel more comfortable sharing their honest opinion. As your change initiative proceeds, consider embedding links to short pulse surveys in emails and websites. A two- or three-question survey can help you get a read from employees about how things are going. Surveys also can help you gather input when your team is weighing multiple options and you need to find out which choice employees prefer. Polling software provides the same benefits, and can be used during large-scale meetings (in-person or virtual) to capture employee feedback in real time.

If your team conducts a survey or poll, be sure to actually use the information you collect. Share a summary of the feedback with survey participants so they know that you have reviewed their input. And let employees know what you have decided to do—and why—now that you know what they think. Employees become cynical when they believe they've taken the time to share their opinion but it appears their feedback has been ignored. Before you ask employees for their feedback, be sure you're prepared to hear and use it!

Actions

Of course, what you do communicates far more than what you say. Does a leader need employees to try the new software? Has he demonstrated that he's trying it himself? Are employees supposed to attend training on a new procedure? Their supervisor needs to ensure they have the time to participate, and she needs to make sure she attends the training too. Did the project sponsor assert in a public gathering that the change initiative is one of the top priorities for the company this year? If so, the company needs to commit appropriate resources, in terms of personnel, time, and funding to the project, to ensure that progress is made.

When employees see actions that conflict with what they've been told about a change initiative, especially when they sense that their company leaders are engaging in behavior that's incompatible with the change, they become cynical. They question why they need to get on board and make any changes themselves. After all, how real can the change be if what they're seeing and experiencing doesn't jibe with what they've been told? Perhaps they should just hunker down for a while and let it pass.

Coach leaders so they appreciate the power of their own behavior. Explain that employees won't commit if they suspect that their leaders aren't committed themselves. Let leaders know that employees are watching them to see how much weight to give to what they've been hearing. Help leaders see that their actions communicate far more than their words.

What If Leaders Aren't Communicating Support for the Change?

For employees to support a change initiative, they need to know that their leaders fully back the change too. Employees need to hear leaders talking about what the initiative means for their organization and why it's so important. They need to see leaders allocating financial and human resources to back up their words. Employees need to know their leaders will provide them with enough time to participate in training, try out new behaviors, and learn how to support the change. And they need to see their leaders engaging in the new behaviors too.

But sometimes that doesn't happen. What action should you take when a key leader isn't doing what's needed to support the change initiative?

It really depends on who the leader is. Are they the project sponsor? If they're the sole sponsor for the project and it looks like their support is wavering, this is a good time for your project leader to check in to see what's going on. Perhaps the sponsor is still fully committed to the project and is just overwhelmed with other priorities. In that case, the project leader and sponsor can discuss which actions the sponsor can engage in to signal their support to employees. Or perhaps the project needs to be put on pause for a while until the sponsor can devote more time. In that case, ask the sponsor to clearly communicate to the project team and the rest of the organization their continued commitment to the project and the rationale for the delay. If the sponsor has expressed concerns about how the project is proceeding, discuss how their concerns can be addressed so the team can regain the sponsor's support.

What if the leader whose support is wavering isn't a sponsor? Depending on the reluctant leader's level and role within the organization, either the project leader or one of the project sponsors should meet with them to hear their concerns. Hopefully, their concerns can be addressed in some way. Remind the leader about the outcomes the change initiative is intended to produce. Discuss with them how, specifically, the initiative will help the organization achieve those outcomes. If possible, focus on the benefits and outcomes the change will generate for the area the leader oversees.

Consider asking one of the leader's peers who supports the project to speak with the reluctant leader. When the leader sees their colleagues getting on board, they may be more willing to show their support too. And if the leader's concerns can't be addressed, the sponsor may need to escalate the issue to whomever the leader reports to and ask them to intervene.

Are you trying to decide which of these approaches to use for your change initiative? Maybe you don't need to choose. Perhaps you should use all of them, in combination, as you address each communication challenge. Consider your options in Table 12-1.

Table 12-1. Communication Tools for Any Purpose

When You Want To . . .	Communication Vehicle to Consider
Inform or update senior leaders or high-influence, highly affected stakeholders, and hear their ideas and concerns	One-on-one and small group meetings that allow plenty of two-way discussion
Hear and address concerns from someone who has voiced objections or is otherwise resisting the change initiative	One-on-one meetings following the structure provided in chapter 14
Ensure that employees who are affected by the change trust what they are hearing and can provide input to how the change is implemented in their area	Department meetings led by their supervisor
Send a message quickly to a large group of people	In-person or virtual town hall meetings or emails, paired with forms of communication that support two-way communication, such as department meetings, polling, and surveys
Inform or update employees who aren't significantly affected by the change	In-person or virtual town hall meetings or emails
Provide access to shared documents related to the change initiative, such as project plans, training plans, and presentations	Emails with embedded links, websites with embedded links, and shared collaboration spaces such as Google Docs, Google Drive, and Microsoft One Drive
Remind employees about actions they need to take related to the change initiative	Informal meetings, emails, websites, social media, videos, and visual reminders
Provide employees with an opportunity to give anonymous feedback or share their opinion about an option your team should pursue	Anonymous survey or poll
Provide opportunities for two-way communication	One-on-one meetings, department meetings, town hall meetings with ample time for comments and Q&A, informal conversations, and surveys/polls
Build employee trust and communicate that the change is really happening	Actions that are consistent with messages sent via other vehicles

Look again at the communication vehicles you're thinking about using. Will they help support two-way communication? Will employees tune in and pay attention to them? Will they remind employees about actions they need to take related to the change? No single communication vehicle addresses every need. Perhaps you really do need to use them all!

Thinking About How to Communicate?

- What are you doing to make sure there's a balance between telling people about the change initiative and listening to what they have to say?
- Who are the high-influence, high-impact stakeholders you need to gather input from before finalizing project-related decisions? Who else do you need to gather input from before proceeding? Which methods of communication will you use to gather input from these stakeholders?
- How will you structure in-person and virtual meetings to ensure employees have ample opportunities to share their ideas, offer feedback, and ask questions?
- Whom can you ask to generate "buzz" about the change initiative through their informal conversations and daily encounters with others? Can senior leaders mention the change initiative during their planned and unplanned interactions with employees? Can transition-monitoring-team members remind co-workers about what's coming and what they need to do to prepare?
- When you send messages via email and video, which other communication vehicles will you use to make sure those messages are received and understood? When you communicate via email and video, what else will you do to provide opportunities for two-way communication?

Pulling It All Together: The Communications Plan

As you and your project team make decisions about who will communicate, what messages will be communicated, and how messages will be shared, organize what you've discussed in a communications plan. A communications plan will help you keep track of the many ways in which communications will occur over the course of your change initiative and will help you monitor progress and make adjustments as your initiative unfolds. Your communications plan can help clarify who needs to hear what, by when, and from whom. The plan also can help ensure that everyone associated with your project understands their responsibilities and commitments as they relate to change communications.

If your organization uses project-planning software, check to see if the tool can be used to create a communications plan. Some software packages include templates for building these plans. But it's also easy to create a communications plan using Microsoft Word or Excel. That's what Sharon did in the PCo case you read about in chapter 11. Table 12-2 shows the plan she started to sketch out.

Table 12-2. PCo Communications Plan

Communication Event	Key Messages	Audience	Sender/ Leader	Start Date End Date	Frequency	Owner/ Creator
R&D Department Meeting	To help manage costs and labor issues, a business manager will be hired for each lab; lab managers will partner with their business manager as co-equals in running the lab	Lab Managers	Ivan and Sharon		Once	Ivan
Town Hall Meetings With CEO	Update on current market status and financials—here's why we need to change and how we're doing To change, we need everyone to be accountable for the results they contribute to	All Employees	Petrina			Petrina

Here are the basic elements to include in your plan.

Communications event. What is the communication action that will occur? For example, is this a town hall event where the change initiative will be announced to a group of affected employees? Is this a regularly occurring status-update meeting with key stakeholders? Is this a pulse survey to gather feedback from affected employees? Is this a quick and informal check-in between transition-monitoring-team members and their peers? Identify the action that's planned.

Key message. What are the specific messages that will be sent during the communication event? For example, the message may be "Our office is relocating on March 3, 2022, to Ypsilanti, Michigan, because . . ." or "Here are instructions for packing in preparation for the move" or "We want your input about which date works best for the move" or "Convey concern for employees whose commute will be longer because of the move." Make sure the message is tailored to the specific audience the communications event is targeted to reach. Remember to be clear about the WIIFM. In your communications plan, you don't need to lay out a detailed script. Just summarize the key points that need to be conveyed, tailored to the specific audience who will be hearing the message.

Audience. Which specific stakeholder group will receive the message? Who will attend the town hall event? Whom will the email be sent to? Who will have access to the website?

Sender/messenger. Who will deliver the message? If it's an email, who is the sender of the email? If it's a presentation, who is delivering the presentation? If it's a department meeting, will frontline supervisors deliver the message, or will you arrange for a senior leader or member of the core project team to attend and speak?

Start/end date. When will the specific communication event begin and end? If it's an announcement email, when will the email be sent? If you plan to send updates via a monthly newsletter, when will employees begin seeing stories in the newsletter? When will these stories end? What else is your organization communicating that may compete with this message for employees' attention? When should you send this communication so employees focus on it?

Frequency. How often will this specific communication event occur for this audience? For example, is this a one-time-only town hall event, or will town hall meetings occur for this stakeholder group once each quarter? If this is a status-update meeting with project sponsors, will this occur monthly? Weekly?

Owner/creator. Who is responsible for preparing the communication? For example, who will create the presentation, arrange the town hall meeting, or draft the email that's planned?

Be sure to identify each communications activity you have planned. List out separately each action that addresses a specific audience with a specific message. That way you can plan and monitor it most effectively. For example, perhaps you're planning a town hall meeting to announce an organizational restructure, and intend to follow up with department meetings conducted in each of the three affected departments. That's four separate communications events to plan and monitor: one town hall meeting attended by all of the affected employees, and three separate department meetings, each led by a different department supervisor and attended by the supervisor's direct reports (Table 12-3).

Table 12-3. Communications Plan Example A

Event	Key Message	Audience	Sender	Frequency
Town Hall Meeting	Announce restructure	Departments A, B and C	Vice President	Once
Department Meeting A	Discuss how restructure affects department A	Department A	Department A Supervisor	Once
Department Meeting B	Discuss how restructure affects department B	Department B	Department B Supervisor	Once
Department Meeting C	Discuss how restructure affects department C	Department C	Department C Supervisor	Once

You can list a recurring action as a single event. For example, if you plan to conduct biweekly update sessions with the transition-monitoring-team members, you can list that as a single event in your Communications Plan (Table 12-4).

Table 12-4. Communications Plan Example B

Event	Key message	Audience	Sender	Frequency
Transition Monitoring Team Update Meetings	• Obtain feedback on how change is working in local departments • Provide update on next steps	Transition Monitoring Team	Project Leader and Change Management Leader	Biweekly

After you've prepared an initial draft of your communications plan, use this checklist to step back and ask:

Does the plan appropriately address who needs to communicate?

- Does your plan reach each stakeholder adequately and appropriately? Take a look at the stakeholder analysis and RACI matrix and then check out the details you have outlined in the communications plan. Are there stakeholders identified in the stakeholder analysis that you don't have any communications events targeted to? Which stakeholders have you indicated in the RACI matrix need to be kept informed, and is that reflected in your communications plan? What needs to be done to address any gaps?
- For each communication event that's planned, have you selected the right sender? Does the target audience view the messenger as credible and trustworthy? If not, is there someone else who is better positioned to send the message?
- How are you involving each person who needs to communicate about the change?
  - Leaders
  - Frontline supervisors and managers
  - Peers
  - The core project team
  - Everyone affected by the change

Does the plan appropriately address what to communicate?

- Do messages convey:
  - The truth
  - The whole truth
  - The good and the bad
  - What you need people to do and achieve

- ○ Something for the heart, the head, and the hands
- ○ Stories
- ○ Successes

Does the plan appropriately address how to communicate?

- Take a look at the stakeholder analysis. Did you capture the forms of communication each stakeholder group prefers, and does your communications plan reflect those preferences?
- How are you leveraging informal communication? Should you ask senior leaders, project team members, and transition-monitoring-team members to mention the change initiative in their day-to-day conversations?
- Does your plan include sufficient actions and enough repetition of key messages for each stakeholder group? Remember, employees won't tune in to each message you send. Be sure to use multiple communication vehicles to send each message. If you've sent a message via email, do you need to follow it up with a mention during a department meeting? Do you need transition-monitoring-team members to check in with co-workers to make sure they've read and understood the email? Are you providing enough reminders?
- Have you provided enough opportunities for two-way communication? Do you need to build in additional small group discussions? Do you need to plan for multiple pulse surveys throughout the course of your project?
- How are you using the different communication vehicles we reviewed?
  - ○ Formal meetings
  - ○ Informal conversations
  - ○ Emails
  - ○ Shared collaboration spaces
  - ○ Websites and social media
  - ○ Visual reminders
  - ○ Videos
  - ○ Surveys and polling software
  - ○ Behavior

With your draft communications plan, check in with stakeholders and members of the transition-monitoring team, if you've established one, for their feedback. And as your change initiative unfolds, keep checking back with them to see which communications are working and which parts of your plan need to be adjusted. Keep adding to your plan as additional communication needs arise and additional actions are identified. Think of your communications plan as an evolving document that will need to be adjusted throughout the course of your project.

What Else Can Sharon Include in the Communications Plan?

Take a quick look back at the communications plan that Sharon drafted for the PCo business transformation case in chapter 11. PCo's CEO intended to communicate her vision for the company's transformation through a series of town hall meetings that she would lead. That's great. But is it enough? What additional ideas could Sharon recommend?

- The concept of accountability that PCo's CEO wants to convey is highly abstract. Sharon could recommend using storytelling to make these concepts more concrete. PCo's CEO can weave stories about how she's seeing accountability in action into the messages she sends at town hall events. These stories should clearly convey what employees can do themselves to support the company's transformation. Employees can be asked to share examples of their own. Perhaps stories submitted by employees can be shared more broadly via a company newsletter.

- PCo leaders need to be enlisted to talk about the transformation during all of their interactions with employees. For example, if the company wants employees to make more financially responsible decisions, PCo leaders need to refer to financial results or ask about financial matters during conversations with employees.

- A key part of PCo's transformation involves generating a greater sense of accountability among employees. Frontline supervisors can play a key role, because through their words and actions, they communicate to employees what they're responsible for delivering—or not. The communications plan could include actions for engaging with supervisors, asking for their ideas about what greater accountability could look like in the departments they lead, and letting them know what they are expected to do and why to support the transformation. Sharon could recommend setting up frequent meetings with frontline supervisors to hear about their needs and challenges, and to discuss ideas for addressing these challenges. And Sharon could provide supervisors with resources to use during their regularly scheduled department meetings that help them generate discussion among employees about accountability. Department meetings can be used to keep messages about the transformation in front of employees and make it clear how they can participate through their concrete actions.

- PCo can provide formal opportunities for employees to provide feedback about the change via short pulse surveys.

These are just a few possibilities. Can you think of more?

About to Begin?

Are you about to begin preparing communications for a change initiative that's happening in your organization? As you develop your plan, ask yourself:

- Have you thought about everyone who is affected by the change? Check your stakeholder analysis and RACI matrix to make sure you've assembled a comprehensive list.
- How will you communicate with each of these stakeholders to ensure you balance telling with listening?
- How will you convey the WIIFM to each stakeholder group, so they clearly understand what's happening, why, and what they're expected to do to bring it about?
- How will you leverage all the communication vehicles available to you?
- Whom will you check with, and how, to make sure your communications plan is working as the change initiative unfolds?

Of course, employees not only need to know what they are expected to do to support a change; they need to know how to do it too. Effective communication is crucially important for your change initiative to succeed, but it's typically not sufficient. Often employees are aware of a change, and really want to actively participate, but they lack the ability to translate their good intentions into action. In chapter 13, we'll address that gap. We'll look at steps you can take to help employees build the knowledge, skills, and attitudes needed to support a change. You'll see that, just like with communications, the actions you plan need to extend far beyond a single training "event." You'll need to provide many training activities that work in combination to help employees build the right knowledge, skills, and attitudes. You'll also see that the impact of what you plan can extend far beyond the current change initiative. The decisions you make about training can influence how employees experience change today and their willingness to embrace changes in the future.

Learn more. Check out:

Greene, R. 2020. *Instructional Story Design: Developing Stories That Train.* Alexandria, VA: ATD Press.

Johnson, E. 2017. "How to Communicate Clearly During Organizational Change." *Harvard Business Review*, June 13.

13

Developing Knowledge, Skills, and Attitudes Needed to Support the Change

Have you ever had a simple routine down pat—something you didn't need to think about, like navigating to your gate at the train station you commute from each day or placing an order on an app you use all the time—and then suddenly things changed? Your gate moved. The app was updated. And for a short time, until you adjusted, you found yourself devoting mental energy to a task that previously had been so easy, something you didn't even need to think about. You might have felt mildly annoyed, unsettled, maybe even aggravated for the minutes or days it took until you settled into your new routine.

The same situation can arise in the workplace when change occurs. Your office relocates and for a few days you need to really focus as you drive there so you remember to get off at the right exit. Email software is updated and you have to think for a second or two to select the right tab to respond to your boss. "Eh, it's all fine," you may figure. Maybe you're even happy with the relocation and the opportunity to use new software. But there's still this slight feeling of disorientation as you work through the change and figure things out, even if it's just momentary.

Sometimes the changes introduced at work are more substantial. A new leader comes on board and sets challenging new goals that require you to work in a completely different way. Your company implements new processes and technology and you have to relearn the fundamental tasks to perform your job. You might feel excited about these changes. You might have even advocated for them. But that excitement likely is also coupled with a sense of unease as you feel somewhat less than competent doing what is now asked of you. You may feel confident that you can learn the new way of working or master the new processes and technology. Or you might not. But there's still this sense of awkwardness—this feeling like, "OK, I don't know what I am doing now."

In this chapter, we'll address steps you can take to help employees navigate through this period of discomfort and awkwardness, whether it's caused by a relatively minor change or a more significant one. You'll do this by helping employees develop the knowledge, skills, and attitudes needed to support the change. You'll see that your task will be to help employees build and maintain a sense of confidence that they can learn what's needed to meet expectations in the new environment. To do that, you'll need to understand how the change affects each stakeholder group and what new knowledge, skills, and attitudes they now need to demonstrate. You'll need to develop a well-thought-out training plan that spells out how employees will learn what's needed in an appropriate timeframe. You'll need to work closely with the project leader who is managing your change initiative, so you can influence project-related decisions that pertain to what employees need to learn and how and when they will learn it.

The actions you take to address the training needs of employees may not only affect the success of your current change initiative; they can also affect the success of future initiatives. When you help employees feel confident they can master the skills required to support the current change, they develop a more generalized sense of readiness and willingness to support other changes that may come in the future.

Training Addresses the Hard Side of Change

As you and the leaders in your organization implement change, actions you take related to employee training can substantially impact the success or failure of your initiative. Here are the hard facts—indeed, the hard-side facts. Your organization won't achieve the outcome it's shooting for if employees don't have the knowledge, skills, and attitudes needed to make the change happen. You won't get the benefits you're expecting from your new system if employees don't understand how to use its features and functionality. Your new process won't make things more efficient or won't produce better customer service if employees don't know what the right steps are or how and when to take them. Managers won't change the way they are leading employees if they don't have the ability to interact with them in the way you need. Employees need the right knowledge and skills to do what's expected of them.

Training Addresses the Soft Side of Change

Employees need the confidence to do what's expected, too. When any organization implements change, it's not uncommon for employees to feel like they have lost their sense of competence. There's a new way of doing things with new expectations. And it will take time for each employee to feel like things are right again—to feel like they know what to do to succeed in the new environment. Depending on the change and on the person experiencing it, that sense of loss may be extraordinarily profound. Or it may be relatively minor. But it almost always feels uncomfortable. I've been there. You've been there. Your employees and colleagues have been there. A sense of disorientation, a feeling of awkwardness, a sense of frustration about things taking more time arises while you learn how to do what's needed to perform your job correctly. Sometimes there's fear and doubt as you wonder if you'll ever learn what's needed. And that can send you spiraling downward as you begin to have questions about your job security. You may begin to wonder, do I have what it takes to succeed here now? It's no wonder employees sometimes resist getting on board with a change. After all, who wants to feel awkward and incompetent?

The actions you and your organization take to address this sense of incompetence—to help employees feel confident they can learn to do what's expected—can determine employees' willingness to make the changes you need.

The Risk of Training as an Afterthought

Here's what amazes me. Despite understanding how training helps address the hard and soft sides of change, organizations sometimes give short shrift to it as they create and execute their project plans. A project leader may tack training onto the end of a project plan, and pay little attention to it until the conclusion of the project is in sight. Or they create a project plan that allocates insufficient time to training development and delivery. As project dates slip, training is cut back to ensure the initiative still launches on time. Opportunities to embed training and learning throughout the course of the project are missed, as the project leader assumes that training can occur only via an "event" scheduled to happen right before launch. The project leader may assign training responsibilities to talent development staff who have been excluded from participating on the core project team. Operating blind, they create training programs that send the wrong message about the rationale for the change or the benefits the organization will accrue. Despite understanding how crucial training can be to the overall success of their change initiative, some organizations still treat training as an afterthought.

None of this is intentional. It happens when training responsibilities for a change initiative are "outsourced" to the organization's talent development function so the core project team can focus on what they consider to be, well, core. It happens when no one is present, as project-related decisions are being made, to advocate for the role that training needs to play in the overall success of the change initiative. It happens when there isn't anyone focused on learning and development who is fully integrated into the core project team.

I know from experience what can go wrong when the talent development function isn't represented on the core project team. One of the most frustrating and challenging projects I ever worked on involved a change that should have been relatively simple and straightforward. The organization was implementing some new features in its HR system. Very easy to use, the technology would provide employees with much greater visibility about the benefits they received at the company. So far, so good. The organization decided to change one of its HR policies at the same time it was implementing the new technology. That meant employees not only needed to learn how to use the new features in their HR system, but they also needed to be able to interpret and abide by the "rules" set forth in the new policy. This made things somewhat more complex, but still manageable. What made the initiative so frustrating and challenging was that I, in my capacity as talent development leader for the organization, wasn't brought into the loop until the very end of the project. Despite my early objections—and I probably didn't protest enough—the project leader insisted that he wanted talent development involved only when he deemed it was time. So when the project leader finally did begin to share project details with me, the entire initiative had already been planned and most decisions had been made. The new policy had been drafted. New "rules" had been programmed into the HR system in accordance with that new policy. The project was almost ready to launch. And what I saw really gave me pause.

I saw that although teaching employees how to use the technology would be a snap, helping employees understand the new policy would be quite a different story. In the new policy, complicated rules governed how and when employees would accrue benefits. I struggled to understand how the various mechanisms of the policy worked, and I anticipated that rank-and-file employees, even after receiving comprehensive training, would struggle too. I also feared that as employees grappled with the new policy, they might begin wondering if the organization had an ulterior motive. Would employees think we were launching a policy that was intentionally confusing so managers could manipulate employee benefits to suit their own whims?

Resigned to the fact that this was a done deal, I created a series of scenarios that explained how the policy worked, and reviewed them with the organization's vice president of HR so she could see what the training would cover. When she complained to me that the scenarios were far too complicated, we decided to review them with the organization's division HR leaders to get their input. As we walked the HR leaders through each scenario, they responded with horror. "How can we ask the average employee to understand the new policy," they complained, "when we are struggling to make sense of it ourselves?"

In the end, the organization went back to the drawing board, revised the new policy, and reprogrammed the HR system to reflect new, much simpler rules. But to do this, the organization needed to push back the project launch date several months. When the system finally rolled out, employees quickly mastered the new technology. They also seemed to have little difficulty understanding the "new" new policy, and few questioned the organization's intent or integrity. So the project had a relatively happy ending. Mistakes were made. Mistakes were corrected. It cost the organization some time and some money for reprogramming. It cost me some aggravating conversations. But overall, things worked out. No harm, no foul.

What was so frustrating for me is that none of this had to happen. Talent development had been brought into the project late in the game. Training wasn't considered until the project was about to launch. And so the project team made decisions that failed to consider employees' ability to learn something that was so extraordinarily complex.

In this case, we got lucky. Even though the planned changes were about to take effect, organizational leaders finally saw—with some prodding from me and some support from other HR leaders that proceeding as planned would be a significant mistake. And fortunately, they acted based on this new realization. But it all easily could have gone the other way. The leaders could have decided to proceed anyway, knowing that they were taking a gamble. And then, we could have ended up spending countless months cleaning up the ensuing mess. The delays and cost and aggravation could have been prevented if the talent development function had been fully integrated into the core project team—or at least represented on that team—right from the start.

Involve Training at the Beginning

I share this story because the same situation occurs far too frequently in organizations as they plan and implement change. As project planning occurs, someone needs to ensure sound decisions are made about what employees will need to learn, what they can learn, and when and how that learning will take place. If you're the person assigned responsibility for developing and delivering training to support the change initiative, this means that you need to partner closely with the project leader who is managing the change initiative. You need to make sure you have full and timely access to project plans and decisions so the training you prepare is accurate and comprehensive. You need to see the stakeholder analysis (see chapter 9), so the training you create is tailored to what each unique stakeholder group will need to know and do. You need access to the communications plan (see chapter 12), so your training program reinforces and sends the same message about the rationale for, and benefits associated with, the change. And you need to make sure enough time is allocated in the project plan (see chapter 4), so employees develop the knowledge, skills, and attitudes that are needed to support the change.

The easiest way to ensure you have that partnership—with full access to all the information you need to develop appropriate training—is by participating in the core project team. Perhaps you already have been asked to wear multiple hats to support the change initiative occurring in your organization. You may be the change management leader assigned to the project, with responsibility for stakeholder engagement, communication, and training and development. If that's the case, be sure that you, in your change management role, work closely with the project leader and participate fully in core project team meetings. Or you may be responsible for creating training and development for the change project, while another individual or team handles some of the other aspects of change management. You may even report to the change management leader for the work you are doing that relates to the change initiative. In that case, be sure to partner closely with that person to ensure your work closely aligns with the other change management tasks they perform. And see if you can attend the core project team meetings anyway, to ensure you have full and timely access to information you need to develop accurate and comprehensive training.

If you're in a situation like I was, where, for whatever reason, you're unable to work as closely as you need with the project leader or change management leader, or can't participate on the core project team, ask to receive project-related documents like the project charter (see chapter 3), project plan, stakeholder analysis, and communications plan, and ask to be included on the distribution list for these documents whenever they are updated. You can glean important information from these documents that will help you get a head start in thinking about the training that's needed.

Need to Convince the Project Leader to Include You From the Start?

- Ask to meet one-on-one with the project leader to clarify expectations, deliverables, and how you'll work together.
- Prepare for the meeting by reading everything you can get your hands on related to the change initiative, including the project charter and related attachments, project plan, stakeholder analysis, and communications plan. Show the project leader that you are interested, informed, and willing to work hard to help the project succeed.
- Focus on the hard side of change. During your meeting with the project leader, convey your enthusiasm for the project and the outcomes it's expected to produce. State that you're committed to helping employees develop the knowledge, skills, and attitudes they need to support the change. Explain that you need to stay informed about project details to ensure the training you create and deliver meets the project leader's expectations and stakeholder needs.
- Focus on the soft side of change. Remind the project leader that people sometimes resist change because they don't want to feel incompetent. Explain that you're committed to developing and executing a training plan that will help employees move through this period of incompetence as quickly as possible. Explain that to do that, there may be opportunities to incorporate training throughout the project. You want to get involved right from the start so you can identify where these opportunities lie and how to best take advantage of them.
- Explain that to stay informed, you need access to the most current version of project documents, and you need to know when these documents change. You also need to be aware of and understand project decisions as they're being made. You need access to the site where project documents are updated and stored, and you need to attend core project team meetings.
- State that you want to be held accountable for preparing and executing the training plan, just like other members of the core project team are accountable for completing tasks that they've been assigned. Ask the project leader to incorporate key details from the training plan in the overall project plan, and ask for time to be allocated in project team meetings so you can report on the status of training.
- As the project unfolds, participate actively in core project team meetings. Show up on time, and prepared.

Training Responsibilities

OK, so you've been assigned responsibility for training and development to support a change initiative that's occurring in your organization. You've arranged to be a member of the core project team, or you've established a strong relationship with the project leader or change management leader. You're confident that you will have full and timely access to project-related information. What is it you're responsible for doing anyway?

For most change initiatives, the person or team assigned to handle training and development for the project is accountable for three main functions:

- Analyzing what each stakeholder group will need to learn to perform their job successfully when the change is implemented
- Preparing and executing a training plan that ensures employees develop the knowledge, skills, and attitudes they need in the new environment
- Advocating for the learning needs and capabilities of stakeholders as they relate to the change initiative

Let's take a closer look at each of these responsibilities.

Analyzing What Each Stakeholder Group Needs to Learn

One of your first priorities will be to analyze the training needs associated with the project. Essentially, your job here is to figure out who needs to learn what and by when. For each stakeholder group affected by the change initiative, what will they need to know, do, and think, and how does that differ from what was happening before? Fortunately, you probably have a lot of resources at hand that can help you answer these questions.

Project-Planning Documents

Look at the project charter to understand what your organization is trying to accomplish by embarking on the change initiative and why that's so crucial for your organization. That's important information you can provide to employees about why the training matters.

Check out the stakeholder analysis to see who is affected by the change initiative and how. These plans provide a quick summary of what is changing for each stakeholder group and how extensive the impact is for each stakeholder. They'll give you a sense of how many groups of employees you need to target training to and a broad idea of what that training will need to cover. The stakeholder analysis should also give you insight into how much, or how little, each stakeholder group supports the planned change. You'll get a sense of the emotional issues and concerns you may need to address in the training you prepare.

Review the project plan. What milestones are planned, and when is work on various deliverables expected to be completed? That should help you identify when training can be conducted, and when enough information will be available for you to begin developing that training.

Go over the communications plan. You'll see what key messages are planned and whom they will target. You'll want to make sure the training you develop reinforces this same messaging.

Ask for any other project documents. They may provide details about the current state, or what each stakeholder group does today, and the expected future state, or what they will need to do when the change is fully implemented. Those details will certainly help you determine the tasks your training program needs to focus on.

Keep in mind that all of these resources—the project charter, stakeholder analysis, project plan, communications plan, and associated documents—likely won't be complete when you first start analyzing the training needs for your project. So make sure you are on the distribution list and stay posted as these documents evolve and change.

People Associated With the Project

Of course, the most significant resource you can tap into to analyze training needs are the people who are working on the project and the stakeholders who are affected by it. Plan on having lots of conversations with the project leader, change management leader (if you aren't also wearing that hat), and members of the core project team. Use these discussions to gather detailed information about what employees will need to know, do, and think, and how that differs from the current state. Ask them what resources you can get access to, in addition to the project-planning documents, that can help you figure out what employees will need to learn. If the project involves implementing new technology, ask if you can get access to the software test site so you can see for yourself how the new system works. Ask if the software vendor provides user documentation and training so you can determine if it can be leveraged to address training needs for your organization.

And plan on having lots of conversations with stakeholders to make sure you clearly understand their current level of knowledge and skill, what they think about the change, the way they learn best, and their availability to participate in training. Meet with employee supervisors to gather their perspective about the content that training needs to focus on most. Supervisors can also let you know what to expect about how quickly employees will be able to master the training content. And they can let you know which methods of training employees are most receptive to and when employees can be made available for training.

If your organization has established a transition-monitoring team, meet with them too to gather their input about what training needs to focus on most, who needs it, and when and how they think it should be conducted.

In your organization, you may already have a formal training needs analysis process that you use to determine general training requirements. Use that process if it will help you gather and organize information about who needs to be trained on what by when to support your change initiative. Otherwise, just keep asking questions:

- Who will need to know, do, or think something differently as a result of this change?
- What tasks will they need to perform as a result of the change? How does that differ from what they are doing today? When will they need to start doing things differently?
- How will performance be measured? How will you know that employees are doing what's expected?
- What benefits will employees receive from what's changing? What will they lose? What are the consequences employees will experience for doing—or not doing—what's expected?
- How receptive will employees be to what is changing?
- What methods of training are employees most receptive to? When are they available for training?

Keep in mind that for the same change initiative, the answers to these questions may vary considerably from one stakeholder group to the next. Some stakeholders may need intensive training because they are significantly affected by whatever is changing. Other stakeholders may require very limited training or training on a very different set of content because the change affects them in a completely different way. Don't expect broad-brush training to meet the need. Change initiatives can fail when training isn't tailored to the unique requirements of each stakeholder group. Find out what each stakeholder group needs to know, do, and think, by when, and how.

Before moving on, as you are analyzing what each stakeholder needs to learn, ask yourself and others two questions: Is training the right solution? And is a more extensive, organization-wide assessment needed? Asking these questions will ensure you don't fall into the role of order taker. For training to be effective—and for the change initiative to succeed—you need to function like a true performance consultant.

Is Training the Right Solution?

During some of your conversations with project team members or stakeholders, you may receive requests to provide training to address a need, but training isn't really the right solution. As you gather information about who needs to know, do, and think what, consider whether training is the appropriate response.

Are employees aware of what's changing and why, and of what will be expected of them after the change is implemented? If not, this need probably is better addressed by adding actions to the communications plan. Training can be used to reinforce key messages about the change. But employees shouldn't be hearing about the change for the first time through training. To understand why the change is important and what they're expected to do to support it, employees need to hear from organizational leaders and frontline managers. Don't let leaders outsource their communications responsibilities to trainers.

Are there obstacles that will prevent employees from doing what's expected? Can the project team remove or reduce the impact of these obstacles by adding some actions to the project plan? It's less than ideal if training has to instruct employees about workarounds they'll need to engage in. I've seen this a lot with technology projects. The core project team makes a decision they know will make the technology more cumbersome to use, and they say, "We'll just train around that issue." See if a better decision can be made—ask if the obstacles can be addressed—so training won't be needed as a "fix." How will you know when the project team is about to make one of these less than desirable decisions? You'll hear them discuss it in a core project team meeting! That's why you need to attend these meetings, even when you're sure there's nothing related to training on the agenda.

Will employees experience rewards and consequences for engaging in or ignoring the behaviors that are expected after the change is introduced? Don't let training take the fall because managers aren't managing. Sometimes a request for training is much better addressed through another approach, such as performance management. In the PCo business transformation case you read in chapter 11, Sharon, PCo's head of learning and organizational development, has an opportunity to do some digging here. PCo leaders indicate that they want employees to show more accountability. Although they haven't asked Sharon (yet!) to create training on this topic (thank goodness!), Sharon probably needs to find out more about how the company's performance management process is operating. Are managers and employees working together to establish performance goals? Do employees understand performance expectations? What happens when PCo employees meet or exceed these expectations? And given PCo's "culture of niceness," what happens when employees fail to meet expectations? Employees need to see that they'll receive tangible or intangible benefits when they engage in behavior that supports the change. Or at minimum, they need to see that by doing what's expected, they can avoid negative consequences. Don't agree to deliver training when performance management is what's really needed.

Have employees had opportunities to share their needs and concerns? Training can derail when employees feel like it's the only vehicle available to them to express their thoughts and ideas. Instead of focusing on the content they need to learn—the specific procedure that's changing or the new technology—they use the training as a gripe session. If you're intentionally using training as an opportunity for employees to share their needs and concerns about the change, make sure that's identified as a stated objective. And if it's the only opportunity for two-way communication that your organization is providing, arrange for organizational leaders and frontline managers to participate in the training so they can hear what employees have to say. For ideas on how to create additional opportunities for employees to share their thoughts, see chapter 12, in which we discuss the communications plan.

Bottom line: When you are analyzing training needs, wear your diagnostic hat. Think about what's needed to drive employee performance. Consider what's needed for effective communication to occur. Many times training will be needed. But sometimes it's not the right solution. Work with your project leader, change management leader, and stakeholders to make sure training is used wisely.

Is a More Extensive, Organization-Wide Assessment Needed?

Sometimes an organization embarks on a change initiative where the impact on what employees know, do, and think is expected to be profound. The organization may be transforming its entire business model and strategy. Perhaps it's attempting to shift its entire corporate culture. With changes like these, the majority of employees working for the organization need to retool and significantly upgrade their skills, acquire new knowledge, or change certain attitudes. In that case, a more formal—and more extensive—training needs assessment may be required. You may need to rigorously evaluate each job in the company to determine how tasks will change and which skills will be required to successfully perform each task. You may need to assess each employee to determine their current skill set and their capacity to develop whatever new skills are needed.

For example, an organization-wide needs assessment may be appropriate at PCo, the company you read about in chapter 11. PCo was overhauling its business practices across the organization, while simultaneously attempting to build a culture of accountability. A comprehensive needs assessment would help PCo leaders understand the skills the company needed to support their transformation and let them know precisely where they needed to intervene. That assessment might show that sales staff need training to engage in consultative selling. Or it might reveal that they already have this expertise from their work at prior employers. The assessment might show that plant managers need the finance and marketing training that PCo's CEO pressed for. Or it might reveal that plant managers need to develop a much broader range of business skills to perform in accordance with the company's new expectations. Without engaging in a comprehensive training needs assessment, PCo might devote resources to training that will have little effect, or they might miss providing training in areas where it's sorely needed.

If your organization's change initiative will have a profound impact on what a significant number of employees need to know, do, and think, talk with your project leader or change management leader about conducting a formal, organization-wide needs assessment. The steps involved in this assessment fall beyond the scope of this book; however, *Needs Assessment for Organizational Success,* by Roger Kaufman and Ingrid Guerra-López, is a terrific resource you can use to learn more.

The good news is that most organizational change initiatives are more limited in scale. If that's true for your project, keep asking: What precisely will employees need to know, do, and think and how does that differ from what happens today? By when do employees need to learn what's needed? How do affected employees prefer to learn? When are they available for training? Is training the right solution to address these needs? As you gather the answers to these questions, you can begin preparing your training plan.

Tips for Analyzing What Each Stakeholder Needs to Learn

Focus on the hard side of change. Ask:

- What do employees need to know, and what do they need to be able to do, when things change? What knowledge and skills will employees need to develop to successfully perform their job responsibilities in the new environment?
- How can employees develop this knowledge and these needed skills? What methods of training are they most receptive to? What else can be done, in addition to providing formal training, to help them develop the knowledge and skills they need?
- How will employees know what's expected of them? How will performance be measured and rewarded?

Focus on the soft side of change. Ask:

- What do employees need to believe and feel for the change to succeed? What attitudes do employees need to convey in the new environment? What will they do that demonstrates they have these attitudes?
- What methods of training can help employees develop these needed attitudes? What else, besides formal training, needs to occur?
- How can training address the emotions employees may experience related to the change? How can you construct training so employees move through the period of incompetence as rapidly as possible? How can you construct training to help employees feel like the organization cares about them and is committed to helping them succeed?

Focus on key messages in the communications plan. Ask:

- What messages do you need to reinforce about the overall vision for the change, what's happening and why, and how the change affects each stakeholder group?
- How can training answer the questions "Why this?" "Why now?" and "Why you?"

Preparing and Executing a Training Plan

In its most basic form, a training plan summarizes whom the target audience will be for training, the objectives the training will address for each audience, how and when training will occur, and who is accountable for ensuring that training is developed and delivered. A well-constructed training plan will help you:

- Coordinate actions that will help employees develop the knowledge, skills, and attitudes they need to meet new performance expectations, given the changes that are occurring.
- Ensure training activities support the objectives of, and align with, the overall project plan and other project-related activities.
- Communicate planned training activities to others on the project team and to organizational leaders.

Table 13-1 shows a quick snapshot of the training plan that Sharon, PCo's learning and organizational development leader, prepared in the case study you read about in chapter 11.

Table 13-1. PCo Training Plan

Audience	Objective	Training Program	Method	Start Date/ End Date	Frequency	Owner/ Creator
Sales Staff	Understanding of and ability to engage in consultative selling process	Consultative Selling Skills	Classroom instruction led by vendor			Sharon and Ed
All Employees	Ability to read and interpret simple financial document	Finance 101	Online tutorial			Sharon and Phil
All Employees	Understanding of what information is confidential and why; ability to treat confidential information appropriately	Ethics 101	Online tutorial			Sharon and Phil
Plant Managers	Ability to make marketing and finance decisions	MBA Boot Camp	Classroom instruction co-led by university faculty and PCo business leaders			Sharon

You can summarize your training plan in a simple Microsoft Word document or Excel spreadsheet. If your organization has a different format in place to create training plans, it's fine to use that too. Just be sure your training plan identifies the target audience and training objectives, summarizes how and when training will occur, and identifies who is accountable for ensuring training is developed and delivered.

Target Audience

By reviewing the project charter, stakeholder analysis, project plan, and related documents—and through your conversations with the project leader, change management leader, core project team members, and various stakeholders—you've begun to identify all the various stakeholder groups who will be affected by the change. You have a sense of which stakeholder groups will need to develop new knowledge, skills, and attitudes to do what's expected of them. List out the various groups who will need training.

Objectives

From your review of the project documents and various discussions, you have a sense of what each stakeholder group will need to know, do, and think differently as a result of the change. Which of these needs can and should be addressed through training?

Create learning objectives that summarize what each stakeholder group should be able to understand or do when they have completed training. Tailor objectives to the unique needs of each stakeholder group. Perhaps your training addresses new technology that all employees need to begin using. Will supervisors use different functions within the software to perform their review and oversight responsibilities? If so, identify supervisors as a separate target audience and list out the unique learning objectives the training needs to address for them.

Make sure training objectives don't just focus on teaching employees how to perform tasks. Your training probably needs to address what employees think and believe about the change too. Or as we said in chapter 12, when we discussed communications, make sure the messages sent through training address the heart, the head, and the hands, so you connect with each employee wherever they are focusing most.

- **Heart:** What do you need employees to believe and feel? You likely will want employees who complete your training to feel confident they can learn and do what the organization now expects of them. You want them to feel like the organization understands that the change may be challenging, but that it is there to support them through these challenges. One objective for your training may be to help employees recognize that they are not alone and that the organization is providing resources to help them learn and do what's needed to succeed in the new environment.

- **Head:** What do you need employees to think and know? One objective for your training is to reinforce messages about the rationale for the change initiative, why your organization is pursuing it, and what the benefits are for the organization and for the stakeholder groups participating in the training. Make sure the training helps each stakeholder group understand the unique way in which the change will affect them. Training should answer the questions "Why this?" "Why now?" and "Why you?"
- **Hands:** What do you want employees to do? Identify the behaviors each stakeholder group needs to be able to demonstrate. By the end of the training, what will each employee be able to do?

Training Program and Method

You've figured out who needs to learn and what they need to learn, and you probably have a sense of when that learning needs to occur. Now you're ready to decide how. How will you structure programs and activities to address the training objectives you have set?

Let's take a quick look at the programs and activities Sharon identified in the training plan for PCo. Here's what she sketched out based on her meeting with the company's leaders:

- A classroom-based MBA boot camp program, led by faculty from a university and the organization's business leaders, designed to help plant managers make smarter finance and marketing decisions
- A classroom-based sales training program, led by a vendor, designed to help PCo sales staff employ a more consultative approach to selling
- Online tutorials designed to help employees interpret basic financial documents and understand their obligations to protect confidential information

These are all fine approaches that probably will address—at least in part—the objectives that Sharon and the executives at PCo identified. They're fairly conventional solutions—classroom training and online tutorials—and they serve their purpose. These training programs will begin to equip employees with knowledge and skills so they can do what PCo expects of them. But do they go far enough?

What I have learned from years of working with organizations as they navigate through change is that whatever training you have planned probably isn't enough. If you have classes planned to teach employees how to operate your company's new technology, that's a great start, but employees probably will need more help to master using that new technology. Employees may walk out of your classes thinking they know what they need to do, but they likely will fumble a bit as they begin using the new technology anyway. If you've prepared an online tutorial to teach employees a new procedure, that's terrific too. But don't be surprised if employees experience frustration during their first attempts at following the new steps they have learned. If, like at PCo, you're offering courses to help employees make better business decisions, or manage more effectively, or sell in a different way, that's a great part of the solution. Hopefully employees appreciate the encouragement and ideas they will receive by participating in your training program. But they likely will struggle, at least for a while, as they try to implement these new ideas back on the job. Classroom training and online tutorials are great, but their impact only goes so far.

The organizations I know that experienced the best outcomes with their change initiatives took a far more aggressive approach with their training plans. They recognized that employees might feel anxious about their ability to master everything they needed to learn to support the change that was coming. They anticipated that employees might feel frustrated as they tried out new behaviors for the first time. They knew that employees might be reluctant to embrace the changes that were planned, because they wanted to avoid that awful feeling of incompetence.

To help employees feel more confident in their ability to learn and then perform what was needed, these organizations structured their learning programs to help move employees through that period of incompetence and frustration as quickly as possible. They found ways to adjust the timing and frequency of learning programs and activities, so employees had the opportunity to receive training as early and often as possible as the change was being implemented. They took steps to reassure employees that support would be readily available to them as they attempted to engage in the new behaviors that were expected of them. And finally, these organizations structured their learning programs to reinforce and extend whatever training was offered through other means. They implemented approaches that ensured employees would continue to build needed knowledge and skills long after the project had officially concluded.

Here are some programs and activities I've seen organizations include in their training plans to achieve these goals. Many of these ideas are exceedingly simple. Others require more planning and coordination. As you create training plans to support change initiatives in your organization, consider if these approaches make sense for you to use.

Approaches That Accelerate the Timing and Frequency of Training

These approaches help ensure employees receive training early and often throughout the change initiative. They ensure that training isn't just designed to be an "event" tacked onto the end of the project plan. Instead, training occurs through a series of activities over the course of the initiative. By helping employees learn early in the project life cycle, the change becomes more tangible. Employees can begin to envision what the future state will be like because they can see it for themselves. By delivering training focused on small chunks of content, employees see that what they need to learn to support the change is actually quite manageable. As they master each small piece of content, they may become more confident in their ability to learn what's needed.

You can do this by embedding training in stakeholder status meetings, conducting training at each milestone and as each short-term win is achieved, and using quality assurance testing to train.

Embed training in stakeholder status meetings. The project team for your change initiative probably meets periodically with stakeholders to update them on the status of the initiative. Allocate a portion of time in each status-update meeting to teaching a small chunk of content that employees need to learn. I've seen an organization use this approach to train employees in preparation for their move to a new location. During each move-update meeting, the company dedicated a small portion of time to teaching employees one new task they'd need to perform at their new site, like swiping into the building's security system or operating the new type of phone that was being installed. A tip sheet for each task was available online, so employees had handy reminders they could access as needed. When the move finally happened, employees didn't have to spend precious time learning these systems and tasks for the first time. Instead, they were able to focus on unpacking and adjusting to their new workspace. Likewise, a large medical center used this approach when they introduced a new electronic patient records system. In each employee meeting that occurred during the months before the system "went live," the center introduced two to three new vocabulary words or concepts employees needed to know to effectively work with the new technology. When training on the full system was conducted closer to launch, employees felt less overwhelmed because they'd already had a head start learning about some of its key components.

Conduct training at each milestone and as each short-term win is achieved. Think about each milestone that is planned for your project. Is there something employees need to learn related to that milestone? If so, see if it makes sense to deliver training when that milestone is reached, instead of waiting until the very end, when all of the project deliverables have been completed. Hopefully your project is planned in a way that delivers short-term wins (see chapter 4 for more on why early wins are so important!). Plan training so that it's delivered as each short-term win is achieved. Does your change initiative involve making 10 new software features available, and two are ready to launch now? Launch them and train employees on how to use them. It's probably easier for employees to learn a few new features at a time rather than having to figure them all out at once. If your organization uses Agile methodology for project planning (see chapter 4 for more on Agile), your change initiative likely is already organized around generating multiple bursts of output that stakeholders will need to learn through-out the project life cycle. Be sure you're ready to provide training as each output or short-term win is made available.

Use quality assurance testing to train. If your change initiative involves implementing a new technology or new process, the project plan probably includes a step where testing will occur to make sure the software or procedure functions as planned. Consider using quality assurance testing as a training oppor-tunity. Invite stakeholders who will need to learn the new technology or process to participate in testing. Provide stakeholders with a brief overview, then give them "scripts" that describe the scenarios to be tested, and the steps they need to follow to conduct the test. The core project team may thank you for providing resources to assist with quality assurance testing. And you'll be ahead of the game by having a group of stakeholders who are already partially trained by the time your formal training program is ready to launch. If you plan things well, you may also be able to incorporate the scripts and scenarios used during testing into your formal training program.

Approaches That Reassure Employees That Support Is Available

When employees first start engaging in the new behavior they have been trained to perform, they likely will need support. They'll try some things they thought they learned, and quickly realize they haven't quite yet mastered what they need to know. These approaches help employees feel confident that assistance will be available to them as they try out new behaviors.

Create job aids and tip sheets. If employees need to learn steps to perform a new task or factors to consider when making a decision, develop job aids or tip sheets they can refer to as they try things out back on the job. Your job aid may cover steps for conducting a productive virtual meeting in your company's new "work from anywhere" environment, or the procedure for accomplishing a task using new software. Maybe your tip sheet addresses factors employees need to consider when deciding how to handle confidential information. For example, Sharon, in the PCo case, might create a job aid that helps employees interpret financial data and understand whom they can and can't share this confidential data with. Depending on your work environment, you can post job aids and tip sheets online, or provide them in printed form so employees can post them in their physical workspace. If the same content is addressed in classroom or online training, be sure to let employees know how to access the job aids and tip sheets that support this training. Your goal is to help employees feel like they have resources they can turn to for support as they try out new behaviors related to the change.

Set up drop-in "clinics." Consider setting up a physical or virtual support center that employees can turn to for help. I saw one organization do this to support a group of employees who needed to begin using new software as part of a larger change initiative. Some employees quickly mastered the new tool, while others who felt far less confident took advantage of the drop-in clinic the organization had established. Employees who needed help brought real work they needed to complete to the clinic, and sat side by side with an expert who provided hands-on coaching until the employee was comfortable working alone. Other employees who needed less support simply called the clinic experts for quick answers to their questions. I've seen this same approach used by an organization that wanted its managers to provide more effective coaching to employees. A virtual "clinic" was established that recently trained managers could turn to for an expert review of the coaching conversation they planned to conduct. Managers role-played with clinic staff the coaching conversations they had planned, and checked in with them to debrief after their actual conversations with employees had occurred.

Train super users. Super users can be a valuable asset for assisting in training other employees. Start by providing more extensive training to one or more users who work in each department or area affected by the change. Let employees know they can turn to these specially trained, "super user" co-workers for expert assistance. This approach is commonly used when organizations are implementing new technology or new work processes. But it can be used effectively to support other changes as well. Is your organization relocating? Consider designating and training a move super user in each department, whom employees can turn to with questions about packing procedures, commuting, resources available at the new location, and so on. Of course, be sure you're not taking advantage of your super users' expertise and generosity. You still need to train everyone else affected by the change. Super users are there to supplement the training you've provided to all affected employees, by providing a little extra help to their co-workers when they need it.

Tap into the transition-monitoring team. We talked about the transition-monitoring team in chapter 7. Review your training plan with them to verify that your plan addresses what each stakeholder group needs to know. Have team members test out your training to make sure it's clear, comprehensive, and focused on the right content in the right way. Provide more extensive training to team members and ask them to serve double duty as super users. They can supplement the training you provide to their co-workers by offering on-site assistance to co-workers when they need it.

Approaches That Reinforce and Extend Training

These approaches help employees continue to learn—and build confidence in their ability to learn—after the project has officially concluded.

Embed training in staff meetings. Employees in your organization probably meet periodically, either in person or virtually, to discuss department business. Ask department leaders or managers to allocate a portion of time in these meetings to reinforcing content that was covered in more formal training. For example, the vice president of sales in the PCo case can devote a portion of each staff meeting to helping sales staff work through the challenges they're encountering as they apply their newly learned consultative selling skills. Provide managers with a discussion guide that helps them generate conversation among employees about how they are applying their new skills. In these meetings, have them ask employees to raise examples of situations they are struggling with or have questions about, and have employees talk through these situations to help one another find solutions. Have managers keep you posted on the topics employees have the most questions about, then update job aids and tip sheets to address these concerns. In an organization I worked with that used this approach, we asked managers to conduct a half-hour discussion during staff meetings each month, using a discussion guide we posted online. Each month's online guide focused on a different behavior the company needed employees to demonstrate more consistently. For example, one month the discussion guide focused on "taking informed risks." The guide asked managers to pose questions like, "What kinds of risks do we deal with in our jobs in this department? How should we decide how to handle that risk? What information should we consider before deciding how to proceed? Who, if anyone, should we talk with before deciding how to proceed?" The discussion guide provided managers with general principles and guidelines they could raise as employees provided their own answers to these questions. In your organization, managers may already use their staff meetings to reinforce material they know employees need to learn. But don't count on all managers to do that. Provide managers with resources, like discussion guides, to help them focus a portion of each staff meeting on learning. Let managers know they are expected to do that. State in your formal training plan that your organization is relying on managers to reinforce training during their regular staff meetings.

Provide booster-shot training and tips of the month. Provide periodic microlearning programs that remind employees about what was covered in formal training or that teach employees how to perform a task at a more advanced level. One organization I worked with reinforced training related to a process change by sending employees an online, two- to three-minute tutorial each month—each focused on a single task previously addressed in classroom training. Another organization that was implementing new technology shared a new tip sheet with employees each month. Although formal classroom instruction was offered to help employees learn the basics, the monthly tip sheets helped employees gradually learn how to use the system's more advanced features.

Remember transition planning. This isn't really an optional approach. You need to do this. Make sure you think through how training related to the change will be maintained after your project has officially concluded. Some employees will have participated in training, and that training just didn't stick. What mechanism do you have in place to help employees who need to repeat training? If training was conducted via classroom instruction, how will employees who missed it get access? If training was conducted online, have you structured enrollment so employees who need to complete the training multiple times can take it again? If some of the content covered in the training needs to change, who will update that content and how will you ensure employees are trained on what's new? As new content for job aids and tip sheets is identified, who will prepare it and how will it be distributed? And how will you ensure that new employees who join the organization after your project officially concludes receive the training they need? As you create your training plan, make sure you think through how you'll ensure that training continues after the project team has disbanded.

Validate Your Plan

Once you have drafted the objectives and training approaches planned for each target audience, circle back to the people you've had discussions with to verify that the information included in your training plan is accurate and complete. Ask your transition-monitoring team for their feedback. Make adjustments as needed.

Throughout the course of your change initiative, and through your ongoing conversations, it's likely that additional stakeholder groups will be identified, or that other training needs related to the change will surface. Timeframes may change too. That's all OK. Keep adjusting your training plan to reflect new information as it emerges.

What Else Can Sharon Include in the Training Plan?

Take a look at the training plan Sharon created for the PCo business transformation case you read in chapter 11. Sharon's plan includes an online tutorial to help employees understand basic financial documents, an online tutorial to help employees understand their responsibility to protect confidential information, a consultative selling course for PCo sales staff, and an MBA boot camp program designed to help plant managers make smarter business decisions. What else should Sharon include in the plan?

- Given the scale and scope of the business transformation occurring at PCo, should Sharon recommend the company conduct an organization-wide training needs assessment? That way, PCo's leaders will have a more comprehensive understanding of the organization's current skill level, and know more precisely where action is needed to intervene. Without that assessment, it's possible the company will devote resources to training where it will have little effect, or might miss providing training in areas where it is sorely needed.
- PCo wants each employee to be able to read and interpret simple financial documents so they can make more informed financial decisions on the job. It also wants employees to understand that financial information shared with them is confidential, and that they need to protect that confidentiality. Perhaps the company can prepare a simple job aid that explains the key

components of the financial documents they plan to share with employees. They can distribute this job aid each time they send financial documents to employees. During town hall meetings where financial information is shared, PCo leaders can spend a few minutes explaining what the financials mean and why they are important. At the same time, they can remind employees that the financial information they're receiving is confidential and discuss why it's important to protect it. Sharon and PCo's finance staff can prepare a discussion guide managers can use during staff meetings to lead a conversation about the types of financial decisions employees make on the job and factors to consider to make smarter financial decisions. Perhaps the company can prepare a similar discussion guide to focus conversation on the types of confidential information employees have access to in their jobs, and actions they can take to protect that information.

- The company wants sales staff to transition to a consultative selling model. Sharon can meet with the vice president of sales to confirm that employees have been informed about these new expectations and that rewards will be adjusted to support the consultative selling process. She can also confirm that employees, in fact, don't currently have consultative selling skills and that training is needed. Assuming sales training is needed, Sharon can work with the VP of sales and the training vendor to create tip sheets and job aids that reinforce the consultative selling practices that will be covered in training. The VP of sales can devote a portion of each staff meeting to discussing and working through the challenges sales staff face as they try out their new consultative selling skills. Perhaps PCo's sale training vendor can send sales staff a short online tutorial every few weeks to help them learn additional consultative selling strategies and techniques.

- PCo plant managers need to make smarter marketing and finance decisions. Sharon can meet with the acting vice president of operations to confirm that plant managers have been informed about these new expectations and that rewards have been adjusted accordingly.

- Given PCo's goal of creating more accountability across the company, Sharon can recommend PCo revisit its commitment to performance management. Are managers and employees working together to establish performance goals? Do employees understand expectations? What is rewarded at PCo? Does PCo need to refocus efforts on performance management, training, or both?

These are just a few ideas. What additional advice do you have for Sharon?

Tips for Preparing and Executing Your Training Plan

Focus on your target audience and the learning objectives for each stakeholder group. Then think broadly about the different methods you can use to address these learning objectives. What can you do besides, or in addition to, offering stand-alone training? How can you make training truly part of the change? Consider:

Accelerating the Timing and Frequency of Training
- How can you embed training in stakeholder status meetings?
- Can you conduct training at each milestone and as each short-term win is achieved?
- Can you use quality assurance testing as an opportunity to train?

Reassure employees that support is available as they perform their jobs:
- Can you provide job aids and tip sheets for employees to refer to as they try out new processes and behaviors?
- How can you set up actual or virtual drop-in "clinics" and "office hours" so employees have resources they can turn to for answers to their questions?
- Can you identify super users who will receive more extensive training, who in turn can coach and answer employee questions?
- Will you establish a transition-monitoring team? Can they help answer questions from their peers?

Reinforce and extend training:
- What resources can you provide to frontline supervisors and managers to help them conduct short, supplemental training sessions during regularly scheduled staff meetings?
- Can you offer microlearning programs or distribute tips of the month to reinforce and extend training and help employees learn continuously?
- Who is responsible for maintaining the training program after your project officially concludes?

Advocating for the Learning Needs and Capabilities of Stakeholders

As your change initiative proceeds, there will be times when you need to assume the role of advocate. Your job will be to ensure the core project team understands what employees need to learn for the initiative to achieve its intended target—and considers how they will learn it—as the team makes project-related decisions. Your role is to make sure the project is planned and executed in a way that allows employees to develop the knowledge, skills, and attitudes they need to do what's expected of them. You need to be proactive, recommending actions that will afford employees appropriate opportunities to learn. And you need to be vigilant, on the lookout for decisions that might compromise employees' ability to learn what's needed in the right timeframe. There may be times when you will need to engage in some difficult conversations, where you present the case for decisions to be reconsidered and where you provide the rationale for more appropriate decisions to be made. But it will be worth it when you see employees grow and flourish and the project succeed.

You'll certainly need to play the role of advocate when project schedules are prepared and timeframes are established for training to occur. Discuss with the project leader or change management leader the amount of time needed to prepare and deliver required training, and work with them to incorporate training-related dates into the overall project plan. Be realistic— and firm—as you explain what is included in the training plan you created and why you established the timeframes that are set forth there. If training activities need to be concluded by a certain date for the project to launch on schedule, be clear about when training will need to begin. Ask how the overall project plan can ensure training begins and ends within the timeframe that's needed. If other project tasks slip that push back the start date for training activities, discuss with the project leader or change management leader how the project plan can be adjusted to ensure appropriate time is still allocated for training to occur.

At times, you may have the opportunity to play the role of advocate as decisions are made about the design of other project deliverables. For example, as the core project team lays out steps for a new process employees will need to follow, take a step back and consider how easy or difficult it will be for employees to learn the new procedure. Is there a simpler way the process could be designed that achieves the same goal, one that won't be so frustrating for employees to adjust to? If so, advocate for a better way. That's the situation I faced when the organization I described earlier was implementing new software and changed one of its HR policies at the same time. I recognized that employees would struggle as they tried to understand the new, complex, and convoluted policy, and would begin to question the organization's motives. And so I stepped in to advocate for a different approach to be taken, one that better matched what employees had the capacity to learn and that better reflected the organization's actual intent. As an advocate, I had to engage in multiple, difficult conversations, but the outcome was worth it.

How did Sharon in the PCo case fulfill her role as advocate for employee learning needs? She advocated for learning—in a way—when she questioned if employees would understand the financial documents PCo's CEO planned to distribute. Sharon may have recognized that without some training or assistance, employees would be ill-equipped to use the information PCo leaders planned to share. She stepped up and questioned if employees would need more support. That's great. But where else does Sharon need to intervene? If Sharon prepares a training plan that merely reflects the ideas PCo leaders proposed during their meeting with her, she is acting like an order taker. Some of the actions contained in the plan may address employees' learning needs, at least in part. But they likely will miss the mark too. The good news is that while Sharon may have felt "dismissed" from the executive staff meeting she participated in, she recognized that her work wasn't done. She knew she needed to question and challenge the ideas PCo's leaders had proposed. She knew she needed to propose alternative—and additional—approaches. Sharon recognized that she needed to step out of the order-taker role and act as an advocate. In your organization, when you engage with stakeholders as a performance consultant—when you seek to understand stakeholder needs, challenge the wisdom of proceeding with ineffective solutions that you've been asked to implement, and propose creative solutions of your own—you're acting as an advocate.

And finally, during training sessions, whether you conduct them in person or virtually, you likely will hear feedback from stakeholders about the change itself. In your advocate role, you can share that feedback with the core project team and organizational leaders. In fact, training participants may fully want and expect you to let leaders and the team know about the concerns and frustrations they're experiencing. As the person responsible for training, you play an intermediary role of sorts. You're charged with conveying important information about the project to employees. And you also have responsibility for conveying employee needs and issues back to the project team. When you conduct training, let participants know what you will and won't share with others. And be clear about what is and isn't confidential. If you establish the norm that "what's said in this classroom stays in this classroom," seek employee permission before discussing with the project team the feedback that you're hearing.

What to Do When Training Goes Wrong

What should you do if your training program is hijacked by employees expressing concerns and frustration about the change? What if the training veers off course because employees have so much to say about the change itself? How can you refocus participants on the content you need to address?

Plan for it:

- Ensure employees have other opportunities—in addition to training—to express their needs and concerns. During training, remind employees about the vehicles for two-way communication you have established for the project. When employees express critical feedback, show empathy, acknowledge their concern, and ask them how they could use one of the other vehicles for sharing. For example, say, "That's an interesting perspective. Is that an idea you'd feel comfortable sharing in next week's town hall meeting?" Or, "It sounds like you're really frustrated by that. Have you shared that with your supervisor?"
- Allocate a set time during the program for employees to discuss their issues and concerns before moving on to address other content. Let employees know you will share what you are hearing back with the project team. Be clear that you can't promise their concerns will be addressed, but you can promise you'll let the project team know what they've shared.

Show empathy. Say things like:

- "I know when I first heard about the change, I felt. . . ." Or, "I wondered about that when I first heard it too. I can see that you're frustrated by that."

Express confidence in employees' ability to learn what's needed to succeed in the new environment and remind them about the support that's available. Say things like:

- "I know that's a lot to learn, but I'm confident you can do it."
- "Remember, you're not alone. There are a lot of people who can help you master this. There's the drop-in clinic. . . . "
- "We know this is a lot to learn. That's why we're going to cover the material again in each department meeting."

Anchor on the rationale for the change and the benefits employees will receive. Acknowledge the challenges too. Say things like:

- "I know it's going to be awkward to have to do this, but you'll also now be able to do. . . ."
- "I hear you. This is going to take a lot of extra work. I'm really looking forward to when we get past that and are able to do. . . ."

> Direct participants back to the agenda and the content that needs to be addressed. Sometimes you just need to ask participants for their permission to move on. Say things like:
> - "I hear you. Right now, we need to cover. . . ."
> - "I can see that there's a lot of interest in talking about that. Can we agree to talk about that after this session is over? Right now, we need to cover. . . ."

Here are two quick tips to help you advocate for employees' learning needs: Use your access to project team members and get support from other stakeholders.

Use Your Access to Project Team Members

So how do you advocate for the learning needs of employees as your change initiative proceeds? The most straightforward way is to just state what's needed and why during discussions with the project leader, change management leader (if you're not also serving that role), and core project team. Have these conversations as early as possible in the project life cycle—ideally while initial project plans are being drafted—so the overall project plan can be constructed to accommodate what's needed. As you spot issues and concerns, discuss them—again, as early as possible—with the project leader, change management leader, and core project team. For you to appropriately serve your role as an advocate for employee learning—for you to hear what's going on and recognize situations where you need to step in—you need to work in close partnership with the project leader or change management leader. Ideally, you should participate in core project team meetings too.

Get Support From Other Stakeholders

To advocate for employee learning needs, you can also leverage the power of other stakeholders involved with the project. For example, if training dates are at risk, or if you're questioning the wisdom of a process design decision, you can recommend gathering input from employee supervisors or from members of the transition-monitoring team. It's possible their recommendations will coincide with and support what you are advocating. That's the approach the vice president of HR wisely suggested in the situation I described earlier, where I had serious doubts about the design of an organization's new HR policy. The VP recommended sharing the new policy design, and associated training, with a broader group of division HR leaders who would need to support the policy and respond to employee questions about it. After receiving their input, the original design was scrapped and new decisions were made that better reflected what employees could learn. I recognize now that the way I performed my advocate role during this situation was imperfect. Although I had raised concerns to the project leader, I gave up at some point. What would have been better is if I, instead of the VP of HR, had recommended gathering input from the division HR leaders. That way, the mess could have been cleaned up even earlier. I should have recognized there was an opportunity to leverage the power of other stakeholders to address the issue I had raised.

As you advocate for employee learning needs, recognize that there are other stakeholders who likely have the same goals and intent as you. Take a look at the stakeholder analysis if you need ideas about whose help you can solicit. Other stakeholders want to make sure employees have the knowledge, skills, and attitudes needed to achieve the project outcome, just like you do. Take advantage of the opportunities to work together with these stakeholders to advocate for those needs.

Tips for Advocating for the Learning Needs and Capabilities of Stakeholders

- Review the project plan. Is enough time allocated for training development and delivery? To meet project deadlines, does the core project team want to shorten the amount of time allocated to training? Step in and explain how quality training is needed to ensure employees can do what's required for the project to succeed. Help your project team consider options other than cutting back on training.
- As project decisions are made, question if employees can master what they will need to learn in the required timeframe. Ask if the new process, procedure, or policy is just too complex. See if the core project team can make it simpler and easier to learn.
- Raise questions when you're asked to implement training that's likely to be ineffective. Propose alternative solutions that better address learners' needs.
- Listen to employees as they express needs and concerns during training sessions. Consider when you should reassure employees, when you should convey what you're hearing to project decision makers, and when you need to do both.
- During meetings with the core project team, stay alert for actions and decisions that might compromise your ability to successfully execute the training plan. If you sense trouble, be assertive and speak up.
- Remember that stakeholders are concerned about their learning needs too! Gather input and feedback from key stakeholders regarding their learning needs. Leverage their power and influence to ensure enough time and resources are dedicated to training.

Training as a Mechanism to Build Change Resilience

In this chapter, we addressed steps you can take to help employees build the knowledge, skills, and attitudes they need to support the change that's occurring in your organization. We talked about analyzing needs so you have a clear sense about who needs training on what and when. We explored ideas for providing training that helps employees learn earlier in the project life cycle and in more manageable chunks. And we looked at actions you can take to reassure employees that the support they need is available as they try out new behaviors back on the job. We looked at steps you can take to help employees continue to build knowledge, skills, and attitudes after your project has officially concluded. And we looked at how important it will be for you to advocate for employees' learning needs throughout the entire course of your change initiative.

Why does training matter so much? On the hard side of change, for your change initiative to achieve its intended outcome, employees need to be able to do what's now expected of them. They need to know how to operate the new technology, how to perform the new procedures, how to make decisions according to new protocols. On the soft side, for employees to support what's changing, they need to feel confident they can learn what's needed in the right timeframe. They need to trust that your organization is providing them with the appropriate resources they need to learn.

In some ways, the training you provide can have an impact that extends far beyond your current change initiative. When employees recognize that they can learn what's needed for the current project, that feeling can generalize to the next change initiative they face, and the next after that. When employees see that your company is providing resources that help them move through the expected period of incompetence as quickly as possible, they may begin to feel like your organization has its act together, that it manages change well. When employees recognize that they can navigate successfully through change, because there's help readily available when they feel lost and disoriented, they become more resilient. The training you provide can help employees learn what's needed to support your current change initiative and more readily get on board with change initiatives to come.

To do this, participate actively on your core project team. Meet frequently with your project leader and change management leader to ensure your training plan fully integrates with other plans. And create and execute training programs that are tailored to the unique needs of each stakeholder group and that take advantage of every training opportunity that's available.

About to Begin?

Are you about to begin preparing training for a change initiative that's happening in your organization? As you develop your plan, ask yourself:

- Do I have access to all the people and documents I need? Can I join the core project team or attend their meetings? Do I have access to project documents like the charter, project plan, stakeholder analysis, and communications plan?
- Have I analyzed the unique training requirement for each stakeholder group? Am I sure training is the right solution to address their needs?
- Does my training address both the hard side of change, or the knowledge and skills employees need to learn, and the soft side, or the attitudes they will need in the new environment?
- Have I found ways to accelerate the timing and frequency of training? Am I delivering training in manageable chunks to help employees feel confident they can learn what's needed?
- Are we reassuring employees that they will be supported after training has concluded? Do I need to create job aids and tip sheets? Should we establish a drop-in clinic or help line? Can we train super users or press the transition-monitoring team into service to address employee questions back on the job?
- What are we doing to reinforce and extend training after formal training concludes? Can we embed training in staff meetings? Should we conduct periodic booster-shot training sessions?
- Have we determined how training will be maintained after the project has officially concluded? Who will be responsible for training new hires and employees who need to repeat training? Who will update training material as the content changes?

Of course, despite these efforts, all employees some of the time—and some employees all of the time—will still feel reluctant to get on board. You've provided opportunities for employees to get involved with your change initiative. You've made sure they understand what's changing and when, and what the impact will be for them. You've helped employees build the knowledge, skills, and attitudes they need to succeed in the new environment. What should you do if they push back anyway?

In chapter 14, we'll take a look at resistance. You may be surprised to learn that sometimes resistance can be a really good thing! There may be times when employee resistance is just what your project needs to generate results! But of course, that's not always the case. Sometimes you should take advantage of the resistance that's occurring, and sometimes you'll need to quiet it down. Or just maybe you need to do both.

Learn more. Check out:

Kaufman, R., and I. Guerra-López. 2013. *Needs Assessment for Organizational Success.* Alexandria, VA: ATD Press.

Rothwell, W.J., B. Benscoter, M. King, and S.B. King. 2016. *Mastering the Instructional Design Process: A Systematic Approach.* John Wiley & Sons.

14

Anticipating and Addressing Resistance

You've probably seen something like this before. Employees smile and nod politely as their manager describes changes that are planned. A few employees ask questions to be sure they're clear on what's happening. A few even volunteer to try things out. But later on, in private, these same employees joke disparagingly with their co-workers. "She's crazy," they're overheard saying. "She won't get far with this. You'll see."

Or, a training manager checks in with employees to see how a new process change is going for them. Her trainees assure her things are great; they just haven't had time yet to try out the new procedures they were trained on. For now, they're still doing things the old way. "I'll do it soon," each trainee assures her. "I promise."

Or, a project leader expresses frustration to the rest of his team after a key stakeholder misses their third status-update meeting in a row. "It's just plain old resistance. That's inevitable," he continues, as he tosses a stack of status reports onto the conference room table. "He'll get on board. You'll see. I mean, what choice does he have?"

You may have encountered similar examples of resistance to change initiatives happening in your organization. And when you saw it, perhaps you wondered, is it just plain old resistance or is it something deeper? Is resistance inevitable? What does it take to really get people on board? And does it matter if employees feel like they have a choice?

In this chapter, we'll take a look at these questions. You'll see that the project leader in our last example was partly right. It is just about inevitable that resistance will arise in some form or fashion with each change initiative you work on. But the project leader was partly wrong too. Resistance isn't something you should just dismiss, assuming that people will eventually fall into line because they don't have a choice. Instead, you'll see that resistance is something you can anticipate, plan for, and sometimes avert. It's something you should deal with, when it does emerge, honestly and straight-on. You'll see that providing stakeholders with choices can help them "get on board." And you'll see that resistance is something you can harness and put to work to help your change initiative produce even better results than you might have otherwise achieved.

But first, let's explore why resistance is so ubiquitous. Why do we encounter so much resistance when our organizations embark on change?

Reasons for Resistance

Resistance happens when employees don't support the change that's affecting them, so they act, intentionally or unintentionally, in ways that interfere with the initiative's success. Sometimes the reasons for their opposition are obvious. Maybe your company faces job cutbacks during lean economic times. Why would someone want to get on board when their job might be eliminated? Maybe office space is being consolidated and reconfigured to help your organization save on real estate expenses. Who wants a smaller workspace and less privacy? Maybe a beloved co-worker is leaving and your organization has hired a replacement. Who wouldn't miss being able to work with a good friend? It's natural for people to feel disappointed by these kinds of changes, and it's normal for them to want to hold back a bit.

But many times the reasons behind resistance are far less clear. Maybe antiquated software is being replaced. Who wouldn't feel excited about that? But some employees still seem reluctant to give it a try. A cumbersome process is finally being streamlined. Who doesn't love it when work becomes easier? Yet some employees are arguing for a return to the old procedure. The new office location is chock full of amenities. Who can't wait to try out the new, gourmet cafeteria and on-site gym? But some employees are advocating for their department to remain behind at the old location. Why?

I've seen employees show real reluctance to get on board, despite the obvious benefits a change will bring, when they sense that something else is amiss. Here are some possibilities to consider.

- **Fear of incompetence.** They worry about how much they will need to learn, or relearn, as a result of what's changing. They don't want to feel incompetent. Sometimes a change causes employees to question if they have what it takes to succeed in the new environment.

- **Workload.** They're concerned their work volume will increase substantially. They know that work will just be harder, at least initially, while they are learning how to perform the new behaviors that are expected. Or they recognize that they will just need to do more—perhaps indefinitely—given the way the new workflow has been designed. They sense that their free time will be diminished.
- **Loss of status.** They're concerned they'll lose competence or prestige because of a change in job responsibilities.
- **Loss of friends.** They're upset about the loss of co-workers after layoffs or a restructuring.
- **Change fatigue.** They're overwhelmed by change. I've seen this in an organization that was establishing a whole new executive team. Employees felt like they were reeling as they tried to understand and adjust to the succession of changes each new leader brought with them to the organization.
- **Pride.** They've created the way work is currently performed, they're proud of it, and they don't want to see what they've built eliminated.
- **Preferred a different approach.** Sometimes employees support the reason for the change, but believe that a different solution should have been selected. I've seen this happen when organizations implement new technology: Sure, everyone agrees the old software had to go. But why didn't they pick the new vendor that I advocated for?
- **Mixed signals.** They don't see their immediate manager, or other organizational leaders, supporting the change.
- **Flavor of the week.** They believe that leaders aren't really committed to the change, because they've seen them introduce idea after idea, only to quickly abandon them. Employees sense that they can survive best if they just hunker down. They've outlasted changes like these in the past, and they can make it through this change too.
- **Prior failures.** The organization doesn't have a good track record in implementing change. After participating in a succession of failed projects, employees don't see why this one will be any different.
- **Change for change's sake.** Employees don't understand the reasons the change is necessary. They feel like things aren't broken, so why fix them? They might believe that things really are OK, but that leaders are just trying to change things to make their mark.

- **Confidence the change is wrong.** They genuinely question how wise it is for their organization to proceed with the change, at least given how the change initiative is currently planned. Sometimes, employees honestly believe that the organization they love, and want to protect, is going down the wrong path. They feel like they have an obligation—maybe even a moral imperative—to prevent the change from succeeding.

How Resistance Is Expressed

In the best case, employees will tell you about their concerns. They'll share with you what they sense is amiss. But with resistance, we typically see opposition expressed in a more oblique way. Resistance might occur in the form of employees establishing barriers, not following through, superficially complying, creating workarounds, avoiding, and disengaging. Let's look at each before we discuss what to do about it.

Establishing barriers. Sometimes, stakeholders put up barriers to stop a project from proceeding, or at least to slow it down. I worked with an organization that was attempting to replace its temporary staffing firm with a new vendor. Stakeholders kept bringing up additional vendors they wanted the project team to check out. After each series of demos was completed, stakeholders would produce another list of temporary staffing firms they "just learned about" that needed to be investigated. This process went on for many years! When it became clear that each and every vendor had been considered, stakeholders presented a new list of requirements they needed each potential supplier to respond to. Stakeholders privately admitted they didn't want the project to proceed and that their strategy was to ensure that it stalled.

Not following through. Sometimes, employees agree to do what's needed but then fail to follow through. They claim they're too busy at the moment, and promise they'll get back on track soon. And soon never comes. Perhaps they're overwhelmed with higher-priority work and can't commit the time needed to complete the task. Or perhaps, intentionally or unintentionally, they're focusing on lower-priority work instead of tasks related to the project that they had agreed to perform. Perhaps their supervisor has directed them not to complete the task. If the lack of follow-through is intentional, it may be a sign that either the employee or their supervisor is resisting.

Superficially complying. Resistance can appear in truly sneaky form. Employees may look like they have complied with the change, when they haven't really changed things at all. I worked with an organization that wanted all employees to use a new, online decision support tool. The CEO actually tracked how many times per day his direct reports logged in to the new system. I checked in with one leader who seemed to be adjusting to the requirement better than most, because the logs showed he was accessing the tool far more frequently than his peers. I was surprised—and somewhat amused—to find that he had programmed a utility to open the new tool multiple times throughout the day, whether he was at his desk or not! He had found a way to comply with the "letter of the law"—he made sure the tool was opened multiple times each day—without actually engaging in the intended behavior!

Creating workarounds. Employees may come up with workarounds to avoid engaging in the new behavior. I've seen more than my share of "shadow systems" created after an organization implements new technology. Instead of using software the organization has just deployed, employees set up and maintain their own spreadsheets so they can keep doing things the old way. "Why does it matter if I use the new system," they ask, "when I can still get you the information you need?"

Avoiding. Sometimes, people just don't show up. You plan a meeting to gather a stakeholder's requirements, and they accept the invite, but then cancel at the last minute. This happens again and again. "I'm just really busy!" they say with a smile and a sigh, as they apologize to you for the umpteenth time. Or they stop responding to emails or phone calls. When confronted, they promise they'll get to it. "I'm just swamped," they claim.

Disengaging. Other times stakeholders show up at meetings but refuse to participate. They come unprepared. They don't contribute anything during discussions, or they passively agree to whatever is proposed. You try to gather information from them, but it feels like you're pulling teeth. Sharon, the learning and organizational development leader you read about in the PCo business transformation case (see chapter 11), noticed signs of this. The company's acting vice president of operations seemed disengaged throughout the entire executive team discussion. He contributed little to the discussion about changes that were planned for his own team. He readily agreed to actions the CEO proposed, but failed to share details about how he would implement those actions. The CEO seemed pleased, because she assumed his silence signaled his agreement. But Sharon sensed trouble. She recognized that the acting VP of operations' disengagement during a meeting could morph into foot-dragging later on. Sometimes resistance is expressed through loud and strident protests. But often it's expressed through disengagement. Don't assume a person's silence means that you have their support.

Resistance really can appear in many shapes and forms. So what do you do when you encounter it? There are three approaches I've seen work most effectively. You can plan to encounter resistance, and take steps to avert it. You can deal directly with resistance when it appears, and attempt to neutralize it. And you can use resistance that emerges to make your project even stronger. Because resistance is so ubiquitous, on most change initiatives you'll probably need to do all three.

Tips for Understanding Reasons for Resistance and How It Is Expressed

Identify why stakeholders resist the change. Ask:

- What could they lose because of the change? Is it something tangible, like their job, a pleasant work environment, access to knowledgeable and friendly co-workers, or free time? Will they lose something intangible, like their sense of competence, status, prestige, or pride? Will work become harder for them because of the change?
- Are they hearing a consistent message about the change? Is their supervisor saying they can ignore the change while senior leaders are saying something different?
- Does your organization have a poor track record implementing change? Have similar changes failed? Have leaders demonstrated a lack of commitment to other changes, so this one feels like it's the newest "flavor of the week"?
- Do they understand why the change is necessary? Have you articulated a clear and compelling rationale for the change?
- Do they genuinely think your organization is going down the wrong path—that it's a mistake to pursue the change or that the change is being implemented in the wrong way? Do they believe that the change, at least how it is currently planned, will do more harm than good?

Identify how resistance is expressed in your organization. Ask:

- Are stakeholders creating obstacles, like establishing requirements that are impossible to meet?
- Are they not following through on commitments to the project team, complying only superficially, or creating workarounds?
- Have they stopped showing up for project-related meetings? Do they show

up but refuse to participate? Do they seem overly passive, agreeing to whatever is proposed but actually doing nothing?
- What else are you seeing that might indicate stakeholders are expressing resistance to your change initiative?

Plan for Resistance

You won't be wrong if you assume that you'll encounter resistance at some point during every change initiative. Someone is going to have concerns and question whether your project should go forward in the way you have planned. It's possible many people will have their doubts.

Given that reality, one of the first steps you can take to prevent resistance from interfering with your change initiative is to anticipate that it will occur. Think through who is likely to resist and why. Plan actions you can take to cultivate their support, or at least moderate their opposition. And identify steps you will take if you see signs of resistance emerge anyway.

Identify Who Is Likely to Resist and Why

Start by thinking about potential sources of resistance. Who might resist the change and why?

If you've conducted a thorough stakeholder analysis (see chapter 9), you've already done a lot of the work here! You've already identified who will be affected by the change initiative and how. Hopefully you had conversations with these stakeholders and have a sense of what their concerns are. You've already begun to figure out who supports your change initiative, who opposes it, and who's in between. You have a sense of the extent to which each stakeholder can influence the overall success of your change initiative. And you've been thinking through how much support you actually need from each stakeholder, given the level of sway they have over the project or over those who are affected by it. If you haven't identified your stakeholders yet, or haven't met with them to understand their concerns, do that now. Conduct your stakeholder analysis.

Then, reflect on the information you've gathered in your stakeholder analysis. Which stakeholders seem to oppose the change initiative and why? Who is on the fence and why are they reluctant to get on board? What are employees potentially losing because of this project? Take another look at the possible reasons listed for resistance that we discussed earlier in this chapter. Is it possible employees will lose their job? Will they lose the prestige associated with being your company's "resident expert"? Are they going to have to take on more work? Did they advocate for a different solution than the one your organization ultimately chose to pursue? Are they just tired from all the change they've recently been through, not all of which has gone well? Is their manager ambivalent about the change? For each stakeholder or stakeholder group, try to anticipate what their core concerns might be that will prevent them from throwing their full weight behind your project.

Decide What Can Be Done to Prevent Resistance

It's often said that the best thing you can do to prevent resistance is to manage your project correctly from the start! Think about actions you and the project team can take, when you're just beginning to plan the change initiative, that address stakeholder concerns. Provide opportunities for stakeholders to participate in project planning and decisions. Which stakeholders should participate in the core project team (see chapter 6)? Who should serve on the transition-monitoring team (see chapter 7)? Which stakeholders should be on the red team (see chapter 8)? Make sure stakeholders are aware of what's changing, why, and what it means for them. Plan frequent status-update meetings and provide plenty of opportunities for two-way communication. Prepare and deliver training that helps stakeholders build the knowledge, skills, and attitudes they'll need to succeed in the new environment. Provide resources that adequately support employees as they're building needed skills. Make sure leaders communicate and demonstrate their active support for the initiative. Do things right from the start and you'll prevent the resistance that can be avoided.

Then, plan additional actions that focus on places where you expect resistance will emerge anyway. Think about those stakeholders who can significantly influence your project's success who seem reluctant to get on board. What's at the root of their opposition? What can your organization do, in advance, to address their concerns? And think about those who have somewhat less influence, but whose resistance might still affect your progress. What can be done, as you and your team plan project-related activities, to address their needs?

Often you can prevent resistance from taking root by providing resisters with opportunities to get involved, offering them options and choices, and finding ways to compensate employees, at least in part, for the losses they will experience as a result of the change.

Involve Resisters

People often resist change when they feel like something is being imposed on them from the outside. Can you find ways for them to get more involved so they feel like they are on the inside? If the person can significantly influence the success of your project, take a step back and consider if they should be included on the core project team. If you really need their active support, can you—and should you—add them to the team now? Can you put their critical eye to good use by asking them to join the red team? Can you involve them by asking them to review communications or training plans before they're implemented? Can they help with testing, when the project reaches that stage?

Perhaps this is an employee with less official influence who you know just likes to be heard. Maybe they're someone who typically has a lot to say during department meetings or who doesn't hesitate to let everyone know what's on their mind. While they may not hold a formal position of power, they may still be able to influence what their co-workers think, or at least what they hear. Can you satisfy their need to be heard by checking in with them periodically to provide updates and to listen to their ideas?

Provide Options to Comply

Employees sometimes resist when they feel "managed," when they feel like they have lost control over how they do their work. Allow employees some choices that will help them feel like they have retained some sense of control. In one organization I worked with, employees felt lukewarm about being reassigned to jobs in a new call center the company was establishing. But their mood brightened when the company set up staggered work hours. Within certain parameters, employees were able to choose the work shift that suited them best. Having a choice about when they worked helped quell some employees' concerns about how they worked. Think about the choices you can provide employees. Can they choose the date they'll attend training? Provide input into how their new cubicle will be configured? Decide which project phase the change will go live for their team? When you offer choice, you can prevent resistance from emerging.

Reduce or Compensate for Losses

And finally, think about actions your organization can take that will, at least partially, restore what employees have lost because of the change, or that compensate employees in some way. I worked with an organization that was relocating to a new building to save on real estate expenses. At the new location, offices and cubicles were smaller, conference room space was reduced, and the employee break room was eliminated. When employees were informed about the move, they complained bitterly. They weren't upset about the reduction in work space. The reasons for the move made sense to them. But they questioned why the company would eliminate the place where they stored lunches and snacks they brought from home. As soon as organizational leaders agreed to install a full-size refrigerator at the new location, complaining stopped. The company found a way to restore something important that employees feared they might lose. For the change initiatives you support, think about actions you can take to reduce the sting of loss. Perhaps your organization can offer more flexibility, different work hours, an extra vacation day after the project launches. From your conversations with stakeholders, find out what's important to them, and see if it can be offered in some way—even if it means installing a refrigerator.

Let's look at some additional situations that can arise during a change initiative and actions you can take to prevent resistance from emerging (Table 14-1).

Table 14-1. Sources of Resistance and Potential Actions

Key Concern/Source of Resistance	Potential Actions to Prevent Resistance
A department manager tells you he's concerned about exposing his department to glitches that will inevitably emerge during a change project. He's concerned project-related decisions haven't been as well thought out as they should. You need his support for his employees to get on board.	Let the manager know you'll consult with him before key project decisions are made. Update your RACI matrix (see chapter 10) to show that this manager has been assigned consulting status.

Invite the manager to participate in red team meetings (see chapter 8) to review—and potentially help improve—key project plans and decisions before they're made.

Offer choice. If the project is rolling out in phases, ask the manager if he'd prefer for his department to be included in one of the earlier waves of implementation. That way, he and his department can help shape how the project team addresses the issues that will inevitably emerge. Or does he prefer for his department to be included in one of the later implementation phases, when many of the issues have already been identified and fixed?

Include in testing. If the change involves a new process or technology, ask the manager to assign some department members to join the testing team. Let him know his team can play a key role in helping to shake out glitches before the change goes live. |

Key Concern/Source of Resistance	Potential Actions to Prevent Resistance
A key stakeholder whose input you need tells you she doubts she'll be able to meet on a regular basis. She's busy.	Meet one-on-one with the stakeholder to see if she has concerns, besides the needed time commitment, that prevent her from wanting to get involved.
	Ask the stakeholder if she can designate a deputy to represent her in project-related meetings. Let her know you'll still need to circle back to her for some key decisions, but that otherwise she is authorizing the deputy to make them for her. Keep her updated on key decisions before they're live, to ensure she agrees with the approach her deputy has advised.
Employees are concerned that their manager doesn't support the change. The employees say they want to engage in behaviors needed for the change, but fear negative repercussions from their manager.	Meet one-on-one to hear the manager's ideas and concerns, and implement their ideas when appropriate.
	Involve the manager in project planning, through participation in the core project team or red team, if appropriate.
	Include the manager in frequent status-update meetings that provide opportunities for two-way communication.
	Ask senior leaders or sponsors to intervene if needed to secure the manager's support. Ask them to meet with the manager to ensure the manager understands the rationale for the change initiative and the impact on their area. Ask senior leaders to convey to the manager what the manager is expected to do to support the change.
Employees are concerned about work volume. They fear work will take longer to complete, or that there will be extra work to perform during the transition, or perhaps even permanently.	Plan for reduced productivity during the transition period, and temporarily adjust employee productivity targets and goals accordingly.
	Consider hiring temporary staff to ease demands.
	Acknowledge the extra demands placed on employees, and assure them, if you can, that it's temporary.
	Let employees know their extra effort is appreciated; consider spot bonuses, additional vacation time, or other rewards/compensation as appropriate.
Employees fear losing prestige. Their job responsibilities or job titles are changing in a way they believe will diminish the amount of respect they receive.	Focus communications on helping employees understand the value their new roles provide to the organization and its overall goals.
	Ask the employees' immediate manager to meet with each employee one-on-one to ensure employee concerns are heard.
	Identify actions that can help compensate employees for their sense of loss. Can work hours become more flexible? Can work-from-home opportunities expand? Can employees be assigned a "working title" that conveys a higher status than the official title assigned in the organization's HR system?
Stakeholders will experience real and tangible loss as a result of the initiative. The change initiative brings few benefits to them, even though it benefits the organization overall.	Ask stakeholders what can be done—short of having the change initiative disappear—that will make things better for them. Identify actions that can help compensate employees for their sense of loss. Can work hours become more flexible? Can work-from-home opportunities expand? Can more social activities be planned? Can a new training program be implemented to help them develop additional job skills? Acknowledge—honestly—that they have experienced a loss. Ask for ideas about what can be done to make things better anyway.

This list isn't exhaustive and some of the ideas likely won't be feasible for your organization. Your project leader will need authorization from the project sponsor or other senior leaders to implement some of these approaches. That's OK. Just make sure that you, the project leader, and core project team are thinking through the various sources of resistance associated with your change initiative. Then identify actions that will work for your organization that can help prevent resistance from emerging.

Prepare a Formal Resistance Management Plan

As you analyze who might resist the change and why and identify actions you plan to take to address resistance, summarize these activities in a formal resistance management plan. The plan will help you monitor and track actions you're taking to prevent resistance. And the plan will help you prepare, so you won't need to react on the spot if and when resistance appears.

You can create your resistance management plan by preparing a simple spreadsheet. Table 14-2 is an example of the plan that Sharon, in the PCo business transformation case, began to prepare for her company.

Does something look familiar? You're right! That's because much of the information you need to include in your resistance management plan already exists in your stakeholder analysis. In fact, rather than creating a completely separate document, you might just add a few columns to your existing stakeholder analysis. That is, you can create one document that serves double duty as both your stakeholder analysis and resistance management plan.

Here's what your resistance management plan should include. Fields of information you can gather from your stakeholder analysis feature asterisks:

Stakeholder or stakeholder group*: Who is affected by the change?

What will change*: What will the stakeholder do or experience that's different after the change is introduced? How are they affected by what's changing?

Level of impact*: To what extent will the change affect this stakeholder? Anticipate resistance from stakeholders whom the change will affect most, especially if that impact will be experienced as some form of loss. The loss may be tangible, such as the loss of time, or intangible, such as the loss of status or prestige.

Level of influence*: To what extent can the stakeholder influence whether the change is successfully adopted? Frontline supervisors may wield considerable influence, because they can instruct direct reports to attend to—or ignore—the change. Well-regarded subject matter experts whom co-workers turn to for "the real scoop" may have a more moderate, but still sizable, level of influence

Table 14-2. PCo Resistance Management Plan

Stakeholder Group*	What Will Change?*	Level of Impact*	Level of Influence*	Key Concerns/ Source of Resistance	Current Commitment	Ideal Commitment	Planned Action
Lab Managers	Need to manage costs and labor issues more tightly May need to work closely with new business manager	High	High	Used to working completely independently; don't want oversight Loss of prestige and authority	Against	Supportive	One-on-one meetings with Sharon
CFO	Need to begin sharing financial data more broadly	High	High	Need to protect confidential information	Against	Supportive	
Finance Managers	Need to begin sharing financial data more broadly	Moderate	Moderate	Need to protect confidential information Loss of prestige when they no longer have exclusive access to financials?	Against	Moderate	
Acting Vice President of Operations	Needs to hold plant managers accountable for financial and marketing decisions	High	High	Unknown	Unknown	Supportive	

over their peers' willingness to comply with project-related requests. You need the support of these, and other, high-influence stakeholders. Stay alert for signs that their support is wavering or that they've actively begun to resist. For example, in the resistance management plan that Sharon created for PCo, she indicated that the company's acting vice president of operations could exert a high level of influence over the success of the transformation. After all, he led one of the areas where significant change was planned, and he could encourage his direct reports to get on board or not. Likewise, she identified PCo's lab managers as high-influence stakeholders. These lab managers might cooperate and collaborate with the business managers the company planned to install. Or they might resist, and undermine the efforts PCo had planned for the R&D function.

Key concerns or source of resistance: Why might this stakeholder resist the change? What might they lose because of the change? What are they concerned about, or what else might be happening, that increases the chance they'll resist the change? Hopefully you've gathered this information while conducting your stakeholder analysis. But continue to refine what you capture based on your conversations with stakeholders and members of the project team. Within a stakeholder group, individual concerns are likely to vary. For example, in the PCo case, Sharon understood that some lab managers would welcome the changes planned for their area, while others might view the change as a threat to their status, autonomy, and prestige. For the purposes of your plan, summarize the concerns you've heard, or that you sense or can anticipate.

Current commitment: To what extent does the stakeholder currently support the initiative? Are they hostile, openly opposing the change? Against the change, but not openly hostile? Neutral, neither supporting nor opposing the change? Generally supportive? An advocate? Expect resistance from stakeholders who are openly hostile to or against the change. For them, something is amiss. They might comply with project-related requests, or they might not. In the PCo resistance management plan, Sharon indicated that some of the company's lab managers might be against the change planned for their area. Perhaps the lab managers would fall into line anyway, despite their objections to the change. Or they might not.

Ideal commitment: Given the extent to which the stakeholder can influence the initiative's success, how much commitment do you need them to demonstrate? Can they exert a high level of influence, so you need them to support or actively advocate for the change? Or do they have less influence, so it's OK if they're merely neutral? When a stakeholder who should be supporting or actively advocating for a change demonstrates signs of resistance, you and your team need to act quickly to understand why their support is wavering and address whatever issue is preventing them from getting on board.

Planned action: What will you and your team do to secure the stakeholder's support to reduce the likelihood that they will resist? What can you do to address, or at least partially mitigate, the reasons they might resist? And what will you do if the stakeholder starts to show signs of resistance anyway? Think about actions that can help the stakeholder feel involved, even if this means you'll just meet with them once, one-on-one, to hear their ideas and concerns. Plan how you can increase the options and choices provided to the stakeholder, so they don't feel like the change has been foisted upon them. And think about actions you can take to mitigate the tangible and intangible loss they may experience as a result of the change. Brainstorm possibilities with the core project team. Ask transition-monitoring-team members for their ideas. And don't be afraid of asking stakeholders who might resist the change for their ideas too. Acknowledge that they may experience some loss because of the change, and ask, "What can make this better for you?"

After you've drafted your plan, take a step back and consider:

- Does the plan identify the high-influence, high-impact stakeholders who might resist the change, the reasons they might resist, and the actions the project team will take to build their support? Does the plan identify what you'll do if these high-influence, high-impact stakeholders start to show signs of resisting?
- Are you providing stakeholders with appropriate opportunities to get involved, to share their ideas and ensure their concerns are heard? Are you providing options and choices? Have you found ways to help compensate stakeholders for the loss they will experience as a result of the change?

Review your draft resistance management plan with members of the core project team and key stakeholders. But make smart choices about who sees the details. Hopefully you're sharing lots of project-related documents with stakeholders during your status-update meetings with them. You may be posting documents on a shared site that everyone in your organization has access to. I generally support making as much information as possible available for your stakeholders to see. It helps build trust. But it can be embarrassing for people to see that they or their co-workers have been labeled in project documents as a potential resister. Employees might even feel manipulated if they see in print the actions you have planned to address their concerns. If you've added columns that address resistance to your stakeholder analysis, consider if they should be removed from view on the documents you share more broadly. If you've created a separate resistance management plan document, make smart choices about whom you share the plan with.

Tips for Planning for Resistance

- Identify who is likely to resist the change and why. Anticipate resistance from stakeholders whom the change will affect the most, especially those who will experience some form of loss because of what's changing.
- Ask project team members, stakeholders, and members of your transition-monitoring team and red team, "Who might struggle to support the change and why?"

- Consider actions you can take to appropriately involve stakeholders who might resist the change. Can you take advantage of their critical eye by inviting them to join the red team? Can someone meet with them one-on-one to ensure their ideas and concerns are heard?
- Where possible, provide stakeholders with options and choice. Can they decide when the change will "go live" in their department? Choose which training session to enroll in? Decide how to configure their screen so they have easy access to the functions they use every day?
- Think of ways your organization can compensate employees for, or help reduce the sting of, losses they will experience because of the change. Ask stakeholders for their ideas about what would make things better for them, given the loss the change will bring about.

Later in this chapter, we'll explore actions that Sharon can include in PCo's resistance management plan. But first, let's look at some steps that Sharon—and you—can take to deal with resistance when it arises.

Deal With Resistance

Despite everything you have planned, resistance will emerge anyway. Its source and form may change as your project moves from initial planning through the various phases of implementation. But resistance will happen. Expect it.

So what do you do about it? What steps can you and your project team take to deal with resistance when it does appear?

Let's start by reviewing what you shouldn't do.

Don't Ignore It

Just because you can expect resistance to occur, doesn't mean you should dismiss it. The concerns employees are expressing may be valid, or they may not be. But they need to be heard and resolved or they'll limit your project's chances for success. Remember, people engage in resistance to slow down or prevent something from happening, and these efforts often work. Resistance usually won't go away on its own, and it can affect the outcomes you're working to achieve. Deal with it.

Don't Punish Employees for Expressing Resistance

Don't make dismissive comments like "You're either on the bus or under the bus." Don't isolate employees or push them to the sidelines just because they've expressed concerns. Their feedback might be spot-on. Even if it's not, punishing employees for resistance can just drive them into the shadows, where you won't be able to see or address what they're doing. Instead of penalizing employees for sharing concerns, seek out their feedback and thank them for sharing.

Don't Get Defensive

Don't personalize the feedback you're hearing or the behavior you're seeing. This isn't about you or your capabilities as a change management leader. In every change initiative, some people will benefit more than others. In every project, some employees will encounter loss. And in every project, mistakes will be made, and people will have ideas about what should have been done to prevent them. Keep focused on helping your project succeed and on making this the best experience it can be, whatever the circumstances are, for the people affected by the change. Focus on them.

Address Resisters' Concerns

What should you do when you see someone whose support you need engaging in resistance?

Most often, the best thing you can do is discuss it with that person. And usually, the best way to have that conversation is by meeting with them one-on-one.

You might even want to have two conversations with each person who is resisting—one conversation focused on hearing the stakeholder's concerns, and a second, a few days later, focused on explaining what can or can't be done to address the issues they've raised. That's the approach that change communication experts Sally Blount and Shana Carroll (2017) recommend in their *Harvard Business Review* article "Overcome Resistance to Change With Two Conversations." Inserting some space between listening to a stakeholder's concerns and responding to them can really help turn around resistance. Stakeholders feel like you have taken the time to hear their concerns and ideas, and they appreciate that you haven't jumped to conclusions or rushed a decision. They realize you are really contemplating what they've said, and they trust that you have checked in with others to see if accommodations are possible or desirable. Here's how it works.

The First Conversation

In the first conversation, start by sharing what you've observed. Say things like:

- "I see you haven't logged in to the new system yet."

- "It was good seeing you at the last status-update meeting. You always have such good ideas, so I was surprised by how quiet your were."
- "From what you said at the last status meeting, it looks like you have some concerns."

Let the person know you want to hear their honest feedback about the change initiative. Ask for their help. Reassure them that there won't be any negative repercussions for what they share. Say things like:

- "I need your feedback about what's working and what isn't. I won't take anything you have to say personally."
- "We're all learning on this project, so what you have to share can really help us make things better."
- "You're really in the know about what goes on day-to-day. I'd love to hear what you're seeing and experiencing."
- "I can promise you no one will get into trouble for what you share."

But don't just stop there. Dig deeper. See if the person is willing to share what's preventing them from getting on board. Ask questions like:

- "What obstacles are you running into on this project?"
- "What makes sense on this project? What doesn't make enough sense?"
- "What are your concerns?"
- "When things go live, what will you lose?"

Let the person take their time as they share their thoughts about what's happening. Don't rush the conversation. Spend the majority of the time listening, rather than speaking. Acknowledge emotions the person is expressing, and don't try to fix them. Say things like:

- "This sounds frustrating for you."
- "I can see that you're upset about that. It would make me upset too."

Ask the person for ideas that will address their concerns. Let them know that you want to hear their ideas and that, with their permission, you will pass them along for consideration. Ask for feedback about options if they're available. Ask questions like:

- "What can be done to make this better for you?"
- "What would you need to see to feel better about this?"
- "Would it be better for you if X occurred instead of Y?"

Finally, thank the person for sharing their concerns. Let them know you will contemplate what they've said and will discuss it with others before checking back with them.

Reflection

Review what you have heard with the project leader or core project team. Look back at your resistance management plan. Are there any ideas for preventing resistance that you considered but chose not to pursue? Are any of these options possible now? Can you get the person more involved in some way? Can you offer them some choices in how they will experience the change? Can you provide anything to address the sense of loss the person is experiencing? What can and can't be done to address the person's concerns? Once you've reflected on this, have a follow-up chat with the stakeholder.

The Second Conversation

In your second conversation, let the person who is resisting know that you've reflected on their ideas and reviewed them with others. Explain what can be different, based on what the person shared, or what can't be handled differently and why.

If nothing can be done to address the person's concerns, acknowledge that the change may be difficult for them. Explain why you need their support, and what you need them to do anyway. Sometimes, the best you can do, if the person simply can't support the initiative, is to ask them not to interfere with it. If their input is needed, see if they can designate someone else to provide input for their area. If they've been a vocal critic in status-update meetings, provide them with updates one-on-one before each meeting, hear their feedback in private, and ask for their help by giving other people an opportunity to speak.

Thank the person again for their feedback. Assure them that you're not questioning their intent. Let them know you believe they're only expressing concerns because they care. And encourage them to speak with you again if they develop additional concerns. Let them know that you consider them to be an ally for the project—someone who is helping make the project and the organization better because of the insight they're willing to share. Be clear you prefer for them to share that feedback with you—because you can actually act on it—instead of expressing it through other channels. And who knows? Knowing that they have your ear, over time the resister may even begin to advocate for the change.

Who should lead these one-on-one conversations? Often, the best person to speak with a stakeholder about their concerns is the stakeholder's immediate supervisor or another manager in their reporting chain. Hopefully, the supervisor or manager is someone the employee trusts. In the best case, the employee believes that their supervisor cares about them and will weigh their interests along with the interests and needs of their overall department. And hopefully, the employee will respond appropriately to their supervisor or manager's request to support the change initiative, or at least to not actively interfere with it. At some point, the employee will need to understand the behaviors they are expected to demonstrate related to the change, and what the consequences may be for not demonstrating those behaviors. And to be heard—to hold the appropriate weight—that message needs to come from someone the employee reports to.

Your change management role, as they relate to these discussions, may be to coach frontline supervisors and other leaders on how to conduct these two-part conversations. Prepare supervisors by reviewing the conversation format with them. Role-play the discussions with them to help them practice. Check in with supervisors after they've conducted the first conversation, to hear about the concerns and ideas the employee expressed. And discuss with the supervisor, project leader, and others what next steps might be appropriate to address these concerns. Check in with the supervisor after the second conversation occurs, and circle back to the project team to update plans as needed.

Some supervisors may be unable or unwilling to have these conversations. In that case, ask for their permission to meet with the employee who is resisting, and then meet with the supervisor to update them on what you have heard.

And depending on the stakeholder who is resisting the change, and their level of influence, sometimes the most appropriate person to lead the conversation will be the project leader or project sponsor. As resistance emerges, meet with your project leader to discuss who is best equipped to conduct these discussions. Consider whom the resister trusts and respects. Whom will they be willing to share concerns with? Whom will they listen to? Sometimes it will make sense for you to meet with the person demonstrating resistance. Often, it will make more sense for the project leader, project sponsor, or the stakeholder's supervisor to take the lead. Help the person leading that conversation by coaching them on how to conduct a productive discussion.

What Else Can Sharon Include in the Resistance Management Plan?

Take a quick look back at the resistance management plan you saw in the PCo business transformation case in chapter 11.

Did Sharon, the company's learning and organizational development leader, identify everyone who was likely to resist and why? And did she identify the right actions the company should take to mitigate resistance? Here are just a few possibilities she might consider. Can you think of more?

- PCo's CEO asked Sharon to meet with the company's lab managers to hear their concerns. The conversations will have far greater impact if they're led by PCo's vice president of R&D, to whom the lab managers report, instead of Sharon. Sharon should coach the vice president of R&D on how to conduct a two-step conversation, where the first conversation focuses on hearing the lab managers' concerns and ideas, and the second focuses on letting them know what will and won't happen and why.

- PCo's CFO seems to be concerned about the CEO's desire to share financial documents with employees. He may have valid concerns about protecting confidential information, or he may feel like his status as a "keeper of the secrets" is being diminished. Sharon can coach PCo's CEO to really listen to the CFO's concerns and to ask him for his recommendations about which documents should and should not be shared more broadly.

- According to PCo's CFO, finance staff enjoy a certain amount of prestige from having access to confidential data that only a few other leaders can see. Will they balk when they perceive that their special status has been diminished? Or will they have valid concerns about the company's need to protect confidential information? Sharon can coach PCo's CFO to meet with his staff to listen to their concerns and ask for their recommendations.

- PCo's acting vice president of operations passively agreed to the CEO's recommendations without offering details for how he would take action. Who knows what he's thinking? Sharon can meet with him to hear his thoughts about the changes. She can also share her observations with PCo's CEO and recommend the CEO meet with the acting VP of operations to hear his concerns and solicit his more active leadership.

Tips for Dealing With Resistance

- Take action. Don't ignore resistance or allow it to fester. Don't punish employees for expressing resistance, and don't get defensive. Instead, focus on finding out why the resistance has emerged and on seeing how it can be addressed.

- Decide who will speak with the person demonstrating resistance. Who has credibility? Whom does the resister trust? Usually, this is the resister's immediate supervisor or someone in their reporting chain.

- Coach the person meeting with the resisting employee to conduct two separate conversations—the first focused on listening to the employee's concerns and needs, and the second focusing on letting the resister know what can and can't be handled differently based on what they shared.

Use Resistance to Make Your Project Stronger

When you deal with resistance, it might seem like you're focusing 100 percent of your time on the soft side of change. After all, you're trying to help people feel involved. You're looking for ways to offer stakeholders choices so they don't feel managed and controlled. You're thinking of steps you can take to mitigate the sense of loss employees might be experiencing because of the change, whether that loss is emotional or more tangible in nature. That's all soft-side stuff, right? But dealing with resistance helps you address the hard side of change too. After all, resistance happens when people do things—or don't do things—to stop the change initiative from progressing, or at least to stop the change from progressing for them. When you deal with resistance, you're taking steps to ensure the change moves forward anyway to produce its intended results. It's just as important as any other action you take that more explicitly addresses the hard side of change. Don't dismiss resistance. Anticipate and deal with it.

But there's more. Some employees resist a change for reasons that have very little to do with their sense of personal loss. They see flaws in project plans that leaders and the core project team haven't yet recognized. They have knowledge about customer needs and expectations that haven't yet been adequately accounted for in the "to-be" state. They sense that the company has turned down a path that will take them far afield from the organization's stated values. Sometimes employees resist out of a sense of loyalty and affection for the organization they love. They struggle as they try to figure out how to protect their company from making a mistake they perceive will be disastrous. And they know they are taking a risk by doing so.

What can you do to accurately recognize this form of resistance when it occurs? How can you tell when employee resistance is driven by their genuine desire to help the organization succeed? How can you know when employees oppose change because they fear for the loss their organization will suffer, not the loss they will suffer themselves?

The reality is, you can't. And so the smartest thing you can do is to approach every situation in which resistance occurs with an assumption of positive intent.

Assume the person opposing your project really is trying to help. Assume they see something or know something that you and your project team haven't yet taken into account. Maybe you already know about the issues the resister has raised, and maybe you don't, but be curious anyway. Recognize resistance as an opportunity to make your project even better. Mistakes do happen. Take advantage of the opportunity to hear the person out. Chances are you might learn something that, if acted upon, will make your project stronger.

Bake into your project plan opportunities to hear from resisters. Invite them to participate in red team meetings. Plan to have resisters join action review sessions (see chapter 16) so you can learn about the "ground truth" from their perspective. Schedule one-on-one meetings with resisters to find out more about what they're seeing. You and your project team might agree with what they have to say, or you might not. But to dismiss them is to miss an opportunity to gather information that could be vital for the success of your project.

Tips for Using Resistance
- Assume positive intent. When someone expresses reservations about your project, assume they're trying to help—that they're acting out of a genuine concern for the organization.
- Seek out resisters and provide them with formal opportunities to be heard. Invite them to participate in the red team. Meet with them one-on-one to hear their ideas about what will and won't work and why. Invite them to participate in action reviews to learn more about what they see happening on the ground.
- Use the ideas shared by resisters to improve project decisions. Be open to the possibility that you and your team have made some mistakes or have missed doing something that could make the project even better. Listen to resisters and be willing to amend plans when they share ideas that can help the project succeed.

About to Begin?

Are you about to begin working on a change initiative in your organization? As you think about the resistance you may encounter, ask yourself:
- Who might struggle with what's changing and why? What actions can we take to help them feel better about what's changing?
- When resistance emerges, and it will, how will we deal with it?

- What opportunities do we have to use resistance to make our project even better? How can we make sure we're seeking out and listening to those who have reservations about what's changing, so we can make more informed decisions and increase the chances our project will succeed?

And still, mistakes will be made. They happen on every project. The core project team will make assumptions that turn out to be wrong. Training will be delivered that misses the mark. A key stakeholder will begin objecting vigorously, and you hadn't accounted for their potential opposition in your resistance management plan. So what do you do?

In section 4, we'll take a look at steps your organization can take to continually assess progress, so you can quickly take corrective action when it's needed. And we'll look at ideas for getting back on track if your change initiative goes off the rails. Despite the best-laid plans, stuff, or something like that, happens. But you can structure your change initiative so mistakes are discovered and addressed as early as possible. And even when mistakes aren't readily addressed, there are actions you can take to recover. Let's explore.

Learn more. Check out:

Airiodion Global Services. n.d. "Change Management Resistance Management Guide." airiodion.com/resistance-management-plan.

Blount, S., and S. Carroll. 2017. "Overcome Resistance to Change With Two Conversations." *Harvard Business Review*, May 16.

Assessing Progress and Making Adjustments

15

The TCW Relocation Case

As Kate, the training and development manager at TCW, waited for the meeting to begin, she shifted uneasily in her seat. This was not going to be an easy discussion. Kate and about 200 of her co-workers from TCW's corporate office had just relocated to less expensive space across town. At first, the project had proceeded swimmingly, and Kate was really glad she had volunteered to represent her department on the project team that was planning the move. But in the end, the relocation hadn't gone well, and the mood around the office was dour. Some employees seemed downright surly.

So when Edie, the space planner who'd led TCW's relocation, called the project team together to conduct a postmortem on the move, Kate wasn't really eager to participate. "Why meet now and rehash all of our mistakes?" Kate wondered. After all, the team had barely met over the five months leading up to the move. No one felt like they needed to get together because things had been going so well. And what purpose would it serve to meet now? The damage was done. Wouldn't it just be better to put everything behind them and move on?

Edie entered the conference room and started to speak before she even sat down. "OK, we want to identify what went well and what went wrong on the relocation," Edie announced to the project team. "And then we'll come up with some lessons that we learned."

Joel, a paralegal who represented the legal department on the project, raised his hand and directed a question to Edie. "So what's going to happen to what we say here today?" he asked. "Why are we meeting?"

Edie sighed loudly. "I think we all know things didn't go the way we planned," she responded. "We're here to show that we're accountable for all this."

Kate winced. That really didn't explain anything. "But 'accountable.' Hmm," she wondered. "Is the blaming about to begin?"

So Kate thought she'd help by trying to get things started on a positive note. "Well, if you want to know what went well," she offered, "we're here in the new location. I mean, the move happened on time. There wasn't a delay."

"Well, maybe we should have delayed," Joel countered. "The conference rooms are still being renovated and there isn't any place in the legal department to hold consultations." Kate saw that Joel was clearly irritated. "We're trying to get work done and can't focus with all the noise and dust and paint fumes," he continued. "This is a disaster. Whose call was it to say we were ready to move?"

Kate had to agree with Joel. Furniture that Kate had ordered for the new training room was on back order, and customer service training had to be rescheduled at the last minute. They probably weren't ready to move when they did.

"If you didn't think we were ready, you should have told me," Edie shot back.

"Don't forget, our systems were down for the first two days," Julia, an accountant in the finance department, interjected. "How did that happen? I mean, who let that happen?"

Zvi, the IT analyst assigned to the project, piped in. "We told everyone that systems would be down. Everyone got an email."

Julia started shaking her head furiously.

Kate wondered where this was going when she saw Aida from the procurement department give her an angry look and begin to speak. "No one prepared employees for this move. I mean, Kate, wasn't that your responsibility? Aren't you HR?" Aida said. "In other places I've worked, HR gave each employee a welcome kit when they moved. You know, fun facts about the new location, commuter tips, restaurant information. Why didn't you do any of that?"

Here it was, Kate thought; her turn to face the fire. "Well, I think preparing employees for the move is everyone's job," Kate responded. "But a welcome kit sounds like a lovely idea. I wish you had shared that with us sooner."

Aida snapped back, "So it's my fault? I should tell you how to do your job?"

Kate turned toward Edie to see if she'd step in to defend her, or at least move the meeting along. But Edie allowed the discussion to continue.

It was Adam, from customer service, who ended up coming to Kate's aid . . . in a way. "Well, Aida," Adam said slowly, emphasizing Aida's name. "If you want to talk about doing your job, why isn't there any furniture in the training room? Wasn't it your job to have everything ordered and delivered on time? Poor Kate had our customer service training ready to launch, and now she's had to reschedule."

Aida glared at both of them. "Well, if Kate had placed the order according to the schedule," she scolded.

This time Kate jumped in to defend herself. "That's not what happened," Kate protested. "If you remember, Aida, when I tried to order the furniture, you said . . ."

And so the meeting continued. Project team members traded accusations back and forth, and it didn't seem like anyone was immune. To distract herself and stay calm, Kate even started to keep a tally as she took notes. In the end, she was blamed for three mistakes, Aida had two, Adam had six, Zvi had one, and Julia had three. And the entire project team saved the most scathing accusations for Edie.

"Was this what Edie meant when she said she wanted us to show accountability?" Kate wondered. And she still couldn't see the point. "We're all going to walk out of here really resenting one another," Kate feared. "Why are we doing this?"

Edie finally signaled that it was almost time to wrap up the meeting. "OK, that was bad, folks," Edie summarized. "But what did we learn from this project? What are our lessons learned?"

Now everyone was quiet.

"Anything? Anything, folks?" Edie asked as she glanced at each team member. The silence continued.

"OK, well then, thanks for your time." Edie exhaled loudly as she shuffled her papers together and quickly exited the conference room.

"I'd run too," Kate mused silently. She lingered for a few moments until her teammates had left the room. "Well, I know the lesson I learned," Kate said to herself. "Don't volunteer. Ever."

Is there a different lesson that Kate could have learned from her participation in the relocation project? After all, the team did appear to make some mistakes leading up to the move. Could they have avoided making any of them? Did they learn anything that could help prevent these mistakes from happening on another project? The team probably made some wise decisions too as their project unfolded. What did the team do well that TCW should repeat in the future?

Unfortunately, Kate, Edie, and the TCW relocation team won't find out the answers to these questions. They were so focused on affixing blame that they missed the opportunity to learn from their experience. If Edie had encouraged the project team to critically examine what happened and why, rather than discussing who made what error, the team might have uncovered ideas that would help them succeed more in the future. And if Edie had arranged for the team to meet throughout the course of their project to discuss progress, ideas, and concerns, instead of waiting until the end for a postmortem, the team also might have learned where adjustments were needed that could have led to a better outcome.

In chapter 16, we'll look at a process that Kate, Edie, and the team could have used to conduct a more productive and less contentious meeting. You'll learn about a change management tool called the action review, and see how you can use it to focus your team on learning and continuous improvement. You'll see that there are plenty of opportunities for you to figure out what's working and what isn't—and to learn and improve—as you work on a change initiative. To take advantage of these opportunities, you'll see that you need to demonstrate some sound project management discipline. You need to focus on the hard side of change. And you'll see that you need to create an environment that supports candid dialogue and a willingness to admit mistakes. To help your team learn from their experience, you need to focus on the soft side of change too.

In chapter 17, we'll explore steps you and your team can take to address problems that may arise as your change initiative unfolds. You'll see that it doesn't help to sweep potential issues under the rug, like Kate and her team may have done as they worked on TCW's relocation. You'll see that the actions you take to fix a change initiative that's going off the rails are similar to the steps you take to address other problems you're experiencing at work and in your personal life. Admitting you have a problem is the first step to recovery. In chapter 17, we'll look at that first step, plus a few more you can take to help get a troubled change initiative back on track. And yes, those actions require you to focus on both the hard and soft sides of change.

16
Learning From Successes and Mistakes

I bet that each day at work, you do lots of things that are successful. And you may also make some mistakes or take some actions that don't turn out quite like you had expected. If you're really disciplined, you pause periodically to reflect on all this. You may ask yourself and others, what am I doing that's working well that I need to keep on doing? And what am I doing that's not working as well that I need to adjust or do differently? You may engage in some soul searching and talk with some trusted colleagues as you try to improve your performance and learn from both your successes and your failures.

The same applies to change initiatives at work. Despite all the challenges you're facing, you and your project team will do a lot of things right. You'll do things that just work out really well. Congratulations! And sometimes you and your team will take steps that don't quite hit the mark. You'll do things on your project that you'll find aren't working at all. You'll be underwhelmed by the results you're getting.

If you and your project team are following sound project management discipline—if you're paying attention to the hard side of change—you'll pause periodically to reflect. You'll meet as a team and maybe ask some stakeholders to join in the conversation. You'll ask yourselves, "What do we need to keep doing because it's working so well? What do we need to adjust because it's not producing the results we need?" You and your team will try to improve the outcomes you're getting on your change initiative by learning from your successes and from your mistakes.

In this chapter, we'll look at a change management tool—the action review process—that you and your project team can use to identify what's working that you should keep on doing and what isn't working that you need to fix. You'll see how you can use the tool to create better project plans, execute your plans more effectively, and increase the chances that your project will lead to the outcomes you had intended. You'll see that for action reviews to work, you need to create a climate in which honest reflection and candid dialogue can occur. You'll see that although the action review process is designed to help you address the hard side of change, for the tool to serve its purpose, you need to focus on the soft side too.

What Is an Action Review?

An action review is a meeting of the key players involved in a change initiative, in which you focus on openly and honestly discussing and documenting the answers to three central questions:

- **What is supposed to happen?** What is the objective we are working toward?
- **What actually is happening and why?** What's working well that we need to keep on doing, and what's not working well that we need to improve? What are the root causes for the results we're getting?
- **What should we do about it?** What actions will we take to ensure we keep doing what's working? What actions will we take to fix what isn't working? And what lessons have we learned that we can apply during this change initiative and to other initiatives we embark on in the future?

An action review is a change management tool that's based on the after action review process developed by the US military during the Vietnam War (Darling and Parry 2000). The military introduced after action reviews to help soldiers and their leaders better understand the "ground truth" about what was happening during training exercises and on the battlefield. During each after action review, soldiers met to discuss and share their observations, from their varying viewpoints, about the operation or maneuver they'd just completed. What were the goals of the operation, and what results did they actually achieve? Which tactics were successful, and which ones weren't? Why? The military also wanted to help its members share what they'd learned on the battlefield across different platoons. What did we discover that we—or others—should do the same? What do we need to do differently to produce a better result? The stakes were high. If you could identify and share lessons learned and ideas for improvement, lives could be saved.

In the decades that followed the war, many for-profit and not-for-profit organizations adapted the after action review process for their own use. Their goal was to improve the outcomes they achieved on projects and change initiatives. Some organizations began using the process before projects even began to anticipate and better plan for the obstacles they thought they might encounter along the way. They conducted before action reviews. And others started conducting reviews periodically over the entire course of their projects, so they could figure out where adjustments and course corrections were needed while their projects were still ongoing. They led during action reviews. Today, organizations use many different names to refer to their after action, before action, and during action review processes. To keep things simple, we'll refer to these processes collectively as action reviews.

Let's now turn to why the review process can be so important to managing change.

Why Conduct an Action Review?

During the crush of a change initiative, it's easy to want to keep things moving forward. As deadlines loom, you and your project team may want to keep plowing ahead so you can stay on schedule. Maybe you tune out feedback that's streaming in from stakeholders. Or you ignore questions that are amassing during software testing. You have a milestone to hit. That makes sense, right? But what if you're rushing down the wrong path? Or what if the path your project is on isn't as efficient as you need it to be? Ignoring these signals and just moving forward won't help you achieve your end goal.

Maybe this was the situation Kate and her team faced in the TCW relocation case you read in chapter 15. They had a deadline to reach. They had a relocation date to hit. So they disregarded the little—or not so little—issues that crept up, and they kept moving ahead with their project plans. Conference room not ready yet? Ignore it and keep going. Furniture for the training room on back order? Forget about it and plow ahead. Need to take critical systems offline during the first two days of the move? No time to discuss it. Just send out a quick email and hope everyone reads and understands it. As the TCW relocation project progressed, the team barely took a breath to consider whether it was delivering the results its members had committed to when they first began work on the project. They just kept pushing ahead to meet the move date. They never paused to discuss which shortcuts and compromises were acceptable and which might not be. So they failed to consider if they were really ready for the move to occur on schedule. And if the date for the move was fixed and couldn't be adjusted, they failed to discuss how they could prepare TCW employees for the challenges they'd experience during their first few days and weeks at the new location, where things weren't quite yet ready.

An action review forces you and your project team to take that pause, even momentarily, to reflect on the objectives you're trying to reach and the results you're getting, so you can make course corrections if needed. It's a process that helps you make sense of all the noise you're hearing on your project, because it forces you to stop and consider what's really happening, what's important, and what to do next. Think of an action review as a comma in a really long sentence. Rather than a full stop, like a period, the soft pause helps you and your team take a breath and understand something that's otherwise pretty complex.

When you pause periodically to conduct action reviews throughout the course of your project, you're creating space to intervene while your actions can still have an impact. You're investing time now to avoid the blame game later. To a certain extent, Kate in the TCW relocation case was right to question why she and her team were meeting to conduct a postmortem well after her company's relocation was complete. Kate and her team missed the opportunity to make things better while their project was in progress. They needed to meet and conduct action reviews while their project was ongoing so they could intervene and make things right.

An action review involves a discussion during which participants share what they see happening and why from different vantage points. So the process also helps you gain a broader perspective about where your efforts are succeeding and where you need to take a different approach. It provides you with a reality check, so you can compare your observations to the experiences and observations of others. Based on what you hear in an action review, you may decide to continue going down the path you were on. Or, you may decide to make some adjustments based on your new, expanded insight.

Maybe you, like Edie, the project manager in the TCW case, think everything is going fine with your project. That may be true, or maybe someone on your project team holds a different view. Maybe they're experiencing a problem that you don't see, because you play a different role on the project. An action review provides an opportunity for you and your team to examine your work from many different points of view. What do you see happening? How is that the same and different from what others are experiencing? Given that broader view, are there decisions you need to revisit?

When you invest time in an action review, you have the chance to bounce ideas off of others and hear their ideas for resolving problems and issues you might be encountering. Maybe you've established an excellent working relationship with a key stakeholder, yet one of your teammates is experiencing more challenges during their interactions with this same individual. An action review provides the opportunity for you to talk this through—for you to say, "Here's what I do during my conversations with the stakeholder that really seem to work. This approach might work for you too." An action review provides a formal opportunity for you, your team, and others to use the power of the team—and your varying observations and experiences—to more accurately determine what's working well, what isn't, and how you can best proceed.

How an Action Review Helped Me Regain Control of My Training Project

We were implementing a new, critically important safety protocol across the organization, and I was responsible for developing the training. It seemed like everyone on the steering team wanted to have their say about what should and shouldn't be included and how the training should be delivered. Lawyers, safety engineers, HR staff, senior executives—everyone weighed in and made their demands. Say this first. Use this word. Show this video, but only at this point in the program. Don't say this. I tried my best to create a program that addressed their varying needs and demands and that still would make sense from a pedagogical perspective. But ultimately I relented. By the time I had incorporated everyone's feedback, I knew I had a mishmash on my hands. The steering team thought that the training program was great. I was confident it was not.

I voiced my concerns one last time, and got the team to agree to a compromise of sorts. We'd pilot the training with a single group of employees, and then immediately conduct an action review that steering team members and a few trainees from the pilot program would participate in.

During the action review, steering team members listened intently as trainees who participated in the pilot program shared their views. This is what worked. This is what didn't work. This is where they paid attention. This is where we lost them. This is what we should do the same and this is what we should do differently going forward. "Terrific," I thought. "More feedback! Just what I need." But the approach the trainees recommended wasn't all that different from the approach I had been advocating for all along. So I felt confident I knew what to do next.

The meeting was about to conclude and I summarized the action plan we had agreed to. As I read my notes aloud, the steering committee chairperson interrupted. "You're the expert," she acknowledged, nodding her head in my direction. "You do what you think is needed to make the program better." And so I did.

Do You Have an Opportunity to Conduct Action Reviews?

Think of a recent change initiative you were a part of where you faced a barrage of complaints about what went wrong.

- Would it have been helpful for you and your team to pause along the way to discuss what was happening and to brainstorm ideas for getting back on track?
- Do you understand all the reasons your project went off the rails? Were there signals you and your team missed or ignored as you worked hard to meet scheduled due dates? What would have happened if you'd paused and considered taking a different approach?
- Are there different perspectives you wish you had considered? Did others see issues or have ideas that you wish you'd had more insight about?
- Do you and your team understand what you should do the same and what you should do differently when you work on your next project?

Now think of a change initiative that was a success, but where you failed to document what went right along the way.

- Do you understand all the reasons your project went so smoothly?
- Can you remember the problems you encountered during the course of your project, and the steps you took to successfully address them? Do you understand what you can do, as you work on change initiatives in the future, to prevent these problems from occurring or to quickly resolve them?
- Do you have a broad enough perspective about what you did that worked so well and why? Would it be helpful to hear from others who might view your work from a different perspective?
- Do you know what you and your team did that worked well that you should repeat as you work on other change initiatives in the future?

How to Conduct an Action Review

Maybe you and your project team already meet for periodic status updates throughout the course of your project. Maybe your organization already conducts postmortems when you reach the end of each key initiative. Are these meetings helping you and your organization hear about what's working and what isn't from different vantage points? Are they helping you understand the root causes behind the results you're achieving? Are they helping you identify and commit to actions that will sustain what's working and fix what isn't? Are they helping you learn from one project to the next, so you and your organization keep improving the way you execute change? As reviews occur, do participants speak openly and honestly? If so, that's great. Keep at it! But if you need ideas for implementing review sessions—or if you need to improve how reviews are conducted so you avoid the blame game and focus more on continuous improvement and learning—consider using the action review format as your guide.

Here are steps you can follow to conduct an action review meeting for your change initiative.

Before the Meeting

Decide on the scope and focus of the meeting. Is this a regularly scheduled status check-in, during which you expect to hear updates from participants about the actions they'd agreed to in the last action review, and plan to discuss any new issues that may have arisen since that meeting? Or are there a few key topics you need participants to focus on and drill down into during the meeting? Perhaps your action review will focus entirely on how training for your change initiative is going. Or you may decide to conduct an action review after you complete the first of many town hall meetings that you have scheduled. The focus of that action review will be to assess what worked and what didn't work during the initial town hall meeting, so you can embed lessons learned in the subsequent town hall sessions that you have planned. Or is this a project close-out meeting—a postmortem of sorts—during which you need everyone to take a step back and consider lessons they learned throughout the project that they can apply to other change initiatives in the future? Help meeting participants prepare by letting them know in advance what the meeting will focus on and what you hope participants will get out of it.

Decide who will participate. An effective action review typically includes all key members of the team working on the change project. This could be your core project team. Or you may want to expand the meeting to include a few key stakeholders too. When deciding on attendees, make sure that all perspectives on the project are represented, but also be careful not to invite so many people that the meeting becomes unwieldy. Typically the meeting includes one or more representatives from each of the functions working on the project. It's important to include attendees who can provide the execution perspective—the ground truth. And it's also important to include leaders who can reflect on decisions that were made and who have the authority to approve any recommended actions. If your project involves internal or external customers, you may want to invite them as well.

If you find you have too many people who need to attend, consider breaking down the action review into multiple meetings. For example, you can have members from each functional area conduct separate action reviews focused on their function's experience. Then a single representative from each of the functional areas can bring the results from their functional action review to a consolidated meeting.

Decide who will facilitate. The most effective action reviews are led by a facilitator who helps to keep the review discussion on track. The facilitator ensures participants understand the objective and scope of the meeting, guides participants through the structure of the meeting, and enforces meeting ground rules. Through their careful line of questioning, the facilitator helps participants reach their own conclusions about what is working well, what needs to improve, and what actions should be taken next. They also work at creating and maintaining an environment in which honest dialogue will occur.

We have all been to meetings where there is little to no participation during the actual meeting, but where attendees engage in heated discussion after the meeting adjourns about "what is really going on." The goal of the action review facilitator is to elicit that honest and animated, but also respectful, discussion during the meeting itself.

For your action review meetings, choose a facilitator who has the skill to create and maintain the appropriate meeting climate, draw out each participant, and keep the discussion focused and moving. If possible, consider rotating who facilitates the action review, providing an opportunity for each member of the project team to lead one meeting over the course of a project. This helps further involvement of team members, provides an opportunity for your organization to strengthen its meeting facilitation capacity, and affords talented team members a chance to lead.

Decide what supporting information participants should review to prepare for the discussion. Depending on the scope and focus of your action review, consider the documents you need participants to read in advance or come prepared to discuss. Should they review the project charter, project plan, or minutes from past action reviews? Should they come prepared to discuss the communications plan, the training plan, or the resistance management plan? Would it be helpful for them to review a template for the action review minutes (Table 16-1), so they'll understand the questions they'll be asked during the meeting? Help meeting participants prepare by letting them know in advance what they should review before they attend. And think about the documents and materials you, or others, should bring to the meeting. In addition to the documents we just discussed, will it be helpful to have the stakeholder analysis on hand? Should you bring the RACI matrix, so you're clear about whose input or authorization is needed before you and your team decide on a new action to pursue?

Table 16-1 Action Review Template

Project Name:	
Date:	

Participants		

What's Supposed to Happen and What Actually Is Happening?

Objectives	Actual Results

Why Is This Happening?

What Should We Do About It?

Actions for Sustaining What's Working

Task or Activity	Person Responsible	Due Date

Actions for Improving What Isn't Working

Task or Activity	Person Responsible	Due Date

Lesson Learned

During the Meeting

Action review meetings typically unfold in four phases:

- The meeting opening
- A quick review of what is supposed to happen
- Discussion about what actually is happening and why
- Agreement about actions that will be taken and lessons learned

Let's review each in detail.

Open the meeting. Open the meeting by reminding participants about the meeting purpose, describing the meeting timing and flow, and helping the team agree on ground rules. Let participants know that the focus of the meeting will be on continuous improvement and learning, not on pointing fingers or assigning blame. Explain that the goal is to understand what's working well so you can keep doing that, and what isn't working as well so you can fix it. Discuss ground rules that need to be in place to ensure full participation and respectful interaction. The facilitator can lead off the discussion by suggesting a few, such as:

- Treat everyone with respect.
- Listen with an open mind.
- Focus on solutions, not blame.
- Leave titles at the door.

Be sure to ask participants if they concur with these, and provide participants with an opportunity to add their own. Because you likely will be holding multiple action reviews over the course of your project, you don't need to spend time establishing new ground rules each time you meet. Just remind participants by reposting the ground rules you agreed on at the initial meeting, and ask participants if they have anything they need to add or change.

What is supposed to happen? After opening the meeting, lead a quick discussion about the overall objective for the change project and the key milestones that should have been accomplished at whatever point you are in the initiative. The goal here is to ensure that meeting participants agree on what is supposed to have happened. Where should we be in the project right now? What should we have accomplished? What results should we be seeing?

This part of the meeting may transpire quickly if participants have already reviewed the charter and project plan that was created for your initiative. If that's the case, you can quickly review objectives, deliverables, and milestones that are stated in these documents and ask participants if they agree that that's what should have been achieved by this point in time.

But don't be surprised if you end up having lots of conversation here. Sometimes a team will discover that they disagree on many of the details of the project objective, deliverables, or project plan, and that they have very different perspectives on what is supposed to happen. Here is where a skilled facilitator can help participants share their concerns and hopefully agree on some common goals. And you and your team may learn some important lessons from this discussion. You might discover that you need to modify or clarify the objectives, deliverables, or milestones that were set for your project. You may find that the original project plan is acceptable, but that considerable work needs to be done to better explain it to your stakeholders. Or you may find that given all the compromises you made and shortcuts you took during the project, you've forgotten what you and your team originally committed to deliver. Imagine if Kate and her team from the TCW relocation case had conducted an action review right before their scheduled move date. Would they agree on all the work they should have completed before proceeding with the move? Would it have been helpful for them to take a step back and ask, "What did we commit to deliver by this point in the schedule? What did we tell employees would be ready before they moved to the new location? What should we have accomplished by this point in the project?"

Remind participants about the overall objectives for your change initiative and what should be happening by this point in time. And, if needed, allow participants time to talk this all through.

What actually is happening and why? In this phase of the meeting, lead a discussion about the results you are actually getting and the progress your team is making, compared with the overall project objective and milestones you have set. And discuss what's working and what isn't working that's helping or hindering your team from achieving the desired results. In this phase of the meeting, you're focused on getting at the ground truth. Given the project objectives and milestones you should have accomplished by this phase of the project, what actually is happening, and what are the root causes for these results?

You may want to start off by quickly reviewing project schedules and budgets and by asking meeting participants to comment on what's on track and what isn't. From there, ask each participant to share their perspective about what is working well and why. The action review is an appreciative process, and you want to make sure you and your team identify steps that are contributing to your success that you should keep on doing. You also will want to ask each participant to share what isn't working as well and probe for root causes about why that is happening.

As the discussion proceeds, capture the key points on a flipchart or in notes that are projected (if you're meeting in person) or shared (if you're meeting online). You are trying to get a comprehensive and accurate sense of what is contributing to and detracting from project success. You don't want to affix blame. So record what was said, not who said it. If needed, go around the room in order, asking each participant to share what they see is working well and what they see needs to improve. Keep the discussion moving. Ask participants to identify the most important issues they think need to be discussed, then focus there.

Ask open-ended questions to clarify details and better understand what participants really have experienced. Ask questions like:

- How did you reach that conclusion?
- Why is that significant?
- What were you assuming when that happened or when you did that?
- Can you give us an example?

Dig below the surface on issues and probe for root causes. Try asking "why" multiple times until it's clear participants have identified something that, if addressed, could have real impact. If you're familiar with tools such as the fishbone diagram or force field analysis, consider using them here to help participants really get at why an issue is occurring. Openly thank participants for sharing, especially when it is clear they are speaking about something they are reluctant to discuss.

What should we do about it? In this final phase of the action review, focus discussion on identifying steps your team will take to keep doing what is working well and to address what isn't working as well. During this part of the meeting, your team might also agree on some overall lessons they have learned about the change initiative, themselves, and the organization. The goal here isn't to generate a laundry list or wish list about what would be nice to have. Instead, as the facilitator, ask participants to share what they think is needed most to keep the change initiative on track or to get the initiative back on track. Participants may list ideas that they can implement themselves without any needed approval. When these ideas come up, ask participants if they in fact can commit to doing them. Participants may list other ideas that they can't implement themselves or that they need approval to implement. Check your RACI matrix to confirm who might need to provide input or authorization before you proceed. If needed, ask for a volunteer to discuss the idea with the person or department that can implement or approve the idea, and ask them to report back at the next action review.

As participants propose ideas, probe and ask open-ended questions to ensure that the actions agreed to will have the intended impact. Consider asking questions such as:

- Why do you think we should do that?
- Why is _____ better than _____?
- How would that affect _____?
- Tell us more about this idea.
- Tell us how that would work.

Remind participants to keep an open mind here. It's not always easy to hear someone recommend ways for you to do your job better! But if you listen, you might discover a way to achieve a whole new level of effectiveness!

Wrap up the action review by asking attendees to share any lessons they have learned—or that the organization should learn—from this change initiative. Sometimes it helps to ask participants to state their lesson learned using the following structure: "When you are doing X, do Y." Or, "If your situation is A, do B." The goal is to identify lessons that members of the project team, or anyone in the organization, can apply as the project moves forward, or when similar projects occur in the future.

After the Meeting

Document your discussion. Summarize what was discussed by preparing and distributing meeting minutes. Consider using the action review template (see Table 16-1). At minimum, document and circulate the action items you and your teammates agreed to complete.

Take action. During an action review, you and your team typically focus on the past. You're looking backwards and asking, what happened? Why did it happen? But the process doesn't serve any purpose unless you focus on the future too. You need to act. What did you and your team agree to do to get your project back on track? Do that. Which stakeholder did you decide you need to re-engage? Meet with them. Which best practice did a teammate share that you agreed to try? Try it. Complete the action items that you and your team agreed to during the action review. And apply the lessons learned that you identified.

Tips for Facilitating an Action Review

Set a distinct period of time for brainstorming. Say something like, "Let's spend 10 minutes identifying everything that's working well, and then we'll spend another 10 minutes identifying everything that isn't working as well." Keep the ideas flowing by asking participants to hold their evaluation and criticism. You want everyone to share their observations and perspectives.

- If someone is dominating the discussion, consider going around the room in round-robin fashion.
- Watch for participants who are silent or who seem disengaged during the discussion. Do they have a point of view that needs to be heard? Should you direct questions specifically to them during the meeting? Or should you check with them during a break or after the meeting concludes?
- Watch for too much consensus and agreement. Are you really hearing everyone's perspective? Has your team really identified what's causing the problem? Will the action you've identified really resolve the issue? Do you need someone to play the role of devil's advocate—or do you need someone from your red team to review what you're proposing?
- Thank participants for sharing their ideas and observations, especially when their views differ from the views of the majority. Encourage honest and candid dialogue by recognizing those who speak openly, respectfully, and with candor.

When Should You Conduct Action Reviews?

When you conduct an action review, you're taking time out of your busy day to reflect on what's working and what isn't working. You're investing time that you assume will pay off as you identify actions that will make your project more efficient and effective. You're committing resources now with the goal of identifying lessons that will improve your performance in the future. Think about when it makes the most sense to invest your time and the time of your colleagues.

Review Both Big and Small Change Projects

You can conduct action reviews during large-scale change initiatives that take many weeks or months to complete, but the process can be useful during smaller change projects too. Just ask yourself, would it help if participants had a constructive opportunity available to talk about what's working well that needs to keep happening and what needs to improve. If the answer is yes, conduct an action review. Maybe all you need is a 10-minute huddle. Maybe you need half a day to review something really large in scale. Adjust the timing of your action review to match the magnitude of your project and the amount of discussion you expect will occur.

Review the Good and the Bad

Sometimes companies plan and conduct action reviews only when things are going off the rails. They think they will save time by allowing projects that are going well to unfold without reviews. This is a mistake. There are lessons you can learn from successful—and less successful—initiatives. It's a lost opportunity if you focus only on what's going wrong that needs to improve. You want to figure out what is going right that you need to keep doing too. And every project, even the most successful ones, experiences some hiccups that represent opportunities to do things better.

You also don't want to create the misperception that your organization devotes time and attention only when bad things occur. Build a habit within your organization of self-reflection, self-criticism, continuous improvement, and learning. Conduct action reviews on change initiatives that are going badly and on those that are going well.

Review Projects at the End, in the Middle, and at the Beginning

Some organizations already have a practice of conducting a review discussion at the conclusion of each change project. After the flurry of project activities has come to an end and people are beginning to settle into their new routine, it's not uncommon for employees to want to look back and talk about what worked well and what could have gone better. Action reviews provide the opportunity for that discussion to happen in a way that is focused on learning and continuous improvement, rather than on assigning blame. It doesn't matter if your organization won't repeat the exact same project again. Each time your organization embarks on changing something—whether it's a technology or a process or a physical setting or an organizational structure—there is much to be learned about how well your organization made decisions, how well those decisions were executed, and how decision making and execution could be improved in the future. When you conduct an action review at the conclusion of your project, you have the opportunity to identify lessons learned that you can readily apply to other types of change.

But beware of falling into the postmortem trap, where you wait until the very end of a change initiative to meet—where you generate a laundry list of what worked and what didn't and wonder if any of it matters anyway. The damage is already done. Isn't it too late to fix anything? That's what happened to Kate and her team in the TCW relocation case. They missed the opportunity to identify actions their project team needed to take while their project was still ongoing, before anyone moved into facilities that weren't quite ready. Organizations with strong change management capability use the action review process throughout their entire project life cycle, meeting at each key milestone or on a regularly scheduled basis, from the very beginning of a project, to support continuous improvement and learning. They ensure their action reviews lead to action, because they conduct them when there's still time to intervene.

Conduct an action review at the start of your project, to set it off on the right course; periodically throughout your project, to help you stay on course; and at the end of your project, to help wrap up loose ends and identify lessons learned that can help you succeed on future change initiatives. Although the basic format for your meetings will be the same, the intent and the structure of the questions you ask will be somewhat different depending on when you hold the meeting (see Table 16-2).

Table 16-2. Conducting Reviews at the Beginning of, During, and After a Change

	At the Beginning of the Change Initiative To identify actions your team will take to set the project on the right course from the very beginning and prevent problems from occurring	During the Transition To identify actions your team needs to take to keep the project on track or get it back on track	After the Change Has Been Implemented To identify final actions your team needs to take to successfully wrap up the project, and to identify lessons learned that can be applied in the future
Open the Meeting	• State the purpose of the meeting. • Inform attendees about the meeting timing and flow. • Let participants know about subsequent action reviews that will be conducted related to this project. • Establish ground rules to use for this meeting and for subsequent action reviews that will be conducted related to this project.	• State the purpose of the meeting. • Inform attendees about the meeting timing and flow. • Review ground rules and ask participants if any changes or updates are needed.	• State the purpose of the meeting. • Inform attendees about the meeting timing and flow. • Review ground rules and ask participants if any changes or updates are needed.
What Is Supposed to Happen?	• Focus discussion on what the team is supposed to accomplish during the change initiative. • Share the project charter and objectives. Ask if any changes or updates are needed. • Share the overall project plan with key milestones and dates. Ask if any changes or updates are needed.	• Focus discussion on what the team is supposed to have accomplished by this point in the change initiative. • Share the project charter and objectives. • Share the overall project plan with key milestones and dates.	• Focus discussion on what the team was supposed to accomplish by the conclusion of the change initiative. • Share the project charter and objectives. • Share the overall project plan with key milestones and dates.

	At the Beginning of the Change Initiative To identify actions your team will take to set the project on the right course from the very beginning and prevent problems from occurring	During the Transition To identify actions your team needs to take to keep the project on track or get it back on track	After the Change Has Been Implemented To identify final actions your team needs to take to successfully wrap up the project, and to identify lessons learned that can be applied in the future
What Actually Is Happening and Why?	• Focus discussion on actions that might help or impede project progress. • Ask about factors and resources the team needs to succeed with this project. • Ask what they anticipate will go well and why that will occur. • Ask what they anticipate might go less well and why that might occur. • Ask about obstacles the team might encounter that will prevent them from succeeding.	• Focus discussion on project results to date and actions taken that are helping or impeding progress. • Ask how results compare to the project charter, objectives and project plan. • Ask what is working well and why that has occurred. • Ask what isn't working as well and why that has occurred. • Ask about obstacles the team has encountered and what it has done about them.	• Focus discussion on final project results and actions taken that helped or impeded progress. • Ask how final results compare to the project charter, objectives and project plan. • Ask what worked well and why that occurred. • Ask what didn't work as well and why that occurred. • Ask about obstacles the team encountered and what they did about them.
What Should We Do About It?	• Focus discussion on actions to get the project started on the right foot. • Ask the team to identify actions they will take to make sure the factors and resources needed to succeed are present on this project. • Ask the team to identify actions they will take to prevent or reduce the impact of obstacles they might encounter.	• Focus discussion on actions to keep the project on track or get back on track. • Identify lessons learned to date and actions the team will take to apply those lessons learned.	• Focus discussion on final actions needed to wrap up the project. • Identify lessons learned and actions the team will take to apply those lessons learned in the future.

Adapted from J.M. Huber Corporation (1998) and New York University (2020).

A Review at the Beginning of a Change?

A group of architects recognized that they needed to change the way they worked with their clients. Their last few projects hadn't gone well, and now they were about to start work on a mammoth renovation project they knew could make or break them. How could they start this project on the right foot, avoid mistakes they experienced in the past, and better address their client's needs? The architects hadn't conducted action reviews before, and they hadn't documented the problems they experienced in prior initiatives. But they agreed to participate in an action review before they started work on their newest endeavor. Here's what they discussed:

- What did they anticipate would go well? They realized the project kickoff sessions they conduct with their clients typically helped get things started on the right foot. They had a good format for these meetings, clients found the meetings to be productive, and the architects got the information they needed to create initial plans. This was something they decided to keep doing as they moved forward with the new renovation project.

- What did they anticipate would go less well? Thinking back to their work with other clients, they admitted to doing a poor job managing architects and space planners that they subcontracted work to. They recognized that on the new project, at least one of them would need to be present whenever a subcontractor met with their client. They saw that in their rush to keep things moving forward, they sometimes would fail to keep clients up-to-date about the status of a project. They committed to scheduling regular status-update sessions with their new client. And they recognized that some key leaders on their new client's team were less than enthusiastic about the project. They committed to paying extra attention to the needs and concerns of these more reluctant partners, so they'd better understand their reservations and hopefully find ways to address them.

The architects met for more than a day, discussing what they anticipated would go well and what wouldn't. In the end, they committed to about a dozen actions—one of which was to conduct periodic action reviews throughout the course of their new project! Yes, they encountered some unexpected hiccups and issues as their new project unfolded, but the architects were pleased to see that, because of their advance discussion and planning, they didn't repeat the same mistakes that had plagued their other projects.

Reviewing Your Action Reviews

After conducting action reviews on several projects, consider doing a second-tier review, during which you read through your notes and documentation from several action reviews. See if you can identify trends in what was discussed, obstacles that were encountered, and lessons that were learned. You may find that the same issues come up over and over again across multiple projects. We discovered that in one company I worked with. In almost every action review employees participated in, they talked about how they failed to establish clear roles and responsibilities at the outset of their project and how that led to lots of problems, delays, and misunderstandings. Once we recognized this trend, we knew we could help teams avoid this issue in the future by teaching them how to construct a simple RACI matrix.

If your organization repeats the same mistake over and over again, you're inadvertently feeding employees' perspective that the organization isn't good at managing change, that change should be resisted, and that "these kinds of projects just don't work." The answers may already be there in your action reviews; it's just up to you and your organization to apply these lessons.

Or you may find that your company is incorporating ideas discovered during earlier change projects into the work plans for subsequent change initiatives. And some of these ideas may really be helping these projects succeed. Good for you! You are building your organization's change management capability. You are also creating employee confidence in the way your company handles change.

How an Action Review Saved Me From Saying "I Told You So"

The business unit was about to embark on a multiyear process and technology change initiative that would affect thousands of employees. Leaders in several departments voiced their opposition. Did it really make sense to invest so much right now? After all, the business unit was still recovering from a recent financial setback. Why did the company select this vendor to partner with? They had advocated for a different approach. And who decided the project should focus on financial systems first? Everyone knew that manufacturing operations was where the business unit really needed an overhaul.

I knew that for this project to succeed, we'd need to assign a project leader who would listen to all these varying viewpoints, help key stakeholders feel involved, and still find a way to keep things moving forward. So when the project sponsor told me who was being considered for the project leader role, I objected vigorously. "He has a reputation for being an autocrat," I protested, "and that's the opposite of what's needed here. He's famous for playing the blame game. He doesn't hold himself accountable for anything. And he leaves a trail of bodies behind him on every project he works on." The project sponsor listened. He confirmed he had heard that feedback from others too. But then he said, "We're moving ahead with him anyway."

"Lucky thing I'm not working on this project," I chuckled to myself. I understood that change management would be led by the vendor, under the direction of the project leader. But still, I feared—I knew—that I'd be called in at some point to help clean up all the carnage. I shrugged as I left the project sponsor's office. "I tried," I sighed. "Oh, well."

I wish I could say my predictions were wrong, but six months into the project, it was clear the business unit had a disaster on their hands. Project meetings deteriorated into name-calling sessions. Employees whose knowledge and skills were sorely needed resigned, leaving the business unit struggling to figure out how to get day-to-day work done, let alone the work of the project. And the project leader kept defending his own misbehavior, claiming he was working with incompetent people, so how could they expect him to meet scheduled deadlines?

In the end, the project was put on hold. The project leader left the organization to pursue other endeavors. And I found myself meeting with the project sponsor yet again. As expected, he wanted me to get involved to help fix some of the organizational damage that had occurred. "Sure, I'll help," I said. "But I need your help too. Every cell in my body wants to say 'I told you so' right now. I warned you about the mess this project leader would create. I told you about the damage he would cause. But you went ahead anyway. Help me figure out what I should say to you now. Because I really want to say 'I told you so.' But I won't." (OK, maybe I did just say it.)

The project sponsor listened intently as I spoke. He nodded and smiled. "Why don't we conduct an after action review?" he proposed. "Just the steering team, me, and you. We'll talk through what just happened here. And why. You know, we thought we picked a great project leader, given the technical skills and experience he brought to the project. But we were wrong. What were the signals we missed? What should we have considered when we were selecting a project leader? And let's talk through why we didn't listen to the people who told us we were going down the wrong path. Maybe we missed what you were telling us. Maybe you could have provided your feedback to us in a different way. Maybe you could have suggested we hire a coach for the project leader. We can do better, and maybe you can do better too." I paused and considered that maybe the project sponsor had a point.

And so we conducted the action review. The steering team members learned some lessons they vowed to apply the next time they selected a project leader. They learned some lessons about listening to their employees. I learned some lessons too. I learned some new ways to communicate with the executive team so my ideas were really heard. I learned that I still had an opportunity to contribute even after—or maybe especially after—a decision is made that I disagreed with. And I learned that conducting an action review means never having to say "I told you so."

Addressing the Soft Side With the Action Review

Although the action review is a tool for keeping projects on track—it helps you focus on the hard side of change—to benefit from using the practice, you need to simultaneously focus on the soft side. You're using the practice to gather input and to generate ideas so your team will make more informed project decisions. But to get that input and those ideas, you need to create an environment in which people feel they can honestly share their observations and perspectives. Here are some tips for creating that climate so your action review meetings can be most productive.

Train employees and leaders on how to engage in productive and respectful dialogue. Consider offering training that helps employees develop their emotional intelligence, so they're better attuned to what others may be feeling and better equipped to manage their own emotions as they process feedback received during an action review meeting. Help employees build skill in conducting frank and honest, yet respectful, dialogue by encouraging them to read *Crucial Conversations: Tools for Talking When Stakes Are High*. Or provide employees an opportunity to participate in Crucial Conversations training (see VitalSmarts .com). Check out the Interaction Management training program offered by DDI (see DDIWorld.com); it's a great resource for helping you build a climate of trust and psychological safety, where honest and candid conversation can occur. And encourage employees to read *Change Your Questions, Change Your Life* before they participate in an action review meeting. They'll see how they can embrace the learner mindset—as opposed to the judger mindset—and discover how to ask more insightful questions of themselves and others so the action review meeting can be most productive.

Conduct separate reviews for each organizational level—the pros and cons. Some organizations conduct multiple action reviews, with participants segregated by organizational level. For example, a company may decide to have one action review attended by lower-level employees, where the focus is on project execution; a second attended by managers, where the focus is on project decision making; and a third attended by a few representatives from each of these groups, where the focus is on integrating these two perspectives. The benefit of this approach is that lower-level employees may feel more comfortable sharing their ground truth, discussing where they could have improved their own performance, without their managers present. And likewise, managers may feel more comfortable critiquing their own decision making without their employees watching on. However, separating participants by level could send an unwanted message about lack of trust between management and employees. Also, there is a rich opportunity for learning that is missed when employees don't hear about the factors their managers weighed when making decisions—right and wrong—and when managers don't hear firsthand from employees about what they experienced as they tried to implement those decisions. Consider what will work best in your organization.

Enforce ground rules. A key responsibility of the action review facilitator is to monitor and enforce adherence to the meeting ground rules. Ground rules can help create the kind of climate that's needed for honest discussion to occur. Keep the ground rules posted throughout your meeting and don't feel shy about referencing them if you begin to see violations. Remind participants that the purpose of the meeting is continuous improvement and learning, not affixing blame. If appropriate, use some humor to gently prod participants back into compliance. Help participants reframe and restate their questions and comments when needed so others are more open to listening to them. Encourage participants to make "I" statements, such as "I was confused when I read the email," instead of "You" statements, such as "You didn't explain things clearly enough in the email."

Identify key issues before the meeting. Do some homework before the action review occurs, meeting one-on-one with key participants, to get a read on the issues that are likely to bubble up—or that need to be discussed but that may be suppressed during the meeting. Check in with a few members of the transition-monitoring team to get a sense of which problems they think might come up—or which issues ought to be discussed—during the meeting. Find out where the sensitivities are. Then, during the meeting, place yourself in the role of empathy expert. Look around the room and ask yourself, "What is this person thinking and feeling right now? What can I say to encourage them to open up here?"

Ask leaders to model self-criticism. Before the action review occurs, meet privately with a more senior member of the team who will be attending the meeting. Ask them to serve as a role model of self-reflection and self-criticism, by admitting during the meeting to missteps they made and by agreeing to take action to address those mistakes.

Consider the connection to performance management. Some organizations are so committed to ensuring honest discussion during their action reviews that they have made this formal commitment to employees: There is no connection between what is said during an action review and an employee's performance appraisal. The thinking is that with that commitment, employees will feel free to engage in honest self-criticism, and will also feel free to openly discuss what their peers—and their managers—are doing that helps and hinders the change initiative. You may want to explore if that approach makes sense for your organization.

Decide if you need an outside facilitator. Typically a member of your project team can facilitate the action review. However, if you expect the action review meeting to be particularly contentious, see if it makes sense to ask someone from outside the project team to facilitate so the appropriate meeting climate is established and maintained. Talent development staff often have strong meeting-facilitation skills and are cued into the sensitivities and political and emotional dynamics that may be present on a project team. Consider asking them to facilitate your action review, if needed.

About to Begin?

Do you need help convincing your organization to use the action review process during change initiatives? Conduct action reviews on your own work and projects and invite internal clients and project sponsors from other areas to participate. You will be exposing other areas to the value of the action review process, and will be doing so in a nonthreatening setting. After all, you will be providing another area with an opportunity to discuss your work—not theirs! Once your internal clients see the value of the action review process, offer to facilitate, or co-facilitate, one or more reviews on the projects they conduct in their areas.

And to build skill conducting action reviews, consider using the practice first on projects that are proceeding fairly well before you move on to less successful, more challenging initiatives. It's likely that employees will be more willing to engage in self-reflection and honest discussion about what might be done differently when things generally are going well. After employees become comfortable with the process, then you can expand it to cover more challenging initiatives, and ultimately make the process a standard for all your change projects. Build a habit of self-criticism and honest conversation when things are less threatening, so employees will be more willing to open up and talk about the tough stuff when it's really needed.

Of course, sometimes things really do go off the rails. Despite your best efforts, you may feel at a loss for what to do to get your project back on track. In chapter 17, we'll take a look at some common issues that can arise during change initiatives. We'll also look at adjustments you can make to get your project moving again on a better path.

Learn more. Check out:

Salem-Schatz, S., D. Ordin, and B. Mittman. 2010. *Guide to the After Action Review.* cebma.org/wp-content/uploads/Guide-to-the-after_action _review.pdf.

17

Dealing With Thorny Issues

Something was different in Gary's cubicle. As I entered to talk about the change project we'd been working on for the past few months, I noticed he had tacked up a poster for the classic movie *Indiana Jones and the Temple of Doom*. Gary and I started to chat about how drained we both were feeling. We had been traveling back and forth each week from New York to Indianapolis to work on our project, and things weren't going well. Our vendor wasn't delivering what it had promised. The vendor missed deadlines creating the software we needed, and the programs it provided didn't work anyway. From what Gary and I could see, the vendor didn't have the capability to make things work. We felt stuck, convinced nothing could be done to fix all the issues we faced, and we believed that the project should be scrapped. But that wasn't our call to make. As I turned to leave, I took a closer look at the movie poster. And then I saw it. Gary had photoshopped in new actors and a new title for the movie that cleverly reflected our experience. Gary, the project team, and I had starring roles in the action thriller *Indiana Drones and the Project of Doom*.

I'm not sure about the drones, but the "project of doom" part was certainly spot-on. Regardless of our efforts, this project was a stinker.

Some of them are. Some change initiatives just seem to be rife with challenges. Thorny issues arise, one right after the other, with no end in sight. It can feel overwhelming and disheartening. And yet, sometimes when projects go off the rails, they can be set right again. Issues can be addressed. Problems can be solved. And your organization can achieve the outcomes the initiative is supposed to generate.

In this chapter, we'll look at the actions you and your project team can take when thorny issues arise that threaten your success. We'll review some general principles your team can follow that will help you identify the source of your team's problems and the path to address them. We'll cover a few specific problems that may arise during change initiatives and actions to consider. You'll see that some actions require a real focus on the hard side of change; they emphasize project management fundamentals, such as conducting action reviews. Other steps focus on the soft side; they involve communication and the restoration of trust. To address most thorny issues, you need a blend of both.

What role can you play to help get an issue-ridden project back on track? After all, you may not have the authority to intervene. That certainly was the case for me in the "project of doom" that Gary and I experienced. I wanted to take steps that just weren't within my purview. But that didn't mean I couldn't do anything, and it doesn't mean you can't do anything either. When challenges arise, you can coach project team members and the project leader on steps they can take to make things better. You can recommend solutions the team and project sponsor can consider. You can facilitate some of the tough conversations that need to happen. And you can advise others on how to create a trusting environment in which those tough conversations can occur. It may not be your call to intervene when a project goes off the rails, but there's still a lot you can do to help set things right.

How to Get Back on Track

You realize that your change initiative is experiencing problems. Where do you begin to fix them? What do you do when it seems like the challenges are insurmountable? Or maybe it looks like the challenges can be managed; they just haven't yet been addressed. What can you do?

Acknowledge Something Is Wrong

You know the old saying "The first step to recovery is admitting you have a problem." That certainly holds true for getting a change initiative back on track. The first step to addressing whatever problems your project is facing is to be honest and acknowledge that things aren't going well.

This starts with the core project team and change management team. It's easy to deny reality when you're devoting so much energy to something and have high hopes that all your efforts will pay off. It's difficult to admit that your hard work isn't producing the kinds of results you had expected, or that despite all those late nights, your project is still behind schedule. But you and your team need to pause periodically, remind yourselves about the outcomes you're trying to achieve, and check to see what's working and what really isn't. That's why the action review process we discussed in chapter 16 is so important. By conducting frequent reviews, during which you compare actual results to what's expected each step along the way, you can identify when minor slip-ups occur before things really go off the rails.

You can intervene early before a small mistake becomes an overwhelming disaster. But even when minor issues are missed and become more significant, you and your project team need to admit to yourselves that there's a problem.

Then you and your project team need to fight every urge to hide that reality. You need to admit to project sponsors, organizational leaders, and stakeholders that a problem exists. Perhaps you've already identified and have begun to implement a solution. If that's the case, let them know that too. But be honest and widen the circle of people who are aware of the challenges you're facing. Leaders typically don't like surprises and don't want to hear through the grapevine about difficulties the project is experiencing. And they may have ideas for resolving the issue that you and your project team haven't thought of yet. The same holds true for stakeholders. Let them know about what's working and what isn't. They may have insight about what's really causing the problem or have recommendations about how to address it.

That's the point that Gary had reached in our "project of doom." As a member of the project team, he felt that the issues we faced were so severe, they couldn't be fixed by the project team alone. He was ready for others to know. And so, when Gary tacked up his poster, he acknowledged—in a very visible way—that our project was in trouble. He wanted the rest of the project team, organizational leaders, and our stakeholders to understand the severity of our issues.

Now, I wouldn't recommend at all the approach that Gary took. His poster was funny but unprofessional. Gary put the team, the project, and himself at risk. But I certainly agreed with his assessment and appreciated his frustration. So I counseled Gary to remove the poster. Then, together, we had a much needed sit-down with the project leader and sponsor. We reviewed the issues we were encountering. We let them know that we were at a loss for ideas about how to fix them. And we admitted that we didn't think the project should proceed. The sponsor and project leader thanked us for being honest with them. They acknowledged that they too had concerns. But they shared with us that we needed to proceed because of contractual obligations with the vendor. Meanwhile they were exploring a range of remedies to address the issues we faced. And so we stayed at it. Gary and I continued to struggle on the project, but at least we knew organizational leaders were aware of the issues and risks. We knew our efforts were appreciated. And we took comfort in knowing our assessment wasn't wrong. Even senior leadership agreed.

If you are coaching project sponsors and organizational leaders, help them appreciate how difficult it can be for project team members to admit that there are issues. The team may feel demoralized. They may feel defensive or embarrassed or responsible for events that fall outside their control. Let leaders know that the project team needs their encouragement and support. The project team needs to hear that organizational leaders appreciate all their hard work. The team may even need to take a short break. Perhaps the team needs to put the project on pause for a week to recharge before moving forward again. Coach leaders so they understand the emotional stress the project team may be facing and actions they can take to help alleviate it. And coach team members too. Help them see that they may need to engage in some emotional and physical self-care. Although they have acknowledged the bad, they need to recognize that some good is happening too. Help your fellow team members put things into perspective.

Assess

After acknowledging that a problem exists, you and your team need to explore what's really behind the issue. Why has the problem occurred? What are the root causes? And to answer these questions, you probably need more input. Ask project sponsors and organizational leaders how they view the issue from their perspective. Ask stakeholders what they think is happening. Meet with transition-monitoring-team members (see chapter 7) and get their ideas. Check in with red team members (see chapter 8) and find out what they're seeing. Or conduct an action review and invite leaders, stakeholders, and members of the various teams to discuss what they see happening and why, and what they think should be done about it. As you engage in these conversations, explore:

Objectives. Take a look back at your project charter (see chapter 3) and the objectives and deliverables that were established for the initiative. Were they the right objectives? If you're encountering obstacles that can't be removed, are there other ways the same outcomes can be accomplished? Look at scope creep. In your efforts to address stakeholder needs, have you added in other deliverables that are keeping you from achieving what was originally intended?

Assumptions. Did you assume you'd receive more assistance and participation from certain stakeholders, but they haven't gotten involved in the way you had planned? Did you assume a leader would actively endorse the project, but it turns out she's voicing concerns? Did your team assume you'd have a certain budget, but only a portion of that funding has materialized? If those assumptions turned out to be wrong, what can be done instead?

Communication. Ask leaders, stakeholders, transition-monitoring-team members, and others about what's working related to communication, and what isn't. What are people confused about? Which methods of communication are working as expected, and which aren't? Do you need to conduct more frequent status-update meetings with stakeholders? Do you need to shift the focus during these meetings to ensure that your team listens more and speaks less? Are leaders effectively fulfilling their communications responsibilities? Where is more communication needed, and how should that occur?

Training. Is your training plan (see chapter 13) helping the right employees develop the knowledge, skills, and attitudes they need to succeed in the new environment? Or are there training needs you hadn't anticipated? What adjustments do you need to make to training content, delivery methods, and audience?

Resistance. Is someone intentionally creating the issue as a stall tactic? If so, how can you address their concerns so you can get things moving again? Check out chapter 14 for ideas.

On my project of doom, the sponsor ended up convening a series of meetings to assess why the project was so compromised and what could be done to set things right. These meetings included members of the project team, senior executives, software developers, attorneys, and sometimes our problematic vendor. Senior leaders confirmed that they were committed to our project objectives. They wanted the software the vendor had promised to deliver, and they needed that software to work. And yet, we also came to see that the vendor lacked the capacity to deliver what it had agreed to in its contract with us. It didn't have enough staff to devote to the project, and the staff it did have lacked the required expertise. And what could we do about it? Well, the contract was pretty clear. Although the vendor was failing, it hadn't failed enough—yet—to allow us to nullify our agreement. As we assessed the situation, organizational leaders came to realize just how big a mess we were in. But we also began to see some potential paths out.

Check In

Next, think about and discuss, as a team, what you have learned from all these conversations. What can and should be done differently that will yield a better result? And can your team actually do what's needed? Consider whom you need support or authorization from to implement solutions. Check the project RACI matrix (see chapter 10), if your team created one. As you consider actions to address the problem, whom do you need to consult with? Whom do you need authorization from? Whom do you need to inform? And check in with your red team. Let them know the problem you've encountered and the solution you're considering. Ask them to tell you why that approach might not work and what unintended consequences your proposed solution might generate. Then decide which options make sense to move forward with to address the problem.

On the project of doom, we decided to assign our own software developers to work alongside the vendor's development team. Where the vendor didn't have enough staff or expertise to get the work done, our own programmers completed the work. This certainly wasn't what our company had expected to do when we signed a contract with the vendor, but it was a path forward. And it was a path our company was willing to invest resources in to bring the project to a somewhat successful conclusion.

Communicate

Let your stakeholders know about the solution your team has decided to pursue. Be clear about what happened, what was learned, what you're doing to fix the issue, and how the new actions affect them. Be honest and as forthcoming as you can. On the project of doom, the sponsor let our project team, our executives, and certainly our in-house software development team and the vendor know why the company decided to assign supplemental resources to the project. He communicated the company's commitment to seeing the project through to its successful conclusion. He acknowledged how frustrated—and exhausted—our team members were, and he thanked us for our continued commitment to such a problematic initiative. He admitted that leadership made a mistake when they selected the vendor. And he shared some insight about why they'd made that mistake and what they'd learned to do differently going forward. We were all still stuck working on this stinker of a project. But at least we felt like our leadership team understood the situation and were committing resources to get us through it. And we appreciated their honesty, humility, and willingness to learn.

Coach leaders to communicate their support for the project team when they talk with others about the problem and its impact on the organization. What leaders say about the issue can influence employees' willingness to participate in future changes. Leaders should convey that they understand that mistakes and problems will happen, and that they view the situation as an opportunity for the organization to improve and grow.

I saw a CEO demonstrate this approach when a project team at his company made a series of blunders during a plant closing. The team had focused communications on employees who were directly affected by the shutdown, and these efforts had been well received. Employees understood why their work location was closing, knew the options they could pursue for continued employment, and felt cared for, supported, and respected. But the project team bungled communications with external stakeholders, which led to some embarrassing articles in the local and national press. The team worked with the local community to resolve the issues. But it didn't stop there. In partnership with local community members, team members took a hard look at the opportunities they had missed to communicate with external stakeholders. They researched best practices they could have employed. And they compiled the lessons they'd learned into a guidebook for managing community relations during a plant shutdown that other teams within the company could access if needed in the future.

Whenever the CEO met with a group of employees across the company, he praised the project team that had managed the plant closing. He commended the team for the actions it took to repair the issue and for its efforts to help others across the organization learn from its mistakes. During one town hall meeting, an employee admitted that he was troubled and confused by the CEO's remarks. "They made a mistake and the rest of us look really bad because of it," the employee challenged. "Why are you rewarding them for screwing up?" The CEO smiled as he responded. "I'm not rewarding them for making a mistake. That was embarrassing. But mistakes will happen. I'm rewarding the team for what they did afterward. It would have been easier for the team just to fix the problem and move on, hoping we'd all just forget about it after some time. But they didn't do that. Not only did they fix the problem, but they found a way to help us all learn and get better. I'm confident that, because of the guidebook they created, other teams won't make that same mistake again. We'll make other mistakes. But we won't make that one. And hopefully we'll learn from the next mistake too."

Reassess

As your team implements the solution, pause periodically to assess the results you're getting. Did the stakeholder who stopped showing up at meetings resume his participation, or do you need to discuss the issue with him again? What are transition-monitoring-team members saying now that you've committed to meeting with them more frequently? Do they feel like they have enough opportunities to provide input, or do they still need more? Does it look like your project is back on schedule since the team eliminated unnecessary distractions, or are you still falling behind? Conduct brief action review meetings with leaders, stakeholders, and members of the various teams to see what's working now that corrective action has been taken, what still isn't working, and what should be done next. A brief check-in conversation may do. Keep making adjustments as you learn.

On my project of doom, the sponsor convened quick check-ins every Friday morning with the project leader and project team until the initiative finally reached its conclusion. Sometimes senior executives would join our meetings. Sometimes these debriefs lasted only 20 to 30 minutes, sometimes longer, depending on the issues we discussed. We talked about the work that was supposed to be completed during the week. What had actually gotten done? Had any new issues arisen? What could we do to address them? Was the new arrangement with our underperforming vendor working? Was it holding up its end of the bargain? Were we? The project was never fun. But we did get it back on track—a different track—and we ultimately got to the end. When we were finished, we conducted lots of action reviews, examining the project and our decision making from a host of different angles. How did we end up in a partnership with this vendor anyway? What was the vendor evaluation process like? What did we miss during contracting with the vendor? What could we have done differently to get the project on a better track earlier on? What should we have done to start the project on a different track in the first place? We all survived the project of doom. And we learned a lot of lessons.

Don't think of these actions as steps your team needs to follow in a prescribed order. Most likely you'll find yourself bouncing back and forth as you engage in each of these actions. Your team will acknowledge the issue exists, you'll do some assessment, you'll widen the circle and inform others about the issue, they'll help you diagnose some more. That's OK. Just make sure you and your team have covered these bases as you work things through.

Tips for Getting Back on Track

Acknowledge something is wrong. Within the project team and change management team, be honest and admit you've encountered a problem. And let project sponsors, organizational leaders, and key stakeholders, including members of your transition-monitoring team, know about the problem too.

Assess what's causing the issue and options for addressing it. Conduct action reviews to gather input from team members, leaders, and stakeholders about why the problem exists and what can be done about it. Ask:

- Are you pursuing the right objectives? And if the objectives still make sense, have you unintentionally lost your focus?
- What assumptions did you make when you started the project, and which assumptions turned out to be invalid?
- How is communication—or lack of communication—contributing to the problem?
- What role does training—or lack of training—play?
- To what extent is employee resistance contributing to the issue?
- What else might be at the root of the problem?
- What options should you consider for addressing it? What are the pros and cons for each potential resolution?

Check in with leaders and key stakeholders for input regarding the solution you've decided to pursue. Review your RACI matrix. Whom do you need to consult with before implementing the solution? Who needs to provide their authorization to proceed? Whom do you need to inform? And check with your red team for their input regarding unintended consequences.

Communicate with stakeholders so they're up-to-date about the problem and the solution. Be clear about what happened, why, what's being done to fix it, how they're affected, and what was learned.

Reassess. Keep checking in to assess the extent to which the solution addresses the problem. Make additional adjustments as needed.

Addressing Some Specific Issues

Now that you have a general framework for tackling thorny issues, let's look at how you can apply it to a few specific challenges.

Employees Are Reluctant to Support a New Change Initiative Because Past Projects Have Failed

When a project fails, there's a double whammy. Your organization doesn't receive the outcomes the current change initiative was intended to produce, and employees may feel reluctant to get on board with future change initiatives. Employees may feel like they worked lots of late hours and slogged through confusion, to what end? Projects like these just don't work. Or perhaps the initiative did produce the results that were expected, but the change process was mismanaged and was just too painful for employees. They may be left feeling disoriented and disillusioned. They may doubt the competence and integrity of organizational leaders. Certainly they're reluctant to experience the same thing all over again.

What do you do when you're about to launch another change initiative in your organization when there is a history of failed projects? How can you encourage employees to give it another go when your organization has previously been so bad at managing change?

When change initiatives have failed or have gone badly, and there's a need to press on with another change, it's important to acknowledge the truth. This begins with organizational leaders as well as the project sponsor and project team for the new initiative. They need to admit to themselves that things have not gone well in the past and that they need to commit to leading differently this time. They may not have been responsible for the errors of the past. Perhaps different leaders and different project teams managed initiatives back then. Perhaps not. But they need to acknowledge that problems have occurred, so they can avoid repeating them.

Leaders also need to let employees know they're aware that past initiatives have been challenging and unfruitful. They need to convey that they understand the toll these initiatives may have had on employees, and thank them for the patience and commitment they demonstrated in spite of these issues. Leaders need to state that they recognize that employees may feel reluctant to give their full support to another change, given what they have experienced. And they need to communicate that they have learned and are committed to doing things differently.

Of course, this assumes you know why things went badly in the past. As planning begins on the new initiative, check to see if someone conducted action reviews on the projects that failed or were otherwise mismanaged in the past. Are notes available from these discussions that your project team can review? Even if a thorough review was conducted, keep probing and diagnosing what went wrong.

Look at assumptions teams made in the past that turned out to be misguided. Did project teams assume stakeholders could commit more time to the project than they really had available? What will be done differently this time? Did they assume leaders needed only 24 hours to review and approve a decision when they actually needed more substantial time? Are you making the same mistake on the new project?

Examine how communications were handled in the past. What worked effectively, and what worked less well?

Look at training. Was it effective in the past? What needs to be handled differently this time?

Ask employees for their assessment. What did they see go wrong, and what would they have wanted instead?

Consider conducting a before action review (see Table 16-2 in chapter 16) with your project team and selected stakeholders, during which you focus discussion on obstacles and issues the team anticipates it might encounter over the course of the new initiative. What actions can be taken to prevent these obstacles from appearing again?

Assemble a red team and ask them to poke holes in your team's plans. Ask them to critically evaluate your plan with an eye toward why your plan won't work, especially given the traps other teams have fallen into in the past. Ask for their honest assessment. Are you doing enough to ensure the new change is really managed differently?

Let employees know what specifically will be done to ensure that the current project will be managed more effectively. And then check in regularly with employees to see if they're noticing anything different. Ask them what looks and feels different and what looks and feels the same. Keep adjusting and rechecking with employees until they tell you their experience has improved significantly.

If you follow these guidelines, you'll be on your way to persuading even the most change-skeptical employee that you've righted the ship.

The Project Sponsor Recommends Terminating the Project

I sure wished someone had pulled the plug on my project of doom. That didn't happen. But it did happen to another initiative I was working on—a project I was leading, a project that was "my baby." The objective of this project was to introduce sorely needed technology to our company's succession management process. Not only had the CEO given the green light for the project, but he was serving as project sponsor. How lucky was I to have the CEO's commitment? But now the whole deal had gone bust.

I was proud of the approach to succession management we had implemented at our company. We used the process to identify up-and-coming leaders and place them into roles that could test and stretch their leadership capabilities. But much of what we did to administer how it worked was manual, time-consuming, and unwieldy, not only for HR staff, but for leaders and line managers whom we collected information from on a regular basis. Now that was about to change. We would introduce technology that would automate the data collection and reporting processes, so we could focus even more attention on what really mattered—providing development opportunities to employees. This would be a real win for everyone!

We assembled a project team that included HR leaders, technology staff, some line managers, and me. I would co-lead the project along with the head of HR information systems, and I would also serve as change management leader for the initiative. We let employees across the company know about the automation that was planned, and they seemed to be really intrigued by what was coming. We gathered input from the CEO, other executives, managers, and HR staff to find out what would be most useful for them. We created mock-ups of how the technology would operate. We evaluated options for purchasing technology or building what we needed within the current HR information system. We reviewed plans with our sponsor, the CEO, to make sure he concurred with all of our decisions. He confirmed we were ready to go.

And then, one morning, our CEO told my project co-leader and me that our project was over—it was canceled. The company had missed some key financial targets, and projections for the foreseeable future seemed tentative. "We can't invest in this project right now," the CEO told us. "Other projects have been canceled too. I'm still committed to succession planning. We're just going to have to continue to limp along without the automation. Wrap things up and let people know the project isn't going to happen."

I was devastated. Upset that our months of planning weren't going to lead anywhere. Embarrassed that I had made commitments to people that I now needed to undo. I certainly didn't look forward to telling everyone who had been so excited about our project that it wasn't going to happen. It was a bust.

Sometimes business conditions change and a project that has already begun needs to be abandoned. Organizational priorities may have changed, or new leaders with new perspectives may have joined your company. Economic conditions may have forced your organization to cut the budget for your project. Or maybe project sponsors have changed their minds about the value your initiative will bring to your organization. What do you do if the project sponsor recommends canceling your project? What do you do when you're in a situation like I was and you've just found out your project has fizzled?

Confirm the decision. Check with your project sponsor to see if they're open to conducting an action review with the project team and key stakeholders, to get their input about terminating the project and to see if any other options make more sense. Consider assembling the red team and asking them to poke holes in the go/no-go recommendation. And check the RACI matrix to confirm who has the authority to terminate the project, and who needs to be consulted before a termination decision can be made. For my succession management project, the decision came from the CEO, so I didn't question who had the authority to make the decision. I also understood that it was final. But that didn't mean my work was over.

Communicate. If a decision is made to cancel the initiative, work with the sponsor to determine how best to communicate the news to organizational leaders, project team members, key stakeholders, and the rest of the organization. Be sure the communication clearly addresses why the organization originally began the project and why it now makes sense not to proceed. Publicly thank everyone who contributed to the initiative, including project team members, transition-monitoring-team and red team members, and employees who supported the change. For my succession management project, our CEO met with the entire project team to explain the decision and thank them for their efforts. And then my project co-leader and I communicated the news to others we had met with over the course of the initiative. We thanked everyone for the input and ideas they had shared with us, and we reiterated the company's commitment to succession management. And the CEO reinforced this message in his formal and informal communications throughout the company. Although we couldn't automate the process—at least not now—succession management was still a key priority.

Identify lessons learned. Conduct an action review with the project team and key stakeholders to reach agreement on what was learned from the project, and share these lessons learned with the rest of the organization. By being transparent with employees about why the project was started and then discontinued and what was learned, you're conveying your organization's willingness to admit when a change is needed and to grow from the experience. You're also letting employees know that organizational leaders weigh their options carefully before deciding to begin an initiative and before deciding to stop it. When employees see leaders engaging in thoughtful decision making, they're more willing to commit to change initiatives that will arise in the future.

To close out my succession management project, our team conducted an action review. During the meeting, team members shared how frustrating it was to do so much work, and to have the CEO endorse that work, only to see their efforts discarded. We commiserated, and maybe that was the best we could do. But a week later, a team member (well, a former team member) stopped by with an idea. Since participating in the action review, she just couldn't stop thinking about our canceled project. And in mulling things over, she stumbled on some simple tweaks that we could make to our existing HR information system that could make our succession management process a bit less cumbersome. It wouldn't really cost anything to make the changes—maybe a day of work. Was I interested? I was. I checked with our CEO, and he was game too. So although our succession management automation project was terminated, it wasn't a total loss. We found a way to make things better—a little bit better. We learned that even when a project is terminated, some good can come out of it. There were still lessons to be learned.

Your Change Initiative Was a Success, but Now the Change Isn't Sticking

You sigh with relief and perhaps a bit of exhaustion, as you and your project team finally—after months and months of late nights—declare the change initiative done. You've checked off the last action item on your project plan. Your project team has conducted its final action review. You may have even enjoyed a project wrap party to celebrate your team's success. Employees are engaging in new behaviors that support the change. And your project is beginning to produce results. Customer survey scores are up, production costs are down, employees are working more efficiently, there's more collaboration across two departments. It's gratifying to see these outcomes because you, your team, and the whole organization have worked so hard. And then you notice employees beginning to stray back to the old behaviors. They aren't following the new procedures they seemed so eager to try just a few months before. They've returned to the old. And old issues the change initiative was supposed to address have started to re-emerge. How do you fix this? What do you do when a change that initially looked so promising just isn't sticking?

It can be a real challenge to admit a problem when you've just celebrated your success. It's easy to ignore the fact that more work is needed after you've announced to everyone that your project is done. But the reality is that change is rarely ever done. Managing change isn't simply a box to be checked off. Don't ignore the issue or hope it will go away. Discuss it with the project leader, project sponsor, or the stakeholder who has ongoing responsibility for overseeing whatever has changed. Acknowledge that something is up that may need to be addressed, and ask for their help to diagnose why employees are slipping back into old patterns of behavior.

As you assess what's happening, consider:

Are employees aware of what's expected? Do employees need to be reminded about what they're expected to do? Do they understand the rationale for these new expectations? Are frontline supervisors continuing to communicate expectations to employees? Are senior leaders continuing to talk about why changes were made and to convey their interest and support?

Are there obstacles that prevent employees from doing what's expected? Do employees have enough time to continue engaging in the new behavior? Sometimes, organizations temporarily reduce productivity targets to provide employees with enough time to learn and begin adopting the new behaviors they're expected to engage in. That works well until the old productivity targets are restored. Check to see if employees need to become more proficient in the new behaviors before productivity targets are increased. Or sometimes, employees discover that a new procedure is just too cumbersome. They may have been willing to try things out for a while, but now they're finding that it's just too challenging to sustain that extra amount of effort. Can anything be done to streamline the procedure so it presents less of an ongoing challenge to employees? Talk with employees and supervisors to find out what, if anything, makes it difficult to continue to engage in the new behavior.

Are there consequences for engaging in the new behavior? Are frontline supervisors recognizing and rewarding employees when they engage in the new behavior? Are they ignoring it? Or worse, are employees, perhaps unintentionally, somehow punished for engaging in the new behaviors? Have employees figured out that to meet the expectations that really matter, they need to ignore the change? Take a close look at the performance management process that's in place. What needs to change to ensure it's aligned with the change initiative?

Do employees understand how to do what's expected? Do employees need refresher training? Have they forgotten some of the content they were trained on? Are there behaviors they never really quite mastered? Does training need to be repeated or extended in some way? How can that be done?

Check to see who has responsibility and authority to take whatever corrective action is needed. If the project team disbanded, you may need to coordinate with multiple parties who now have responsibility for day-to-day oversight of the change. Remind these individuals about the outcomes the change initiative was intended to produce and why these outcomes matter for your organization. Let them know that you need their support to address whatever is causing employees to revert back to old behaviors. And as actions are taken, help them communicate with employees about why the additional steps are required.

Tips for Addressing Your Own Thorny Issues
- Are employees skeptical about a change because other change initiatives haven't gone well in the past? What are you doing to ensure that this change will be managed differently? How are you helping employees see and experience the difference?
- Have you worked on a project that was canceled or postponed midstream? What did you do to help stakeholders understand what happened and why? What did you do to ensure you learned from the experience anyway?
- Have you seen employees lapse back into old behaviors after your change project had officially concluded? What did you do to assess the cause of that lapse, and what did you do to address it?
- What are some thorny issues you've faced during a recent project? What steps did you take to acknowledge, assess, check in, communicate, and reassess that helped you address the issues?

The Hard and Soft Side of Fixing Thorny Issues

In some ways, when you address a thorny issue that has arisen during a change initiative, you're embarking on a mini change project. You're exploring how to change the way you're changing. And perhaps the flipside is true too. When your organization embarks on a change project, you're really just trying to solve some big thorny issue. Either way, you're using the same tools as you weave together the hard and the soft to devise a solution. You're employing sound project management discipline to help your organization achieve the outcomes it's striving toward. And you're helping to build an organization where collaboration, honest communication, and trust are the norm. Whether change is happening or not, those are worthy goals to pursue.

About to Begin?

Are you facing a thorny issue on a project? Ask yourself:
- Would it help to acknowledge that things just aren't going right? Would it help to let your project leader know about the problem? Your project sponsor? Other key stakeholders? Could they help you view the issue from a different perspective and possibly help you identify options for addressing what isn't working?
- How can you assess why the issue is happening and actions you might take to fix it? Who can help you conduct this assessment?

- Whom do you need to check in with before proceeding with a solution?
- Whom should you communicate with about what happened, why, what you're doing to address the problem, and how they're affected?
- How will you reassess to make sure your solution is actually working?

Learn more. Check out:

Carucci, R. 2019. "Leading Change in a Company That's Historically Bad at It." *Harvard Business Review,* August 6.

18

And Then Everything Changed

Much of this book was written during 2020, while the world—and the workplace—struggled to adjust to the realities of the coronavirus pandemic. The changes we navigated through during that time were devastating for some and profoundly distressing for just about everyone. We grieve with those who lost loved ones under the most tragic of circumstances. The more fortunate among us—and at times, it was hard to feel truly fortunate—wrestled with the loss of income, the loss of connection, and the loss of routine.

In the workplace, adjusting to the realities of a global pandemic meant implementing stringent new safety protocols, connecting to the office from home, navigating new policies and procedures, learning new technology, and dealing with furloughs and layoffs for some and overwork and exhaustion for others. Everything related to work seemed to be changing all at once. And it never seemed clear what the end state would look like, when we would reach it, or what our role would be when we got there. The phrase "new normal" took on an entirely new—and often insidious—connotation.

And yet, we mobilized quickly as we recognized the urgent need to do things differently to maintain our own health and protect the safety of others. We adopted new work practices, paused periodically to reflect on what was working and what wasn't, and adjusted as we figured out what we could do differently that would work even better. We discovered new ways to keep everyone up-to-date about policies and procedures as they changed from day to day and week to week. And we developed new skills to meet each challenge as it presented itself. We learned how to convert a trash bag into protective gear and how to teach a class via Zoom.

During 2020, we came to see that—at least for a while—we would need to live in a persistent state of uncertainty. We recognized that whatever we were doing to survive during the pandemic, we would need to keep adjusting as conditions changed. The virus would subside and safety protocols would relax, or maybe they wouldn't. Sales would return to pre-pandemic levels and hiring would resume, or maybe not. Restrictions would ease and employees would return to their offices, or maybe the virtual workplace would remain for the foreseeable future. As we navigated through our work, we came to appreciate how little we knew about what would come next.

What is certain—what we can be confident about—is that the way we work will continue to change. Hopefully the source of that change won't be another global pandemic. But in whatever our "new normal" turns out to be, we will continue to incorporate technological advances into how we perform our jobs. There will be new procedures to adopt. We will work in organizations where the labor force expands and at other times contracts. New employees will join and bring with them different perspectives on how our organizations should operate. Customers will pressure our organizations to innovate, and competitors will force us to closely manage costs. Government regulations will continue to change and the workplace will adjust accordingly. Change, in whatever form we experience it at work, will be a constant.

And we also can be confident that all of us—our organizations, our co-workers, and us personally—will continue to wrestle with change as it occurs. We may support and embrace the changes happening around us, or we may resist them. We may be in the driver's seat, leading the change, a committed navigator, helping to bring the change about, or a passenger, wondering what the destination will be like when we finally arrive. But it won't always be easy to incorporate whatever needs to change into our work environment and our day-to-day work lives. We will wrestle with the hard side of change, as we struggle to find a path to keep us moving forward toward the outcomes we're shooting for. And we'll wrestle with the soft side of change, as we face days where we contend with ambiguity, disorientation, and feelings of incompetence.

Knowing all of this, how can we help our organizations—and our co-workers—retain their footing? How can we ensure that the changes occurring in our workplace are successful, and help our co-workers feel valued and involved? What can we do when we're not in the driver's seat? The driver may not have even asked for our assistance. How can we help guide change anyway?

We can start by developing our own change management competence. And that can mean applying the tools addressed in this book to our own work. Are you about to begin a project, perhaps as a member of a team or perhaps on your own? Even a small one will do. Create a simple project charter, where you document the rationale for your project and the results you're trying to achieve. Discuss the charter with a few people who will be affected by the project in some way—perhaps your manager and a few fellow team members. Confirm that you're all in agreement about what your project in supposed to accomplish before you proceed.

Prepare a project plan, where you lay out the milestones you're working toward. Then reconsider. Is there a way you can incorporate short-term wins into your project, so your organization will benefit from your work even sooner than originally planned? Think about who will benefit or otherwise be affected by your project.

Conduct a stakeholder analysis. Meet with stakeholders to ensure your work addresses their needs and concerns. And think about how you can involve stakeholders so they actively participate in what you are creating. Can you enlist a few stakeholders to serve as an informal focus group—a transition-monitoring team of sorts—to review and provide input? Can you enlist a few others to serve as your red team, critically evaluating and poking holes in your plans to help you make them even better? As you plot out the key tasks and decisions you need to make, create a RACI matrix and review it with a few stakeholders. Is there agreement regarding who is responsible for completing each task, who is accountable for key decisions, whom you need to consult with, and whom you need to keep informed?

As you demonstrate to yourself and to others the value these change management tools provide, volunteer to help colleagues with the change initiatives they're supporting. Offer to create a communications plan for a project that's about to begin in your organization. Think about what senior leaders need to convey about why your organization is embarking on the change at this time, what they're hoping to accomplish, and how the project will affect employees. Consider how you can leverage peer-to-peer communication and frontline supervisors to reinforce these messages.

Volunteer to assess training needs and to create a training plan for a project. Recommend ways to help employees build knowledge, skills, and attitudes throughout the entire initiative, instead of just waiting until the end for a single training "event."

If you're aware of a project that's struggling, see if there's an opportunity for you to speak with the project leader about sources of resistance that may be affecting their plan. If appropriate, provide coaching to the project leader about steps they can take to mitigate resistance, or possibly turn it around to make the project even stronger.

If they're open to it, volunteer to facilitate an action review to help project team members and stakeholders discuss what's happening and why and plan steps to address the issues they're facing.

In your own work, and in your conversations with co-workers about theirs, blend the hard with the soft. Apply sound project management discipline, and ensure that trust and robust dialogue are the norm. Keep your organization moving forward on the outcomes you're all working so hard to achieve, and create an environment where it's safe to share views about why the project shouldn't proceed at all. Build excitement about the benefits change will bring to your organization and invest time and resources to help employees navigate through their feelings of threat and loss. Recognize that successful change requires structure and management. But it also can be quite messy and devoid of anything that looks like management at all. To guide an organization through change, you need to have a clear sense of where you are going and a willingness to walk down paths you hadn't considered.

And finally, demonstrate your own willingness to change. Research new approaches to integrate into your own work. Volunteer to try out a technology your IT department is considering. Agree to implement a new practice your manager or colleagues are advocating for that you aren't quite sure about. Show that you're willing to experience ambiguity and to feel incompetent, at least temporarily, as you explore something new that may—or may not—provide you with any benefit. Be inquisitive, doubt, make mistakes, and stumble. Experience the draw of just wanting to finish the job, the desire to make steady progress toward the end goal and just be done. And then rest in the mess for a while and sit with the confusion and disorientation. How does it feel? What's it like to feel hesitant and uncertain, but know that you need to move forward anyway?

This is the place where change happens. And this is the place where having empathy for others as they consider change occurs too. Feel the tension between the hard, disciplined side of change and the soft, emotional side, and recognize that you can live with both simultaneously. Breathe it in.

Now you're ready to lead yourself and others as you step forward into the dance of change.

"The only way to make sense out of change is to plunge into it, move with it, and join the dance."—Alan Watts

Acknowledgments

To manage change, we need to involve the right people in the right way. Writing a book about change is no different. As I navigated through the project of writing *The Hard and Soft Sides of Change Management*, I was so fortunate—truly blessed—to have the right people supporting and guiding me in all the right ways.

Thanks to Sophie Oberstein, who first approached me with the idea of writing this book. Sophie listened to my ramblings and reviewed draft after draft of rough outlines, helping me transform what started out as an assemblage of loose and disparate concepts into something with a more coherent structure. Sophie helped me establish the vision for this endeavor and the path to walk on to bring it to fruition. Thanks also to Jack Harlow, development editor at ATD, for his guidance, insight, and kindness. Sophie and Jack, you were my transition-monitoring team, providing recommendations and ideas for how I could make each draft of this book even better. And you were my red team, letting me know when I was straying down a path that you knew just wouldn't work. Thank you both for your candor and generosity.

Over the years, I have been fortunate to learn about change management by witnessing the work of some truly masterful practitioners. Thanks to Arshi Chaudhry for showing me how managing change can be done right, and for demonstrating extraordinary patience and forgiveness when I tried far too many approaches that turned out to be just plain wrong. Thanks to Susan Lippman, Caroline Langer, and Eric Loffswold, masters of their craft, who helped me learn alongside them. Thanks to Kevin Hanks and Sharon Banks for demonstrating that it's possible to focus simultaneously on both the hard and soft sides of change. Each day, you keep moving the ball forward while engaging with others in a way that feels inclusive, encouraging, and respectful. I marvel at your talent. Thanks to Dawn Cocco and Joan Beebe, my partners in crime at TCW, who helped me discover how to keep learning—and laughing—through our fortunes and misfortunes. And thanks to Peter Francis, who encouraged me to think big, but to also focus. Thank you for showing me what visionary leadership really looks like in action.

Finally, I am blessed to have the support and encouragement of my wonderful family—my project sponsors of sorts. Thanks to my parents, Henry and Edith Kolb, who helped me develop the confidence to travel down a few unconventional pathways. And thanks to my beloved husband, Howard, and to Julie, David, Bonni, Max, and Will. Through your love and support, you helped me—an admitted digit head—learn that life on the soft side is truly sweet.

Appendix

Project Charter Template
(See chapter 3)

Project Charter Template

Project Name	
Start Date	
End Date	
Objective	• • • • •
Deliverables	
In Scope	• •
Out of Scope	• •
Benefits	• •

Key Deliverables and Timeline

Major Milestone or Deliverable	Estimated Timeline

Project Team and Key Stakeholders

Project Sponsor	
Project Leader	
Core Project Team Members	
Change Management Leader	
Key Stakeholders	

Attachments:
- Statement of Work
- Stakeholder Analysis
- Project Plan
- Stakeholder Engagement Plan

- Communication Plan
- Training Plan
- Budget

Signatures

Project Sponsor:	
Project Leader:	
Change Management Leader:	

Project Plan Template
(See chapter 4)

Project Plan Template

Task Name	Start Date	Finish Date	Duration	Percent Complete	Owner	Comments
Milestone 1						
• Task 1						
• Task 2						
• Task 3						
• Task 4						
• Task 5						
• Task . . .						
Milestone 2						
• Task 1						
• Task 2						
• Task 3						
• Task 4						
• Task 5						
• Task . . .						
Milestone 3						
• Task 1						
• Task 2						
• Task 3						
• Task 4						
• Task 5						
• Task . . .						

Team Competency Matrix Template
(See chapter 6)

Team Competency Matrix Template

Potential Candidate	Candidate 1	Candidate 2	Candidate 3	Candidate 4	Candidate 5	Candidate 6	Candidate 7	Candidate 8	Candidate 9	Candidate 10	Candidate ...
Competency											
Competency 1											
Competency 2											
Competency 3											
Competency 4											
Competency 5											
Competency 6											
Competency 7											
Competency 8											
Competency 9											
Competency ...											

P = highly proficient
M = moderately proficient
Blank = not proficient

Stakeholder Analysis Template
(See chapter 9)

Stakeholder Analysis Template

Stakeholder Group	What Will Change?	Level of Impact	Level of Influence	Key Concerns	Current Commitment	Ideal Commitment	Preferred Method of Communicating	Planned Action
Stakeholder 1								
Stakeholder 2								
Stakeholder 3								
Stakeholder 4								
Stakeholder 5								
Stakeholder 6								
Stakeholder 7								
Stakeholder 8								
Stakeholder 9								
Stakeholder 10								
Stakeholder …								

Stakeholder Impact Influence Grid Template
(See chapter 9)

Stakeholder Impact Influence Grid Template

RACI Matrix Template
(See chapter 10)

RACI Matrix Template

Stakeholder	Stakeholder 1	Stakeholder 2	Stakeholder 3	Stakeholder 4	Stakeholder 5	Stakeholder 6	Stakeholder 7	Stakeholder 8	Stakeholder 9	Stakeholder ...
Key Task or Decision										
Task 1										
Task 2										
Task 3										
Task 4										
Task 5										
Task 6										
Task 7										
Task...										

R = Responsible
A = Accountable
C= Consulted
I = Informed

Communications Plan Template
(See chapter 12)

Communications Plan Template

Communication Event	Key Messages	Audience	Sender/ Leader	Start Date/ End Date	Frequency	Owner/ Creator
Event 1						
Event 2						
Event 3						
Event 4						
Event 5						
Event 6						
Event 7						
Event . . .						

Training Plan
(See chapter 13)

Training Plan

Audience	Objective	Training Program	Method	Start Date/ End Date	Frequency	Owner/ Creator
Stakeholder 1						
Stakeholder 2						
Stakeholder 3						
Stakeholder 4						
Stakeholder 5						
Stakeholder 6						
Stakeholder ...						

Resistance Management Plan Template
(See chapter 14)

Resistance Management Plan Template

Stakeholder Group	What Will Change?	Level of Impact	Level of Influence	Key Concerns/ Source of Resistance	Current Commitment	Ideal Commitment	Planned Action
Stakeholder 1							
Stakeholder 2							
Stakeholder 3							
Stakeholder 4							
Stakeholder 5							
Stakeholder 6							
Stakeholder . . .							

Action Review Template
(See chapter 16)

Action Review Template

Project Name:	
Date:	

Participants:		

What's Supposed to Happen and What Actually Is Happening?

Objectives	Actual Results

Why Is This Happening?

What Should We Do About It?

Actions for Sustaining What's Working

Task or Activity	Person Responsible	Due Date

Actions for Improving What Isn't Working

Task or Activity	Person Responsible	Due Date

Lesson Learned

References

Adams, M. 2015. *Change Your Questions, Change Your Life.* Oakland, CA: Berrett-Koehler.

Airiodion. n.d. Change Management Resistance Management Guide. airiodion.com/resistance-management-plan

Association for Talent Development. 2019. "The Talent Development Capability Model." Association for Talent Development. d22bbllmj4tvv8 .cloudfront.net/18/5b/1142b292431fb5393f2193211e1b/talent -development-capability-model-definitions.pdf.

Aston, B. 2019. "Write a Project Charter: How-To Guide, Examples & Template." The Digital Project Manager, July 5. thedigitalprojectmanager .com/project-charter.

Aziz, E.E., and W. Curlee. 2017. *How Successful Organizations Implement Change: Integrating Organizational Change Management and Project Management to Deliver Strategic Value.* Newton Square, PA: Project Management Institute.

Blackburn, S., L. LaBerge, C. O'Toole, and J. Schneider. 2020. "Digital Strategy in a Time of Crisis." McKinsey Digital, April 22. mckinsey.com /business-functions/mckinsey-digital/our-insights/digital-strategy-in-a -time-of-crisis.

Blount, S., and S. Carroll. 2017. "Overcome Resistance to Change With Two Conversations." *Harvard Business Review,* May 16.

Bridges, W. 2003. *Managing Transitions: Making the Most of Change.* Cambridge, MA: Perseus.

Carucci, R. 2019. "Leading Change in a Company That's Historically Bad at It." *Harvard Business Review,* August 6.

Conrad, A. 2019. "5 Steps to Writing a Killer Project Plan." Capterra, May 29. blog.capterra.com/how-to-write-a-project-plan.

Crawford, L., and A.H. Nahmias. 2010. "Competencies for Managing Change." *International Journal of Project Management* 28:405–12.

Darling, M.J., and C.S. Parry. 2000. *From Post-Mortem to Living Practice: An In-Depth Study of the Evolution of the After Action Review.* Boston: Signet Consulting Group.

DDI. "Interaction Management." DDIWorld.com. ddiworld.com/solutions /leadership-development-program

Dickson, G. 2019. "10 Reasons the Change Management Process Fails (And How You Can Succeed)." Workzone, April 18. workzone.com/blog/10 -reasons-the-change-management-process-fails-and-how-you-can-succeed.

Ewenstein, B., W. Smith, and A. Sologar. 2015. "Changing Change Management." *McKinsey,* July 1. mckinsey.com/featured-insights/leadership /changing-change-management.

Greene, R. 2020. *Instructional Story Design: Developing Stories That Train.* Alexandria, VA. ATD Press.

J.M. Huber Corporation. 1998. *After Action Review Guidebook.* Edison, NJ: J.M. Huber Corporation.

Johnson, E. 2017. "How to Communicate Clearly During Organizational Change." *Harvard Business Review,* June 13.

Kantor, B. 2018. "The RACI Matrix: Your Blueprint for Project Success." *CIO,* January 30.

Kaufman, R., and I. Guerra-López. 2013. *Needs Assessment for Organizational Success.* Alexandria, VA: ASTD Press.

Kotter, J.P. 1996. *Leading Change.* Boston: Harvard Business School Press.

Kovic, M. 2019. "What Is Red Teaming, and Why Do You Need It?" Medium, March 15. medium.com/arscognitionis/what-is-red-teaming -and-why-do-you-need-it-31a6d4087d2e.

Kulkarni, R. 2018. "The Need for Managing Change." Human Capital Online, June.

Mautz, S. 2018. "Want to Better Manage Change in Your Workplace? Learn From Google and Start With These Questions." Inc., August 2. inc.com /scott-mautz/google-is-revolutionizing-how-to-manage-change-starting -with-these-4-questions.html

Millar, C.C.J.M., O. Groth, and J.E. Mahon. 2018. "Management Innovation in a VUCA World: Challenges and Recommendations." *California Management Review* 6:5–14.

Murphy, J.D. 2011. "The Red Team: A Simple but Effective Method to Improve Mission Planning." HR Toolbox, May 1. hr.toolbox.com/blogs/james-d-murphy/the-red-team-a-simple-but-effective-method-to-improve-mission-planning-102711.

Neeb, J. 2020. "The Benefits of the Red Team for your Strategic Business Plan." *Afterburner.* afterburner.com/the-benefits-of-the-red-team-03.

New York University. 2020. "Conducting Successful Projects Using After Action Reviews (AARs)." nyu.edu/content/dam/nyu/hr/documents/Projects_123-AAR.doc.

Patterson, K., J. Grenny, R. McMillan, and A. Switzler. 2002. *Crucial Conversations: Tools for Talking When Stakes Are High.* New York: McGraw-Hill.

Percy, S. 2019. "Why Do Change Programs Fail?" *Forbes,* March 13.

Project Management Institute. 2017. *A Guide to the Project Management Body of Knowledge (PMBOK Guide).* Newtown Square, PA: Project Management Institute.

ProSci. 2020. "What Is Change Management and How Does It Work?" *ProSci.* prosci.com/resources/articles/the-what-why-and-how-of-change-management.

Purohit, S. 2018. "6 Essential Roles in Project Management." *Elearning Industry,* September 22. elearningindustry.com/roles-in-project-management-6-essential.

Rittenhouse, J. 2015. "Improving Stakeholder Management Using Change Management Tools." Paper presented at PMI Global Congress 2015, Orlando, FL. Newtown Square, PA: Project Management Institute.

Robson, B.P. 2020. "Organizational Change Management in Successful Companies." *The Business Value-Oriented Principles Journal,* March 6.

Rock, D. 2009. "Managing With the Brain in Mind." *Strategy + Business,* August.

Rothwell, W.J., B. Benscoter, M. King, and S.B. King. 2016. *Mastering the Instructional Design Process: A Systematic Approach.* Hoboken, NJ: John Wiley & Son.

Russell, L. 2015. *Project Management for Trainers,* 2nd ed. Alexandria, VA: ATD Press.

Salem-Schatz, S., D. Ordin, and B. Mittman. 2010. "Guide to the After Action Review." cebma.org/wp-content/uploads/Guide-to-the-after_action_review.pdf.

Sanchez, P. 2018. "The Secret to Leading Organizational Change Is Empathy." *Harvard Business Review*, December 20. hbr.org/2018/12/the-secret-to-leading-organizational-change-is-empathy.

Shannon, E. 2020. "Change Management: What the Coronavirus Crisis Revealed." *CPA Practice Advisor*, May 6. cpapracticeadvisor.com/accounting-audit/article/21136982/change-management-what-the-coronavirus-crisis-revealed.

Sirkin, H.L., P. Keenan, and A. Jackson. 2005. "The Hard Side of Change Management." *Harvard Business Review* 83:108–18.

Smith, L.W. 2000. "Stakeholder Analysis: A Pivotal Practice of Successful Projects." Paper presented at Project Management Institute Annual Seminars and Symposium, Houston, TX. Newtown Square, PA: Project Management Institute.

Society for Human Resource Management. 2020. "Managing Organizational Change." Society for Human Resource Management. shrm.org/resourcesandtools/tools-and-samples/toolkits/pages/managingorganizationalchange.aspx.

Tarne, B. 2017. "Applying Agile Techniques to Change Management Projects." In *How Successful Organizations Implement Change: Integrating Organizational Change Management and Project Management to Deliver Strategic Value,* edited by E.E. Aziz and W. Curlee. Newton Square, PA: Project Management Institute.

University of Georgia. 2017. "Change Champions." University of Georgia. onesource.uga.edu/_resources/files/documents/uga_change_champions_responsibilities.pdf.

Vitalsmarts, "Crucial Conversations." vitalsmarts.com.

Zenko, M. 2015. *Red Team: How to Succeed by Thinking Like the Enemy.* New York: Basic Books.

Zenko, M. 2018. "Leaders Can Make Really Dumb Decisions: This Exercise Can Fix That." *Fortune*, October 19.

Index

Page numbers followed by *f* and *t* refer to figures and tables, respectively.

A

accountability, 34–35, 132
action reviews, 255–277, 299
  addressing soft side with, 274–277
  to address problems (*See* thorny issues)
  conducting, 260–268, 263*t*
  reviewing, 272–274
  template for, 263*t*, 314*t*
  timeframes for, 268–272, 270*t*–271*t*
  value of, 257–260
actions. *See also* hands (actions)
  communicating change information
    via, 180–181
  for getting back on track, 280–287
  to prevent resistance, 232, 234–236,
    234*t*–235*t*
  stakeholders impacted by, 125–126
advocacy, for stakeholders' learning,
  216–221
Agile method, 50–51, 210
assessing progress and making adjustments, 15, 16
  dealing with thorny issues
    (*See* thorny issues)
  learning from successes and mistakes
    (*See* action reviews)
  TCW relocation case, 251–254
Association for Training Development, 10
authority, designating. *See* RACI matrix

B

barriers to change, 228
benefits of change initiatives, 38
Blount, Sally, 241
booster-shot training/tips, 213
Bridges, William, 93
building awareness, understanding, and
  support
  anticipating and addressing resistance
    (*See* resistance; resistance manage-
    ment plan)
  communicating about change (*See*
    communication; communications
    plan)
  developing knowledge, skills, and
    attitudes to support change (*See*
    training; training plan)
  PCo business transformation case,
    143–152, 150*t*, 151*t*

C

Carroll, Shana, 241
change, vii–xiv
  and COVID-19 crisis, viii–ix, 297–300
  demonstrating willingness for, 300
  external factors causing, vii–viii
  increasing positive outcomes from,
    x–xii
  responses to, viii–x

for stakeholders, summarizing, 120–121
change champions, 92, 106
change management, xi–xiii, xiii*t*, 1–20, 298
    balance of hard and soft sides of, 9
    competencies for, 18–19
    definitions of, 10
    hard side in, xi–xii, 1–5, 2*t*, 13–17 (*See also* hard side of change management)
    integrating hard and soft sides of, 17–18
    soft side in, xi–xii, 5–9, 11–13 (*See also* soft side of change management)
    themes of, 10*f*
change management leader, 40
change management team, 72, 83–89
    collaboration of core project team and, 87–89, 87*t*–88*t*
    communication of change by, 162
    competencies of, 84–85
    responsibilities of, 83–87, 87*t*–88*t*
    staffing of, 85–87
Change Your Questions, Change Your Life, 275
Cocco, Dawn, 169
commitment, 125, 238
communication, 153–183
    of both the good and the bad, 167–168
    by change management team, 162
    of complete picture about changes, 169–170
    by core project team, 163
    by everyone, 155
    by frontline supervisors and managers, 158–161
    to get back on track, 284–285
    of goals, 14
    by leaders, 155–158
    by peers, 161–162
    of red team purpose, 108–109
    with stakeholders about changes, 120–121, 125
    with stories, 170–172
    tools for, 182*t*
    of transition-monitoring team purpose, 96–97
    of the truth, 165–167
    of what you need people to do and achieve, 168–169
communications plan, 183–189, 299
    assessing, 186–188
    organizing information into, 183–186, 184*t*–186*t*, 188–189
    template for, 311*t*
competencies, 18–19
    of change management team, 84–85
    of core project team, 76–81, 79*t*–80*t*
    template for, 307*t*
compliance, 228–229, 233
Conrad, Andrew, 46
consultation, in RACI matrix, 132–133
core project team, 71–82, 87–89
    addressing soft side with, 81–82
    collaboration of change management team and, 87–89, 87*t*–88*t*
    communication of change by, 163
    identifying competencies of, 76–81, 79*t*–80*t*
    informal conversations by, 176
    in project charter, 40
    recruiting members for, 77–81, 79*t*–80*t*
    responsibilities and roles on, 72–76, 87*t*–88*t*
Corning Cable Systems, ix–x
COVID-19 crisis, viii–ix, 297–300
Crucial Conversations, 275

D

decision-making authority. *See* RACI matrix
defining change and how to get there
    creating path to change (*See* project plan)
    DBZ applicant tracking system case, 23–29, 24*t*–25*t*, 27*t*–28*t*
    determining what's changing (*See* project charter)
deliverables, 37–39, 39*t*

Deloitte, ix
disengagement, 229
documentation, 40–41, 198–199
drop-in "clinics," 211

E

emails, change information via, 176–177
end date, project, 37
extending training, 212–214

F

follow-through, lack of, 228
frequency of training, 209–210
frontline supervisors and managers, 158–161

G

getting back on track, 280–287
goals, 14, 104
Google, ix, 33
Greene, Rance, 171
Guerra-López, Ingrid, 203

H

hands (actions), 172, 175, 187, 206, 207
hard side of change management, xi–xii, 300
  addressed in stakeholder analysis, 127
  addressed in training, 192
  addressed with transition-monitoring team, 99–100
  balance of soft side and, 9
  Bervin Cares example, 1–5, 2t
  challenge of, 13–17
  integrating soft side and, 17–18
  and ProxyCo example, 8–9
  with thorny issues, 294
head (reasons), 172, 175, 187, 206, 207
heart (feelings), 172, 175, 187, 206
How Successful Organizations Implement Change (Tame), 51

I

impact on stakeholders, 121–124, 123t, 236, 309t
influence of stakeholders, 122–124, 123t, 236, 237, 309t
informal conversations, 175–176
informing others, in RACI matrix, 132–133
Instructional Story Design (Greene), 171
involving right people in right way, 15, 16
  accounting for key stakeholders (*See* stakeholder analysis)
  designating roles, responsibilities, and authority (*See* RACI matrix)
  generating advocacy on the ground (*See* transition-monitoring team)
  JCo acquisition case, 63–69, 67t
  leading and managing change (*See* change management team; core project team)
  listening to opposing views (*See* red team)
  in project plan creation, 55–57

J

job aids, 210–211

K

Kantor, Bob, 132
Kaufman, Roger, 203
Kotter, John, 52, 173, 176
Kovic, Marko, 105

L

Langer, Caroline, 153
leaders. *See also individual leader roles*
  communication of change by, 155–158
  lack of support for changes by, 181–182
  and project charter, 35, 39–40

M

managers, 158–161
Managing Transitions (Bridges), 93

Mautz, Scott, 33
meetings
    action review, 260–268, 263*t*
    to communicate change information,
        173–175
    embedding training in, 209, 212–213
    of red team, 109–113
    of transition-monitoring team, 97–99
milestones, 39, 39*t*, 49, 209–210

N

name of project, 36–37
Neeb, Joel, 105
*Needs Assessment for Organizational
    Success* (Kaufman and Guerra-López),
    203

O

objectives, 37, 206–207
organization-wide training needs assess-
    ment, 202–204
"Overcome Resistance to Change With
    Two Conversations" (Blount and
    Carroll), 241
owners of tasks, 50

P

peers, communication by, 161–162
preventing resistance, 232, 234–236,
    234*t*–235*t*
problems with change initiatives. *See* red
    team; thorny issues
project charter, 31–43, 298–299
    creating, 36–42
    template for, 304*t*–305*t*
    using, 42–43
    value of, 32–35, 46–47
project leader, 39, 73–74, 197
Project Management for Trainers
    (Russell), 57
project name, 36–37
project plan, 45–59, 299
    addressing soft side in, 51–58
    components of, 47–50
    template for, 306*t*

    value of, 46–47
project sponsor, 39
    in change management, 74–75
    and project charter, 35, 36, 41, 42
    project termination recommended by,
        289–292
project team members, 75–76, 220
ProSci, 10

Q

quality assurance testing, 210

R

RACI matrix, 131–140
    addressing soft side with, 137–138
    constructing, 133–135, 134*t*
    defined, 132
    elements of, 132–133
    in involving stakeholders, 135–137
    template for, 310*t*
red team, 103–114
    addressing soft side with, 113
    choosing members for, 106–108
    communicating purpose of, 108–109
    conducting meetings of, 109–113
    role of, 104–106
reinforcing training, 212–214
resilience, building, 222–223
resistance, 225–231
    because past project have failed,
        287–289
    expressions of, 228–230
    preventing, 232, 234–236, 234*t*–235*t*
    reasons for, 226–228
    used to strengthen project, 246–247
resistance management plan, 231–248, 299
    to deal with resistance, 240–246
    and expressions of resistance, 228–230
    identifying likely resistors and reasons,
        231–232
    involving resistors in, 233
    preparing, 236–240, 237*t*
    to prevent resistance, 232, 234–236,
        234*t*–235*t*
    providing compliance options, 233

to reduce or compensate for losses, 233–234
template for, 313*t*
responsibilities
of change management team, 83–87, 87*t*–88*t*
of core project team, 72–76, 87*t*–88*t*
of project leader, 73–74
of project sponsor, 74–75
of project team members, 75–76
in RACI matrix, 132 (*See also* RACI matrix)
of red team, 106
for training, 193–194, 198–201
of transition-monitoring team, 93–95
Rock, David, x
role(s)
of change management team, 162
in communicating changes, 155–164
on core project team, 72–76, 87*t*–88*t*
designating (*See* RACI matrix)
of project leader, 73–74
of project sponsor, 74–75
of project team members, 75–76
of red team, 104–106
on transition-monitoring team, 93–94, 96
Russell, Lou, 57

S

scale of change, 37–38
scope, 16, 37–38
shared collaboration spaces, 177–178
shared understanding, 34
short-term wins, 52–55, 209–210
signatures, to project charter, 41
social media, 178
Society for Human Resources Management, 10
soft side of change management, xi–xii, 300
addressed by training, 193, 275
addressed in action reviews, 274–277
addressed in project plan, 51–58

addressed with core project team, 81–82
addressed with RACI matrix, 137–138
addressed with red team, 113
balance of hard side and, 9
and Bervin Cares example, 4–5
challenge of, 11–13
integrating hard side and, 17–18
ProxyCo example, 5–9
with thorny issues, 294
staffing teams
change management team, 85–87
core project team, 77–82, 79*t*–80*t*
red team, 106–108
transition-monitoring team, 94–96
stakeholder analysis, 115–129, 299
addressing hard side with, 127
identifying level of impact, 122–124, 123*t*
identifying level of influence, 122–124, 123*t*
identifying stakeholders/stakeholder groups, 117–120, 118*t*
information to include in, 124–126
and new stakeholders, 127–128
purpose and use of, 116–117
summarizing what will change, 120–121
template for, 308*t*, 309*t*
for training needs, 198–204
stakeholders
advocating for learning needs/capabilities of, 216–221
identifying, 117–120, 118*t*
involved in project plan, 55–57
new, 127–128
and project charter, 40, 42, 43
RACI matrix for involving, 135–137
start date, project, 37
stories, communicating with, 170–172
successes, communicating, 172–173
super users, training, 211–212
supervisors, 158–161

support
    in advocating for employees' learning
        needs, 220–221
    for changes, 156–158, 181–182
    reassuring employees of, 210–212
surveys, 180

T

Tame, Bob, 51
target audience, for training plan, 206
tasks
    owners of, 50
    in project plan, 48–49, 57–58
    soft side, 57–58
    timeframe for, 49–50
thorny issues, 279–295
    actions for getting back on track,
        280–287
    after change initiative is finished,
        292–294
    hard and soft sides of, 294
    resistance because past project have
        failed, 287–289
    sponsor recommends terminating
        project, 289–292
timeframes
    for action reviews, 268–272,
        270t–271t
    for milestones/deliverables, 39, 39t
    in project plan, 49–50
    for training, 195–197, 209–210
tip sheets, 210–211
training, 191–204
    to address hard side of change, 192
    to address soft side of change,
        193, 275
    as afterthought, risk of, 193–195
    analyzing stakeholders' needs for,
        198–204
    at beginning of change project,
        195–197
    to build change resilience, 222–223
    evaluating appropriateness of, 201–202
    responsibilities for, 193–194, 198–201
training needs assessment, 198–204
training plan, 204–224, 299

accelerating timing and frequency of
    training, 209–210
advocating for stakeholders' learning,
    216–221
creating objectives for, 206–207
preparing and executing, 204–221,
    205t
reassuring employees of support,
    210–212
reinforcing and extending training,
    212–214
target audience for, 206
template for, 312t
training programs and methods,
    207–208
validating, 214
for when training goes wrong,
    219–220
transition-monitoring team, 91–100
    addressing hard side with, 99–100
    choosing members for, 94–96
    communicating purpose of, 96–97
    conducting meetings of, 97–99
    informal conversations by, 176
    for peer-to-peer communication,
        161, 163
    reviewing training plan with, 212
    value of, 93–94
transition planning, 213–214
truth, communicating, 165–167

V

videos, 179–180
visual reminders, 178–179

W

Watts, Alan, 300
websites, change information on, 178
WIIFM (What's in it for me), 169–170
workarounds, 229

Z

Zenko, Micah, 104

About Kathryn Zukof

 Kathryn Zukof is a learning and organizational development practitioner and educator with more than 30 years of experience in industries ranging from manufacturing, to higher education, to technology services. Her work focuses on helping organizations create and implement innovative approaches to leadership development and succession management, foster an environment of continuous learning, and plan and navigate through transformational change. Before she transitioned to a career in L&OD, Kathryn held management roles in client relations, product development, and marketing in the technology services sector.

Kathryn has a PhD in social psychology and an MBA in marketing. She has taught graduate and undergraduate courses in industrial and organizational psychology, research methods, and marketing.